Crosscurrents / MODERN CRITIQUES

Harry T. Moore, *General Editor*

American Dreams, American Nightmares

EDITED BY *David Madden*

WITH A PREFACE BY
Harry T. Moore

Carbondale and Edwardsville
SOUTHERN ILLINOIS UNIVERSITY PRESS

FEFFER & SIMONS, INC.
London and Amsterdam

For Three American Dreamers

WRIGHT MORRIS

In the dry places, men begin to dream. Where the rivers run sand, there is something in man that begins to flow.—The Works of Love

ROBERT PENN WARREN

Soon now we shall go out of the house and go into the convulsion of the world, out of history and into history and the awful responsibility of Time.—All the King's Men

GRANVILLE HICKS

Some time there will be a generation with both the opportunity and the will, and the better world we hope for will be created. . . . You may see the American Dream come true.—I Like America

Contents

Preface

American Dream: the first time the phrase hit many of us was in 1933, an ironic enough time for it, when George O'Neill (1898–1940) used it as the title of a play which the Theatre Guild produced with Douglass Montgomery. I haven't seen the play since (or read it—is it in print?), but remember several things about it. In the colonial New England part, the young man who was to be the chief beginner of the family whose fortunes the play followed over the centuries, stood up with his demure girl friend (who of course wore a white collar and a little white cap) and said, "Father, we have known each other"—known, that is in the "biblical" sense; and so the family was really starting. In the 1849 section, a descendant of the "knower" stood in the farmhouse doorway and said, in a line I've remembered across the years as being good theater-poetry, "Was there ever a land that leaned so to the West?" He went in the direction of that leaning and made the family fortune. His portrait dominated the parlor of the mansion in which his descendants lived, and in one effective Prohibition Era scene the embittered, family-haunted protagonist threw a martini glass at the portrait, saying, "Here's to my grandfather—the son of a bitch!"

Daring stuff in the thirties, but only a very minor play; it did however, at least call attention to the American dream and nightmare, about which a number of distinguished critics and historians write trenchantly in this collection which David Madden has brilliantly assembled. His own Introduction is so rich and full that it really precludes the necessity of any Preface except for a few beamish words; besides, this book is so large, for our series, that I've been told to write only a few lines here.

And there is just room enough for two statements. One is that it is a pleasure to pick up a book in today's America and find such deservedly notable writers as Robert B. Heilman, Leslie A. Fiedler, Louis Filler, Maxwell Geismar and others (I merely named the authors of the first four chapters), along with a number of newer critics who have their own thing to say and say it well; and the volume closes impressively with Ihab Hassan and Oscar Cargill. It's a superb selection of writers, just to begin with.

The other statement concerns the range of their presentation. We find not only fine general essays, but also valuable fresh studies of numerous writers, including two on Scott Fitzgerald. We also have pieces on Herman Melville, Ralph Ellison, the two-little-known Abraham Cahan, Sinclair Lewis, Henry Miller, and others. Oh yes, and Arthur Miller: one wonders just why he is here, though Chester E. Eisinger does show us how thoroughly Miller dealt with the American Dream in Death of a Salesman. Yet Mr. Eisinger is properly critical: Willy Loman, he points out, is not a tragic figure, and the play is sentimental and confused. I need hardly say that we have, in other sections of this volume, similarly perceptive criticism. I can only say further that this is one of the finest collections of criticism I've seen in a long while and that its angle of approach gives it a special value.

HARRY T. MOORE

Southern Illinois University
April 26, 1970

Notes on Contributors

DAVID MADDEN is the author of *Wright Morris* and of two novels, *The Beautiful Greed* and *Cassandra Singing*. He edited *Tough Guy Writers of the Thirties* and *Proletarian Writers of the Thirties* for the Crosscurrents series, and Southern Illinois University Press published a collection of his essays, *The Poetic Image in Six Genres*, in 1969. His literary essays have appeared in *Prairie Schooner*, *Antioch Review*, *Journal of Aesthetics*, *Modern Fiction Studies*, *Critique*, *Literature and Psychology*, and *Journal of Popular Culture*. He has published film criticism in *Film Quarterly* and *Film Heritage*. His stories and poems have appeared in such publications as the *Kenyon Review*, the *Southern Review*, *Botteghe Oscure*, *Playboy*, the *Southwest Review*, the *Northwest Review*. His stories have been reprinted in *Best American Short Stories 1969* and *Best Magazine Fiction*. Louisiana State University Press published *The Shadow Knows*, a collection of his stories, in 1970. His prize-winning plays have had many productions and several have been published. Former assistant editor of the *Kenyon Review*, he is Writer-in-Residence at Louisiana State University and conducts its creative writing program.

ROBERT B. HEILMAN, Chairman of the Department of English at the University of Washington, is the recipient of a Guggenheim fellowship and of numerous awards in literary criticism. He has published *America in English Fiction, 1760–1800*, *This Great Stage: Image and Structure in King Lear*, *Tragedy and Melodrama: Versions of Experience*, and many essays on Shakespeare, Henry James, and the English and American novel.

LESLIE A. FIEDLER, Professor of English at the State University of New York at Buffalo, has taught and lectured at many universities in the United States and abroad, and has received several awards and fellowships. His works of criticism include: *An End to Innocence*, *Love and Death in the American Novel*, *No! In Thunder*, *Waiting for the End*, and *The Return of the*

Vanishing American. His fiction includes: *The Second Stone,
The Last Jew in America*, *Back to China*, and *Pull Down Vanity*.
He contributed an essay to *Proletarian Writers of the Thirties*.

LOUIS FILLER, Professor of History at Antioch College, is the
author of *Randolph Bourne* and *The Unknown Edwin Markham*.
He edited *The Anxious Years* and three books on Mr. Dooley
and Wendell Phillips, and he has published essays on Chatter-
ton, S. S. McClure, Dreiser, Susan Lenox, A. H. Lewis, Edward
Bellamy, John Chamberlain, and on folklore and political literature.

MAXWELL GEISMAR, having taught for a decade at Sarah Lawrence College, became a free-lance writer and lecturer in 1946;
he has received Guggenheim and National Institute of Arts and
Letters grants in literature. His books include *Writers in Crisis,
The Last of the Provincials, Rebels and Ancestors, American
Moderns, Henry James and the Jacobites*, and *Henry James
and His Cult*. He has edited volumes on Wolfe, Whitman,
London, Lardner, Melville, and Sherwood Anderson. He is a
contributor to many of the major magazines and is a senior
editor of *Ramparts*.

IRVING MALIN teaches at City College of New York. He is the
author of *William Faulkner: An Interpretation, Jews and Americans, New American Gothic*, and *Saul Bellow's Fiction*; he has
edited books on American-Jewish literature, Capote's *In Cold
Blood*, Bellow, Isaac Bashevis Singer, and psychoanalysis in
American fiction. He contributed an essay to *Tough Guy Writers
of the Thirties*.

MARVIN FISHER, Professor of English at Arizona State University,
is the author of *Workshops in the Wilderness* and of articles on
the American Renaissance and nineteenth-century technology
and its impact on the American imagination. He is preparing a
book on Melville's short stories.

JULES CHAMETZKY is Professor of English at the University of
Massachusetts, and coeditor of the *Massachusetts Review*. He
contributed an essay on Edward Dahlberg to *Proletarian Writers
of the Thirties*. He has published numerous essays on modern
British and American fiction, especially on the literature of
immigration and of the thirties.

JAMES C. AUSTIN, Professor of English at Southern Illinois University in Edwardsville, has published books on Artemus Ward,
Petroleum V. Nasby, and Bill Arp.

RICHARD LEHAN is Professor of English at the University of California, Los Angeles, and acting Chairman of the Department of English. He has published several dozen essays on modern literature and books on F. Scott Fitzgerald and Theodore Dreiser.

FRANK KINAHAN recently received his doctorate from Harvard, where he was a student of Harry Levin. He has been studying Yeats, and his essay on Swift's *Tale of a Tub* was published in *Journal of English and Germanic Philology*.

RICHARD P. ADAMS, Chairman of the Department of English at Tulane University, has twice been a Fulbright Lecturer. He is the author of *Faulkner: A Critical Interpretation* and his essays on Emerson, Stephen Crane, Whitman, James Jones, Twain, Hawthorne, Emily Dickinson, Edwin Arlington Robinson, James Gould Cozzens, Eugene O'Neill, Hemingway, and the American Renaissance have appeared in leading scholarly journals.

ALAN TRACHTENBERG is the author of *Brooklyn Bridge: Fact and Symbol*. A fellow in 1968–69 at the Center for Advanced Study in the Behavioral Sciences, he teaches at Pennsylvania State University. He contributed an essay to *Experience in the Novel*, and his essays and reviews on American literature and culture have appeared in *American Quarterly*, the *Kenyon Review*, the *Massachusetts Review*, the *Nation*, and *Critique*, and elsewhere.

C. HUGH HOLMAN, former Dean of the Graduate School and Provost, is now Kenan Professor of English at the University of North Carolina. His books include *A Handbook to Literature* (with Thrall and Hibbard), *Thomas Wolfe*, *John P. Marquand*, *Three Modes of Modern Southern Fiction*, *The American Novel through Henry James*, *Southern Fiction: Renascence and Beyond* (with Louis D. Rubin and Walter Sullivan), *The Letters of Thomas Wolfe to His Mother* (ed. with Sue F. Ross). He has been a Guggenheim Fellow and is now writing a study of W. Gilmore Simms.

FREDERIC I. CARPENTER is the author of *American Literature and the Dream*, *Emerson and Asia*, *Emerson Handbook*, *Robinson Jeffers*, and *Eugene O'Neill*. His essays on Wright Morris and other contemporary American writers have appeared in many scholarly magazines. He has taught at the University of Chicago and Harvard, and is now Research Associate in English at the University of California.

CHESTER E. EISINGER, Professor of English and Chairman of the Committee on American Studies at Purdue University, has had several Fulbright Fellowships. Author of *Fiction of the Forties,* he has published articles on the freehold concept, contributed an essay to *Proletarian Writers of the Thirties,* and is editor of the forthcoming volume on the 1940's in Documents of American Civilization Series.

ALVIN GREENBERG, Associate Professor of English at Macalester College, is editor of the *Minnesota Review.* He has published essays on the modern novel in *Wisconsin Studies in Contemporary Literature, Criticism,* and *Paunch.* He has also published a novel, *The Small Waves,* and a book of poems, *The Metaphysical Giraffe.*

ALLEN GUTTMANN, Associate Professor of English at Amherst College, has published *Wound in the Heart: America and the Spanish Civil War* and *The Conservative Tradition in America;* he has edited books on the Spanish Civil War, the Cherokee nation, the Korean War, and communism. His essays on Washington Irving, Jewish writers, and political ideals and the military ethic have appeared in the *American Scholar* and *American Literature.* He wrote about proletarian poetry for *Proletarian Writers of the Thirties.*

IHAB HASSAN, Benjamin L. Waite Professor of English and Chairman of the Department at Wesleyan University, was born in Cairo, Egypt. He is the author of *Radical Innocence: Studies in the Contemporary American Novel, Crise du Héros Américain Contemporain,* and *The Literature of Silence.* He contributed the chapter "Since 1945" to *The Literary History of the United States.* Recipient of two Guggenheim awards and a Fulbright lectureship to France, he is currently at work on a study of the avant-garde in the twentieth century.

OSCAR CARGILL, Chairman for many years, now retired, of the Department of English at New York University, is the author of *Intellectual America, Thomas Wolfe at Washington Square, The Novels of Henry James,* and *Toward a Pluralistic Criticism.*

Introduction

True Believers, Atheists, and Agnostics

Seven years ago, in Washington, D. C., Martin Luther King told 200,000 civil rights marchers: "I have a dream. It is a dream deeply rooted in the American Dream. I have a dream that one day in the red hills of Georgia, sons of former slaves and the sons of former slaveowners will sit down together at the table of brotherhood." The night before he was assassinated, King said: "God has allowed me to go up the mountain, and I have seen the promised land." Raised in two decades of nightmare, the generation that has seen prophets of the American Dream shot down, may well ask: What do you old folks mean by this Madison Avenue phrase? "I don't believe in the American Dream," a Negro student leader told Humphrey, who had been perpetuating the tradition of Dream oratory, "because the American Dream doesn't believe in me. The American Dream for the black man is nothing more than a nightmare. If elected, what will you do to restore my and my people's faith in the American Dream?" A few weeks later Robert Kennedy was assassinated. Contradictory events have not made the dream rhetoric mute. In his inaugural address, President Nixon chimed in, "The American Dream does not come to those who fall asleep." In 1969, an ad invited the readers of the *New Republic* to join a Committee for Fulfillment of the American Dream. Inescapably, we are all members of that society, for even in the darkest fields of the republic, American dreams have always been the nation's bumper crop. In small towns and megalopolises, you see them, symbolically enough, at stop lights—bumper stickers on Joad-like jalopies, station wagons, and Cadillacs, declaring: I HAVE A DREAM. Traffic lights turn green, and the cars move on, following an impossible dream which, some have persistently said, leads only to a precluded dead end. The Great Gatsby saw a green light at the end of Daisy's dock. He ended up shot to death in his magnificent swimming pool in West Egg—and again later in a limousine in Dallas, on a veranda in Memphis, in a hotel kitchen in Los Angeles. Mixing metaphors is an old American custom. We reap what we sow, pride goeth before a fall, make the world safe for democracy—the banners endlessly unfurl. But for how long and how far? Other bumper stickers demand: SAVE OUR GUNS. Still, on July 20, 1969, in the midst of nightmares, it was an American, speaking from Tranquility Base in the name of all nations, who said, "The Eagle has landed," thus fulfilling a dream all men have shared since the beginning of civilization.

I began writing about American Dreams and nightmares in my study of the works of Wright Morris; later, this became a dominant theme in my examination of the works of James M. Cain and of the tough guy and the proletarian writers of the thirties; it recurs often in the essays I commissioned for the two volumes I edited for the Crosscurrents Series in 1968. *American Dreams, American Nightmares* is, then, a fuller examination of themes and literary problems explored in *Tough Guy Writers of the Thirties* and *Proletarian Writers of the Thirties*. The contributors to the present volume were asked to focus on the imaginative literature that has come directly or indirectly out of the realities which these terms have both illuminated and obscured. In most instances, I requested essays on a specific work or author or topic, but some of the contributors suggested their own approaches. The book opens with five general essays; the remainder of the collection is arranged chronologically—essays that focus on one work alternate with general essays on a single writer or on a distinct facet of the Dream concept. These introductory observations and questions represent my own involvement with the concepts and are related to the essays written in response to my requests.

Today, in our collective field of vision, in which we perceive mainly the nightmare, "the American Dream" is a cliché, symbolic of the Dream defunct. But "every cliché," says Wright Morris, "once had its moment of truth," factual and imaginative. The literary mind that produces labels so assiduously is reluctant to perpetuate labels already in use. "The American Dream" may be a cultural label, but a cavalier rejection of a term simply because it is a label or a cliché that offends our craving for fresher rhetoric entails the risk of substituting one superficiality for another. Almost daily, through one medium or another, we encounter the term "American Dream"–"American nightmare" less frequently, but its synonyms come rapid-fire. Terms with such inflationary currency issue from cold realities, not from some academic cloudland. In his essay, "The Dream Metaphor: Some Ramifications," Robert B. Heilman examines the key term itself, discussing works by Wright Morris, Hawthorne, Robert Penn Warren, Mailer, Albee, Arthur Miller, Eugene O'Neill, and Tennessee Williams.

What was the American Dream and how did it evolve into nightmare? The edenic promises of the American land helped shape aspects of the American character; ironic and paradoxical tensions between romantic and idealistic elements in that character, as it experienced the land, helped produce the American Dream. The substance of that mythic concept is elusive. But American writers from the beginning have projected visions of dreams and nightmares. No *single* Dream has bemused us from the beginning, no single nightmare has haunted us. There are many American Dreams and nightmares. Those who say yes to the Dream have their own nightmares; those who say no have their private dreams.

"In dreams begin responsibilities," wrote the poet Delmore Schwartz. To most Americans this has meant a responsibility to transform the Dream into realities. To others it has meant a responsibility to expose ways in which the Dream has failed. Despite nightmare realities and prospects, many voices have said YES in thunder to American Dreams, trying to make rain in Eden. Despite dreams that have come true and future possibilities, many voices have said NO in thunder, a prophetic bang in an Eden transfigured into a Valley of Ashes. Those who say yes I call the true believers. They help make and remember heroes. Those who say no I call atheists. They help make and encourage victims. But arching like one of Roebling's suspension bridges over the true believers and the atheists are the agnostics, who say maybe. The agnostic contemplates the interaction between dubious heroes and their vulnerable witnesses.

Numb though we are from the constant assault of nightmare voices, perhaps we can still hear the voice of Cotton Mather speaking in 1702 of "the wonders of the Christian Religion flying from the deprivations of Europe to the American strand" at "the ends of the earth." Christ delivered us, he said, into the American desert, for a purpose. Over the racket of young whites and blacks demonstrating and rioting against nightmare contradictions of the Dream, perhaps we can still hear J. Hector St. John de Crèvecoeur, who cultivated his own garden as a New York farmer, speaking in his letters to his fellow Frenchmen in 1782: "What then, is the American, this new man? He is an American who, leaving behind him all his ancient prejudices and manners, receives new ones from the new mode of life he has embraced . . . [His] labours and posterity will one day cause great changes in the world. Americans are the western pilgrims. . . . They will finish the great circle." In 1835 another Frenchman, de Tocqueville, with his prophetic vision, expressed more clearly still the dream dimension of the Great Experiment: "America is a land of wonders, in which everything is in constant motion and every change seems an improvement."

Compared with other national dreams the American Dream is unique because the settlers, fleeing the nightmare of European history, made, in the name of all Western man, a new beginning in a new Garden of Eden; thus "Americans became the heirs of all civilizations." There has never been a purely American Dream, because in the beginning all Europe lay down in "the American Dream bed" and dreamed *universal* dreams. To old bitch Europe, the new continent was a fountain of youth. In Virgin Wilderness, where all things seemed possible, the New Adam could recreate his lost paradise by the sweat of his brow. In his Brave New World, the young American Adam did indeed transform the Great American Desert into the Garden of the World. Pathfinder, deerslayer, noble savage, this mythic Adam reinstated a primitive innocence in Western civilization as he hacked trails into the wild West. There were visions in those early voices.

Behind James Fenimore Cooper's Pathfinder came another American Adam, the farmer, who reinstated *pastoral* innocence, on the eve of the Industrial Revolution in Europe. A creative witness to the heroic Pathfinder, the agrarian Adam cultivated the Virgin Land, apparently justifying Jefferson's agrarian utopianism and the experimental idealism of Emerson and Thoreau. Historian George Bancroft, a major spokesman of faith in America's mission, declared that "the Spirit of God breathes through the combined intelligence of the people." Transcending nightmares, "humanity has always been on the advance, gaining maturity, universality, and power." Emerson preached the "infinite of the private man," the doctrine that "the individual is the world." Out of this belief he hoped to see the rediscovery of the hero, who would release the energies and possibilities of his witnesses. But "no individual" is "great, except through the general"; justice must be done to "the unexpressed greatness of the common farmer and laborer." The man of the age was the workingman. Through him, nature would be humanized, "until the landscape has human figures that are as good as itself." Emerson exhorted the common man: "Hitch your wagon to a star." To express this new life, what was needed was a national literature, an American scholar, a poet, who "shall draw us with love and terror, who sees through the flowing vest the firm nature, and can declare it."

In "The Significance of the Frontier in American History" (1893), Frederick Jackson Turner declared that "up to our own day American history has been in a large degree the history of the colonization of the Great West. The existence of an area of free land, its continuous recession, and the advance of American settlement westward" explain the development of American character. The Midwest, particularly, he said in another Dream essay, could be for America "what the Mediterranean Sea was to the Greeks," for "if the ideals of the pioneers shall survive the inundation of material success, we may expect to see in the Middle West the rise of a highly intelligent society where culture shall be reconciled with democracy in the large." But just as the romantic Pathfinder had surmounted the last and highest of the mountain barriers, the eastern machine invaded the western garden. And Turner delivered an elegy: "And now, four centuries from the discovery of America, at the end of a hundred years of life under the Constitution, the frontier has gone, and with its going has closed the first period of American history." If the hopeful, innocent frontiersman and homesteader were twin American Adams before the fall, the spidery railroad, which Thoreau heard at Walden, was the diabolical source of knowledge. Now easterners could exploit the West without ever having been frontiersmen or homesteaders, and the sons of frontiersmen and homesteaders could return East where dreams were realized more easily. Believing that the material progress of America caused most people to "live lives of quiet desperation," Thoreau, exemplifying the influence of Oriental mysticism upon American Dreams, said yes to the spirit: "Be a Columbus to whole new continents and worlds within you, opening new channels, not of trade, but of thought" (*Walden*, 1854).

Despite dominant phases of nightmare, many voices have continued to speak of the American Dream of ideal democracy as a constant process working toward reality. For them, the rise of industrialism created a new source of energy, making other and perhaps even greater achievements possible; perhaps the old frontier values of individuality and self-reliance would continue to operate in new forms in a modern technological civilization. Walt Whitman's inner spirit, unlike Thoreau's, reached out to the masses in a collective dream vision: "One's self I sing, a simple separate person, / Yet utter the word Democratic, the word Enmasse." If Columbus' own life ended in nightmare, Whitman commemorated the fact that "Centuries after thou art laid in thy grave, / The shore thou foundest verifies thy dream." Although in *Democratic Vistas* (1871) Whitman lamented America's failure to fulfill its promises, he declared: "I raise the present on the past and project the history of the future." Some true believers have seen American dynamism as the source of an ideal of perpetual change and renewal, of an extended genesis for the American Adam. In *The Bridge* (1930), Hart Crane, feeling that he was Whitman's witness and successor, said no to Spengler's *Decline of the West* and Eliot's *Waste Land* visions; Whitman's heroic spirit guided Crane's epic poem: "thy vision is reclaimed!" Living his own personal nightmare while writing the poem, Crane was not blind to the encompassing nightmare: "Dream cancels dream in this new realm of fact." Technology sends man underground, daily, in the subway, but the Word is made flesh in the bridge. From the same window where Roebling, the visionary architect and engineer, watched its construction, Crane contemplated the mythic meaning of the bridge that vaulted "the prairie's dreaming sod" as it flowed into the sea: "Unto us lowliest sometimes sweep, descend / And of the curveship lend a myth to God." The Brooklyn Bridge is one of our many mythic icons, and Crane's epic poem, which both soars and sinks because of its subjective contraries, is one of the most sublime attempts in the machine age to embody the myth in an "aesthetic image." Thomas Wolfe kept the Whitman Dream mission alive, though he, even more than Whitman and Crane, was himself at the center of his song and perhaps saw the nightmare more consistently than either. In his focus essay, C. Hugh Holman sees Wolfe's last novel, *You Can't Go Home Again* (1940), as an expression of the conflict between "Agrarian Dream and Industrial Nightmare." It is in this novel that Wolfe's vision of America is most succinctly declared: "I believe that we are lost here in America, but I believe we shall be found. And this belief . . . is . . . America's everlasting, living dream. . . . I think the true discovery of America is before us."

It is certainly true that the voice of most serious American literature since the Industrial Revolution got rolling has been a thunderous NO to the machine as a fabricator of American Dreams. But from the beginning, American Dreams have been based on fact: the factual results of exploration, of the frontier experience, of the invention of the steam engine, of the building of railroads and bridges, the perfection of space rockets—and of the invention of the motion-picture camera and projector and of the radio, disseminators of facts and fantasies. Certain dreams and nightmares are peculiar to periods in which ships dominate, in which trails or wagons or railroads or automobiles or airplanes dominate. In the pursuit of both the best and the worst of dreams, American pragmatism and idealism have interacted, producing nightmares in public fact not quite as persistently as in literary vision. The American dreamer is unique among dreamers, for he has often, by necessity or inner compulsion, been a doer. Boone, Roebling, and Lindbergh were dreamers but they were practical and peculiarly American dreamers. Individual inventors and scientific experimenters have stimulated material manifestations of the American Dream. Inventions that appear nightmarish to "atheists" have eventually fostered temporary reinvigorations of the Dream. The Great American Desert was a nightmare myth until the railroad transformed part of it into an actual garden and traversed the barren western plains to reach another garden on the western coast.

Capitalizing on the work of other materialists, such as the explorers and inventors, businessmen too, say some true believers, have contributed to the American Dream, positively as well as in Babbitt booster rhetoric. Seen from one angle of vision, the business spirit produced "a success myth that was a grand but impossible dream" (Kenneth Lynn, *The Dream of Success*, 1955). Periods of great natural abundance coupled with commercial ebullience have stimulated the active pursuit of *attainable* American Dreams. But the fact is that few American poets or novelists of stature have spoken *for* this spirit. The voice of the American businessman—his social, political, cultural values—has been popular culture, with its various business-controlled, mass-media organs. A century old now, the Horatio Alger novels, though no longer read, still exert their influence through the mass media.

In our higher culture, who speaks for democratic capitalism, the major Dream force in America today? The strongest voice, among the very few that speak in novels with the slightest claim to critical attention, is, unfortunately, Ayn Rand's. In *The Virtue of Selfishness* (1964), Rand insists that "the term 'individual rights' is a redundancy; there is no other kind of rights and no one else to possess them. Those who advocate laissez faire capitalism are the only advocates of man's rights." In *The Fountainhead* (1943) architect Howard Roark declares: "A self-sufficient ego. Nothing else matters." "The world is perishing from an orgy of self-sacrificing. I recognize no obligations toward men except one: to respect their freedom and to take no part in a slave society." This is the Dream-rhetoric of the rugged individualist—who causes, say many atheists and agnostics, most of our collective nightmares. In *Atlas Shrugged* (1957), Howard Roark's spiritual twin brother John Galt, leading men of genius in a strike against a world of "second-raters" and "victims," answers that charge: "If there is more tragic a fool than the businessman who doesn't know that he's an exponent of man's highest creative spirit—it's the artist who thinks that the businessman is his enemy." Rand's is a coldly visionary and pseudophilosophical view of the success of capitalism and its ideal potential. Amazement, not blasphemy, makes me couple Norman Podhoretz, editor of the liberal Jewish weekly *Commentary*, with Ayn Rand. He expressed a new honesty about our attitudes toward material success and literary fame in his autobiography *Making It* (1967). "A contempt for success is the consensus of the national literature for the past hundred years and more," but the intellectuals' and artists' own desire to achieve success is a "dirty little secret." It is strange indeed to discover Saul Bellow indicting the American intellectual in words startlingly similar to those of Ayn Rand. (Compare pages 386–87, 392 of the Fawcett paperback edition of *Herzog* [1964] with page 4 of *For the New Intellectual* [1961].) Such parallel conclusions drawn from essentially opposed sensibilities help to explain the confusion in our understanding of contemporary American literature.

For many years during the Industrial Revolution, one constant source of reinvigoration of the Dream, almost as potent as experiencing one frontier after another, was the waves of immigrants that pounded against our eastern shores. Each wave of immigrants experienced a miniature recapitulation of American history. "Each man," remarked G. K. Chesterton, "discovers America for himself." American possibilities reinvigorated tired Europeans, and their sons invested the American Dream with new hope. Though hordes of immigrants perished in vast urban nightmares, many individuals contributed to the industrial and business Dream-machine and introduced new forces and notions into the Dream process. In *The American: The Making of a New Man* (1943), popular historian James Truslow Adams (whom Allan Nevins in in his recent biography calls "the historian of the American Dream") said, "America has been the great adventure" for the millions of immigrants, "not all of them understanding the meaning of the American Dream. Yet on the whole, although the material which the spirit of America has had to work with has been the common, not the uncommon, man, it has been the sort of common man who has glimpsed in the 'New World' a really *new world* in which he could throw off the trammels of the Old and rise to his full stature as a man." On this extraordinary landscape, common men expected the extraordinary of themselves.

Most of the great migrations within America were forced marches propelled by nightmare conditions. The Cherokee Indians, marching to Oklahoma along the Wilderness Road, fell into even blacker nightmare. But often, migrants fled a nightmare in pursuit of a dream—as did Steinbeck's Okies. The migration of the individual dreamer who leaves the small town by train or bus or by hitchhiking is the most common sort in American literature, from *Winesburg, Ohio* (1919), the archetype for such stories, to *North Toward Home* (1968), in which Willie Morris, thirty-three-year-old editor of *Harper's Magazine*, chronicles his own migration in pursuit of fame and fortune; dreaming of a cultural utopia, the intellectual liberal southerner migrates North. *Moving on*, a major act in the American experience, is being replaced today by the cop-out.

In various historical periods, each region has contributed its own version of the American Dream (based often on an outmoded Old World model): New England and Virginia during the periods of settlement and colonization and during the Revolutionary War, the frontiers during the periods of exploration, the South before the Civil War, and the Midwest since 1900. Climate and geography have been significant factors in determining the way a region contributes to the national character. W. J. Cash, in *The Mind of the South* (1941), observed: "There was the influence of the Southern physical world—itself a sort of cosmic conspiracy against reality in favor of romance." The contributions of the humid South and of the cold North, of the Mississippi River and the Appalachian Mountains to the formation of the American character is no less fascinating for being obvious. American landscapes transform American inscapes, as many of the novels of Wright Morris, a Nebraskan, show. In *The Great Plains* (1931) Walter Prescott Webb conceptualized the historical contrast between one kind of landscape and another: "east of the Mississippi civilization stood on three legs—land, water, and timber; west of the Mississippi not one but two of these legs were withdrawn,—water and timber,—and civilization was left on one leg—land." But the influence of physical and social regionalism as a force affecting the character of American Dreams and nightmares is a thing of the historical past. With the dawn of the Moon Age, one wonders what prospects exist in outer space for a renaissance, a transformation of the Dream-as-nightmare into a new Dream.

In the history of America, the phrase "a sense of the past" has meant many things. Looking back today, many atheists interpret the past as a series of nightmares, culminating in Dallas, Memphis, Los Angeles, Chicago, Vietnam. But the past is both fact *and* symbol, reality *and* myth; Americans lived *one* past and willed, through acts of imagination and faith, another. At times the brevity of our past and the shallowness of our traditions have made Americans exaggerate their importance. In *The Inhabitants* (1946), Wright Morris says: "There never was a people who tried so hard—and left so little behind as we do. There never was a people who travelled so light—and carried so much." But if the memory of a hopeful, Dream-dominated past has blinded some yea-sayers to present realities, the American Dream temperament has generally searched for a *usable* past, while trying to avoid an abuse of the past. Americans have always asked, What next?—more inclined to dream into the future than to rest upon traditions of the past. Alluding to the works of Melville, Poe, Twain, Faulkner, Nathanael West, Nabokov, Barth, Eliot, and Hemingway, Leslie Fiedler discusses this phenomenon in his essay "The Dream of the New."

One thing that kept American Dreams flourishing at a time when America had no substantial history or tradition but was only a historical process, was oratory—political, evangelical, and then cultural—and, later, in the early labor movements, social reform oratory. The force of rhetoric casts a spell over the listener and beguiles him into acting; in American history, word and act functioned simultaneously, because America's changing civilization was always on the move, and saying it was like reaching for it.

The thunderous NO's charge that there has been one dream in the rhetoric, another in the action. If serious fiction has, in the main, been an indictment of American society for its failure to translate the Dream into reality, or for its obstinate pursuit of the wrong dreams, popular culture has been the multifaceted medium of American sunlit daydreams. Our journalistic nonfiction, our travel literature, our exploration journals, our advertising certainly, often affirm the validity of American Dreams. Popular fiction, as only one arm of the octopus of mass culture, has been an affirmation of the Dream, though not necessarily of the realities of materialism. Western novels, and the more universally popular cowboy movies, affirm the heroic past; the cowboy movie is our export Dream image (its obverse is the gangster movie), and the intensity of its acceptance in Europe and Asia reinforces our own submission to the mythic image. Our popular war novels reaffirm the Dream. Leon Uris' *Battle Cry* expresses one aspect of the American national Dream, just as his *Exodus* expresses the national dream of another young nation. If the popular escape novel (the historical romance, the detective novel, the religious novel) is an indirect affirmation that all is well, it is, simultaneously, an unconscious declaration that conditions exist from which we must escape.

Listening to atheists of the American Dream, we hear that if the American Adam is not pure myth, he has certainly fallen, he has lost his chance to regain paradise, there is no redemption, no resurrection. To the atheist, the suburbanite is simply the logical nightmare dead end of the frontiersman, the farmer, the simple laborer. The Civil War, the closing of the frontier, the Industrial Revolution, America's wars and depressions, the technological and the present electronic revolutions have caused actual nightmares that only illusory dreams have softened. The Great American Adventure has become the Great American Monotony, while the Great American Desert continues to exist where it *always* has, within each individual. In his play *Christopher Columbus* (1927), Michel Ghelderode, one of many who offer us the foreigner's vision of the nightmare, has Columbus say much the same thing in symbolic terms: "I shall return to the very place from which I set out, because the earth is round." Today, the atheist looks back upon the concept of the Green Breast of the New World, the virgin land, and sees its end in California, continent's end, where bizarre inversions and apings of the worst of the eastern wasteland culture proliferate.

The atheist sings songs not of innocence but of experience, of bitter knowledge. He intones a variable black mass:

Pastoral ideals and the Second Chance for mankind in a new Eden have been defeated by a nightmare of closed systems and electronic preclusions; human resources have gone from budding to blight.

America has gone from a time of explorers to a time of tourists, with Polaroid snapshots.

America has gone through a century of cultural mobility, followed by fifty years of stasis, ending in our present paralysis.

The Dream of Empire has resulted in the rape of natural resources and the nemesis of the Dust Bowl and the Silent Spring.

America as a nation has gone from the concept of service and progress to mere production as an end in itself.

Individuals once acted out the national experience, but the loneliness of the mass man, the organization man, prevails today; grand-scale scientific research has replaced the individual inventor and experimenter.

In the conflict between material and nonmaterial dreams, the spirit always loses, and one's daily consciousness pursues material success as though that could satisfy all a man's dreams.

Even those who make the Horatio Alger dream come true become restless, heartsick, ulcer- and anxiety-ridden.

The abundant wilderness shaped American character, encouraging dreams; but today's limited aspirations cramp the spirit.

America's visible and invisible class structures shape false dreams and actual nightmares.

Men on trails, dirt roads, even on macadam, could dream, but men confined to sidewalks and superhighways are submerged in nightmares.

The large families of the farms, villages, and small towns nurtured abortive dreams, but dispersion of the family has resulted in discord in suburbia and the megalopolis; American cities were once mere camps in the wilderness, but now the urban novel indicts the Dream for spawning nightmares with assembly-line regularity and efficiency.

The religious impulse to the Dream has often been pernicious in its effects.

The little red schoolhouse was the temple of phony dreams, but mass education and the multiversity can only produce nightmares of conformity and desperate rebellion.

The obsession with novelty, the general aversion to antiquity, the haste to be first are contemptible traits in the American character.

Commitment to false dreams has resulted in indifference, withdrawal, cop-outs, disaffiliation, alienation.

America's past sense of mission and purpose was hollow enough, but today she strives only to maintain her image and prestige through rationalization and self-justification;

the transcendental ideal became manifest destiny and has now become international responsibility, with its concomitant homicidal hypocrisies.

In its wars, at home and abroad, America's apparent invincibility could only encourage impossible dreams and occasion overreaching redefinitions, while the atheist has always been aware of the nightmare consequences.

The violence—military, social, criminal, racial—in American history is so dominant that Father Groppi and Rap Brown could say in the summer of 1967 that "violence is as American as apple pie."

All these facets of the American Dream were once most effectively elaborated in religious and political oratory, then in newspapers, but now it is public relations agencies, advertising and TV (with its pseudo and predicted events) that disseminate the Dream seeds, most of them dead; the "American experiment" has failed, and the American adventure is confined to the TV and movie screens.

In the years before mass communication, Americans *lived* history, but the mass media are merely news-gathering, and, more and more often, newsmaking forces.

Dreams, ideals, visions, myths, legends are now easily exposed as nightmares, frauds in disguise. Symbol has been raped by fact, and computerspeak will replace symbol-expression.

The worship of success has so sickened the atheist that he can only make a cult of failure, and cultivate such preachments as the preceding.

How has the average American lived with and endured beyond these nightmare contradictions of the Dream through phase after phase of our history? In "Gift to the World," the general essay that concludes this volume, Oscar Cargill examines the Dream concept in the attitudes of the average American regarding world events of recent years. Louis Filler examines even darker machinations of the public mind in "Machiavelli for the Millions: Some Notes on Power Structures," and provides a broad political and cultural background for the more literary essays.

Today, says the atheist, the world looks to "the American Dream bed" as the place where demons writhe in nightmares of technology—bombs and napalm—though, reluctantly, the atheist admits that the Apollo exploits are exciting; and now it is not America alone, but Europe and Asia that wake up screaming. Perhaps agnostic F. Scott Fitzgerald, who didn't survive his personal crack-up, described the atheist's version of American history when he said of himself in *The Crack-Up* (1945): "I began to realize that for two years my life had been drawing on resources that I did not possess, that I had been mortgaging myself physically and spiritually up to the hilt. What was the small gift of life given back in comparison to that?—when there had once been a pride of direction and a confidence in enduring independence."

Since Hawthorne, the atheist has proclaimed that Puritanistic, Calvinistic concepts of evil and sin poisoned most American Dreams and condoned nightmares from the beginning, so that there never was a natural innocence. From the inception of one of the first historical nightmares—the Industrial Revolution—the epic American Dream vision was offset by the visions of men like Hawthorne, Melville, and Poe, who explored inner hells and nightmares. "From childhood's hour" they saw clouds "that took the form . . . of demons in [their] view." With close scrutiny of single works by Cooper, Irving, Poe, Hawthorne, and Melville, Irving Malin analyzes a distinct manifestation of the Dream, "The Compulsive Design." In a focus essay, Marvin Fisher sees Melville's "The Two Temples" as expressing "The Denigration of the American Dream." Maxwell Geismar's essay, "The Shifting Illusion: Dream and Fact," surveys the Dream concept in American literature past and present.

Henry Adams in his *Education* (1907) compared two kingdoms of force: the Virgin (Love) and the Dynamo (Power). "To Adams the dynamo became a frightening symbol of infinity. . . . Before the end, one began to pray to it." "All the steam in the world could not, like the Virgin, build Chartres." But it could provide raw material for atheist writers, reacting against it, insisting that the dream of love has been raped by the nightmare power of the dynamo. In the Gilded Age, when rugged individualism was paying off for a few individuals, even the winning of success had its horrors, as Henry James showed in his depiction of Newman, the wealthy American businessman abroad: "It was our friend's eye that chiefly told his story; an eye in which innocence and experience were singularly blended." "You are the great Western Barbarian, stepping forth in all his innocence and might, gazing a while at this poor effete Old World, and then swooping down on it." And so on, and on, page after page—insights into American character and Dream, from the American who *seemed* to have turned his back on America.

Over the cult of success hovers always the specter of failure on lower levels. Dreiser, editor of *Smith's Magazine*, which published stories in the manner of Horatio Alger and Frank Merriwell and other popular founts of American Dreams, *believed*, apparently, in the grand and impossible success myth, but recorded nightmare disillusionment when social injustice and a cruel environment prevented common people such as Clyde Griffiths in *An American Tragedy* (1925) from realizing it. The classic expression in the short story of the common man's dream of success is Sherwood Anderson's "The Egg" (1921). "The American passion for getting up in the world took possession of them," the narrator says of his parents. "[Mother] read of how Garfield, Lincoln, and other Americans rose from poverty to fame and greatness and as I lay beside her—in the days of her lying in—she may have dreamed that I would some day rule men and cities." The anonymous narrator himself "dreamed I was a tiny thing going along the road into a far beautiful place where there were no chicken farms and where life was a happy eggless affair." The nightmare dead-end evolution of Anderson's go-getter is Willy Loman. Chester Eisinger examines Arthur Miller's *Death of a Salesman* (1949) as a play about "Wrong Dreams."

The concept of the American Dream gone wrong is reflected in politically oriented social protest literature—the proletarian novel of the thirties, for instance—and, paradoxically, in purposeless tough guy violence as well. In some popular fiction, a critique of the American Dream is submerged. The tough guy novel seems to offer mere escapist violence, but it is also a negative picture of the present, balancing the Western's dream-vision of the past. Crime, real and fictive, testifies to the volcanic vitality of submerged nightmare. Look at America during the Depression through the eyes of the tough guy: the mobster in Ira Wolfert's *Tucker's People* (1943); the hard-boiled private eye in Dashiell Hammett's *Red Harvest* (1929) and in Raymond Chandler's *Farewell, My Lovely* (1940). For Chandler, L. A.

represented the American scene as "the Great Wrong Place." In *Serenade* (1937), *Mildred Pierce* (1941), and *Double Indemnity* (1936), James M. Cain depicted the high hopes of the romantic, violent, dramatic westward movement collapsing on the Pacific shore. Lacking the context of significance that "justified" the proletarian novels, Cain's novels show the failure of the Dream by a camera-cold recording of the nightmare of the thirties. The simplest Dream fable is *The Postman Always Rings Twice* (1934). Frank's and Cora's extreme insecurity accounts in part for their lack of conscience; somewhat like Bonnie and Clyde, they lay down in "the great American Dream bed" of the lurid twenties, only to wake up in a living nightmare in the thirties.

Poverty, of course, has always contradicted the Dream of Success. Many novels and movies have come out of the various American migratory exoduses; the classic proletarian novel of the migratory worker in the thirties is Jack Conroy's autobiographical novel *The Disinherited* (1933), though *The Grapes of Wrath* (1939) is better known. Today, the laborer who became a union man and through violence and deprivation opposed the boss faces the anonymous nightmare of automation. For most of the hopeful immigrants fleeing European poverty, America became a nightmare of ironies. Even some of the anarchist, socialist, and communist immigrants came to America believing in the dream of freedom, equality, justice. Perhaps, they expected, as in a dream, a sudden utopian realization of all the ideals the European nightmare had spawned. The disillusionment must have been brutal, and thus some returned to anarchist activities. Other immigrants, stunned by disillusionment, drifted into crime. Michael Gold said, in his autobiographical novel *Jews Without Money* (1930): "It is America that has taught the sons of tubercular Jewish tailors how to kill." "America is so rich and fat, because it has the tragedy of millions of immigrants." Those who survived the melting-pot experience eventually became acculturated; the vitality and freshness of the waves of immigrants no longer stimulates the Dream. Jules Chametzky discusses Abraham Cahan's *The Rise of David Levinsky* (1917), one of many immigrant novels, as a bitter tale of success.

From the beginning, the Indian and the Negro have been

the most visible contradictions of the Dream. While Ken Kesey's *One Flew Over the Cuckoo's Nest* (1962) is not primarily a depiction of the plight of the present-day Indian, his allegorical use of the Indian who tells the story results in a nightmarish image of the American-as-Indian. Most of the literature of the Negro since Richard Wright has been a literature of overt protest, of the outsider saying NO in Thunder to the American Dream fraud. The dominant Negro response to the Dream today comes from James Baldwin, Eldridge Cleaver, and LeRoi Jones. But the finest novel by a Negro is still Ralph Ellison's *Invisible Man* (1952); it concludes that to achieve individual selfhood is more imperative than defining oneself positively or negatively in terms of a public myth. "I am nobody but myself. But first I had to discover that I am an invisible man." Ellison says of himself as a novelist, "I wasn't, and am not, *primarily* concerned with injustice, but with art." Allen Guttmann's essay focuses upon *Invisible Man* as a novel about "the American Nightmare." In "Choice: Ironic Alternatives in the World of the Contemporary American Novel," Alvin Greenberg examines Ellison's along with many other contemporary novels.

Many atheists escaped the dream-machine to Europe, the mother of nightmares. Henry James came back to America and gave his account of the return of the creative native in *The American Scene* (1907). He observed "the trudging silences of the universal will to move, move, move, as an end in itself." "What was the case but magnificent for pitiless ferocity?" One of the bitterest views of the American urban nightmare is expressed in exile Henry Miller's autobiographical books. In his essay "Henry Miller's American Dream," Alan Trachtenberg looks at Miller as a man making "history on the side."

If some American writers — James, Hemingway, Eliot, Miller — exiled themselves from "the American Dream cheat" to Europe by a physical escape, others on the American scene itself escaped by withdrawing into themselves. Since the forties, two trends have been converging: the literary tendency to render the subjective life of adolescents (*A Member of the Wedding, Other Voices, Other Rooms, A Catcher in the Rye*); and the cultural tendency to indulge, if not to worship, youth as a virtue in itself. All frontiers of the American outer experience being defunct, outer space reminds us of the saharas of inner space. The shock of the nightmare of everyday life in adolescence forces a mental withdrawal. In the forties, this was a Poe-like withdrawal, into fantasy and gothic subjectivism. Generally, the subjective novel constitutes a rejection of the striving that the cult of success dictates. When they reveal themselves in outward behavior, these outsiders suffer social ostracism; but usually they are harmless enough, and tolerated.

But other sorts of outsiders, the dope addict and the alcoholic, are not tolerated: fleeing the bland, banal nightmare of everyday, standardized, conformist American life, he inflicts upon himself a nightmare that is both physical and mental. William Burroughs' vision of America, *Naked Lunch* (1959), is as fantastic in a way as Edgar Rice Burroughs' visions of Mars. Frederic I. Carpenter sees Eugene O'Neill's *The Iceman Cometh* as a brutally ironic play in which the iceman has already come for the disillusioned alcoholics.

The beat generation writers of the 1950's, last of the old-fashioned romantics, banded together in small groups and set out upon Whitman's open road, escaping false American Dream values and civilization by encountering the sort of experiences that only the American road can provide. In *On the Road* (1955), Jack Kerouac, a transitional figure between the true believers and the agnostics, is a witness to the hero, Dean Moriarty, one of the last American "frontiersmen." Many beat outsiders, looking in, saw only nightmare, and saw themselves and their friends as persecuted victims of "square" orthodoxy. Allen Ginsberg howls: "I saw the best minds of my generation destroyed by madness. . . . angelheaded hipsters burning for the ancient heavenly connection / to the starry dynamo in the machinery of night." "Nightmare of Moloch. . . . Moloch who frightened me out of my natural ecstasy." Kerouac's Dean Moriarty becomes Ginsberg's Carl Solomon; hero and witness are both helpless victims of a nightmare conspiracy against the dream of love. Like "Howl" (1956), Hubert Selby's *Last Exit to Brooklyn* (1964) and John Rechy's *City of Night* (1963) not only describe sexual perversion and debasement, but project a larger nightmare vision of America—the "real" you and me. If Transcendentalists made use of Oriental mysticism to prophesy America's Dream future in the realm of the spirit, in the late fifties and early sixties the beat generation used Buddhism, along with jazz and narcotics, as a means of dropping out of the success rat race.

From Queen Elizabeth, in the early era of exploration, to the Statue of Liberty, who proved to be Mom in a bedsheet carrying not a torch but a knife for castration, a woman has often personified the Dream for the man. But Gatsby's Daisy proves to be a bitch goddess of success. By girls like her, the hero in pursuit of his dream is betrayed, as in Norman Mailer's *An American Dream* (1964). Sex and marriage have provided many of the obstacles to the male's realization of the Dream, and it is the wife, the mom, the girl, who often precipitates him into nightmare. On a popular level, America experienced the dream of sexual freedom in historical undress in *Forever Amber* (1944), a franker version of *Gone with the Wind* (1936), but today this freedom is used mainly to prove how pagan the all-American virgin's libido really is. In *Lolita* (1955), Nabokov provided us with insights into the American girl as nymphet. "It was she who seduced me," says the middle-aged, world-weary European, Humbert Humbert. "Gradually the odd sense of living in a brand new, mad new dream world, where everything was permissible, came over me." *Lolita* is not just a vision of Candy before her time, but a black-comedy critique of American mass culture as well. *Candy* (1964) is Terry Southern's pornographic black satire on the mythic innocence of the American child virgin. In *The American Dream* (1961) Edward Albee presented Candy's spiritual brother and translated Philip Wylie's preachments about monarchy into absurdist terms. Grandma says to the athletic young man: "You're the American Dream, that's what you are." A perfect specimen physically, a blank mentally and spiritually, he is Mom's invention, Dad's abortion. When the dreaming male was an active hero, conquering the wide-open spaces, the female was subservient—so the story goes, as told by atheists—but now, disillusioned with the equal status she has finally secured, the American female is out to get revenge on the male for abdicating his supremacy in the American Eden.

The Western tall tales and frontier humor and sidewalk wisecracks that enabled dreamers to endure and survive heartbreak, nightmare, and disillusionment, gave way to the topical satire of Sinclair Lewis, who announced, "Main Street is the climax of civilization." In his essay, James C. Austin sees Sinclair Lewis' humor, influenced by humor in western newspapers, as a kind of antidote to the nightmare. Today, the nightmare is so visible and oppressive that humor, too, must be pushed hysterically to the limit. Satire degenerates into put-down ridicule, Barbara Garson's *MacBird!* (1967); sick humor, Ronald Tavel's *Gorilla Queen* (1967); black comedy, Michael McClure's *The Beard* (1968); and absurd comedy, Arthur Kopit's *Oh Dad, Poor Dad* (1960). Frontier tall talk was a source of legendary history about heroes; gossip columns about heroes created by press agents have taken over that function for the masses. American Dreams were born out of traditional forms of expression—folk as well as institutional—but the iconoclasm that has dissolved those so-called hollow forms leaves no forms, no norms at all, nothing but eclectic, camp gestures, expressive almost exclusively of the nightmare—though often satire masks sentimentality and nihilism masks nostalgia.

In Greenwich Village bohemia of the twenties, in the San Francisco beat renaissance of the fifties, avant-garde experimentalism sought new forms of expression to make one strident statement—that America is a nightmare of mistakes, and the only good American is a dead American. But the hippie subculture dispenses with all forms of individual expression and retreats into herd warmth by such means as LSD. Atheists to the Dream have consistently charged that technology would transform us all into robots in a civilization where everything comes easily with the simple push of a button. But agnostics would argue that use of the easy, instant nirvana of LSD is the cop-out of a robot. The beats were hero-witnesses to each other as they moved across the American landscape, hounded by inner and outer nightmares; but hippies and yippies, moving across an internal landscape of synthetic love, are more inclined to worship nonheroes and victims. The beatnik's open road dead-ends in hippie camps. The hippie movement has produced few individuals—Bob Dylan and Joan Baez are transitional figures— few poets, few novelists; it has produced mainly mass singer-groups, and group, corporate theatre efforts, such as New York's Open Theatre, which presented *America Hurrah* (1967), a satire of the Dream. Product of middle-class suburban conformity, the hippie is the banal conformist in disguise. Few poor slum kids and few Negroes run with them. Hippies are sedentary; theirs is a community-living culture, basically similar to suburbia.

This is the generation raised on Salinger's *Catcher in the Rye* (1951), Golding's *Lord of the Flies* (1955), and Tolkien's fantasies. But one can cite no single book that all kids are reading today. Instead, there are electronically augmented songs for the push-button generation. Music in America has always expressed both dreams and nightmares: Negro spirituals, folk songs, country music, blues, jazz, protest songs, and, not least, popular songs, but hand in hand with the new seriousness comes a new sentimentality of vicarious depression and artificial sensuality. As a medium of popular culture, fast becoming a serious art form as well, the cinema has always reflected and sometimes criticized the American Dream temperament: *Greed* (1923); *A Modern Hero* (1934); *Mr. Deeds Goes to Town* (1936), *Mr. Smith Goes to Washington* (1939), and other Frank Capra movies; *The Great McGinty* (1940); *Grapes of Wrath* (1940); *Sullivan's Travels* (1941); *Kings Row* (1941); *The Best Years of Our Lives* (1946); *All the King's Men* (1949); *The Hustler* (1961); *Bonnie and Clyde* (1967); *The Graduate* (1968); *2001: A Space Odyssey* (1969). Atheists listen eagerly to the voices of doom and despair in the darker of these and other movies; such films encourage alienation postures that turn away from "the American Dream cheat" and reassure atheists that all effort and aspirations, even rebellious, Icarus-like flights toward the sun, are futile.

Ginsberg has *his* vision of the World War II generation. But others saw the best minds of their generation infatuated with defeat and despair, embracing the antihero, celebrating suicide as self-justification, opposing the square's enslavement to false American Dreams by submitting to Moloch in an ecstasy of self-immolation, thrilling to every manifestation of nightmare. At a time when man has walked on the moon (for the early romantic hero the symbol of his imagination's flight), many American writers wallow in the labyrinth, whining in the shadow of the minotaur. They assert their existence mainly as victims of the nightmare; their identity is defined mainly in terms of the false dreams they oppose.

Does a nightmare threaten *every* dream? Haven't some

dreams come true? Many critics of "the American Dream cheat" aggravate the nightmare which they claim is produced by *the others*. Writers who criticize only in black terms the capitalistic, middle-class society were shaped by that society, took their values from it, especially when they were kids— fed on children's books and mass-media popular culture— and possibly, they still believe in most of the values, but react against the fact that many people in power fail to personify those values. Atheists criticize the idealism of the Dream itself. But by criticizing the dreamers for failing to make the Dream come true, they suggest that they, also, believe in the Dream. Confusion for dreamer and critic results. It is often those who want to believe in the Dream, but most intensely see the impossibility of making it come true, who wish to see the Dream immolated in nightmare. Ironically, the intellectual, being American, must see *results*, even for thinking; and in taking greatest delight, perhaps sublimated sexual delight, in destruction—which is quicker than creation—he is *most* American. In a sense, the dreamer turned revolutionary is the worst sort of materialist. Impatient, irrational, impulsive, heedless, he is the twin brother of that ugly, success-mongering American who is interested more in immediate results than in morality and immutable ideals. Serious American literature readily exposes the fraudulence of the "spiritual" and ethical rhetoric that various institutions spout in the service of meretricious dreams; but it is much more difficult for students of literature to detect instances of fraud and hypocrisy in the alienation rhetoric of liberal intellectuals, as Norman Podhoretz points out in his much-maligned, despised, and resented autobiography. Long ago, in "Earth's Holocaust," Hawthorne, himself a nay-sayer, warned against the surrender of the intellectual, of the artist, to the power of blackness. "If we go no deeper than the intellect, and strive, with merely that feeble instrument, to discern and rectify what is wrong, our whole accomplishment will be a dream, so unsubstantial that it matters little whether the bonfire . . . were what we choose to call a real event and a flame that would scorch the finger, or only a phosphoric radiance and a parable of my own brain."

The American Dream, negatively or positively, affects lives; it is in *that* way *real*. And so is the nightmare, for the rhetoric that promotes the nightmare affects the sensibilities of those who write and speak it as well as those who consume it. Word has a way of becoming flesh. "Words are also actions," said Emerson. "To think is to act." Saying it *can* make it so. Hayakawa talks of the "self-fulfilling prophecy." Serious literature, like popular literature, is full of lies, distortions, and half-truths. Examining a typical issue of the *Reader's Digest*, one may laugh at the pandering pro-American Dream endings to all the articles, but can one deny that the *New Republic* and the *New York Review of Books* are just as predictable in the way they flatter the assumptions, preclusions, and prejudices of their own dedicated readers?

Of course, no is often a hysterical way of saying yes, as every has-been virgin remembers. One may scream no out of an impotence to overcome the forces that prevent yes from becoming flesh. To the man who knows that trying to make the Dream come true is more difficult than surrendering to the nightmare, opportunities for easy, moral one-upmanship are very attractive.

What is the psychological basis for the development of dreams and nightmares? What in human nature explains the flowering and withering of American Dreams? What in man wilfully perverts the Dream into nightmare? What, even in the most fervent dreamer, prevents realization of the Dream, or even wishes it to fail and celebrates its decline or death? These are, of course, the most difficult questions of all, for American Dreams and nightmares begin in the psychological makeup of *individuals*. Carson McCullers' *The Heart Is a Lonely Hunter* (1940), the work of a twenty-one-year-old dreamer, is a lucid and prophetic demonstration of the universal psychological and spiritual dilemma that prevents the individual American's dream from coming true.

Is it only that the nightmare eclipses the Dream, or can the Dream also eclipse the nightmare? If particular dreams provoke concomitant nightmares, perhaps particular nightmares stimulate dreams. Does the nightmare always kill off the Dream or might it not, in some instances, keep the Dream alive, or do both simultaneously, and thus keep it in suspension, dangling, or paralyzed, rather than render it entirely defunct? American history has been a continuously dynamic experience actively involving America's various regions, groups, and races, so that some kinds of dreams and nightmares have been dominant in periods of storm and stress, others in periods of quiescence—"to sleep perchance to dream." In some phases of American history, dreams and nightmares interacted productively; in other phases confusion between dreams and nightmare prevailed.

One of the most powerful psychological sources of energy generating pursuit of both Dream and nightmare is *guilt*. What is the function of guilt over the treatment of minorities in the shaping of dreams and nightmares? Pursuing their own dreams, white men exterminated the Indians in the Wilderness, enslaved the Negroes to cultivate Eden, and mistreated the Jews who had been driven to refuge in American metropolises by European nightmares. The general guilt of the American over his infliction of nightmares upon others —including the bombing of Hiroshima to preserve a national Dream—can be a negative impetus to pursuit of the Dream, for public guilt may make a people feel obligated to achieve their nobler aspirations. *Private* guilt can be the mainspring for an *individual's* pursuit of his particular American Dream. We need to scrutinize the various forms of *expiation* for guilt to see how they function in the shaping of dreams and nightmares. A subtler problem is the function of guilt by complicity: the feeling that we all killed Lincoln and the Kennedys and Martin Luther King because we all helped produce Booth and the other assassins. And it may be profitable to study the various kinds of suicide in America and ask what dreams frustrated into nightmares they express. For instance, what does it mean that some suicides choose to plunge from the Empire State Building, others from the Brooklyn Bridge? Most of us may succumb to nightmare, but for a few, the interactions of guilt and expiation may work toward the realization of dreams. America's serious literature so far, however, has been mainly concerned with depicting the *nightmare* results of public and individual guilt.

It appears that there are two major American Dream myths: the Old Testament idea of a paradise hopelessly lost, followed by endless nightmare suffering; and the New Testament idea of a paradise that a new American Adam will eventually regain. Most serious fiction is slanted against the New Testament vision; hope for clear vision lies in the ambiguous area between Paradise Lost and Paradise Regained.

The agnostic dilemma lies in the struggle to avoid remaining in a suspended state, a moral and literary limbo. The agnostic asks, What is the role of the individual, the hero and his witness, in the American Dream process, compared with anonymous groups? There were, after all the debunking is done, genuine as well as merely legendary or bogus heroes in the American past: explorers, missionaries, and dreamers who were doers—Columbus, Washington, Boone, Crockett, Jefferson—to mention a few not yet forgotten names. The sixteenth, seventeenth, eighteenth centuries were times of legends; the nineteenth a time of biography—the lives of great men fascinated the witnesses who wanted to get easily what the heroes had earned through risk; and the twentieth century is appropriately a time of autobiography—mere witnesses must assert their reality at a time when history rejects the individual. The time of heroes and the time of mere celebrities, human pseudo-events—Gary Cooper, Marilyn Monroe—have passed. Now even celebrities can't survive the blinding glare of TV lights, the on-the-spot coverage wherever the group action is, or, inspired by the presence of cameras, might be. With the passing of the hero, precedence replaces the cult of experience as source of authority. Security and the computer mentality replace self-reliance and self-confidence. The individual was the vanguard of liberty, but equality produces the mass man and his desire for security. Out of the interaction between hero and witness in the past came dreams; but in a nightmare world of little men, witnesses produce only victim-mongering. What happens to energy, vitality, exuberance, enthusiasm, sheer joy—those heroic American qualities—when the opportunity for their expression is gone? The American past produced audacity and improvisation, but the present produces caution, standardization. Aggressiveness and competitiveness were perhaps the nightmare consequences of the reign of the rugged individualist, but a programmed career is hardly a dream come true. Many American intellectuals have rejected absolutes and embraced paradoxes and contradictions; but the resulting relative values encourage too often the gray mediocrity which is in even the best of us. What is the role of the group in the American Dream? Can groups dream? Can groups that dream act creatively *as groups*? Individualists wrecked early attempts at American utopias; perhaps now bland utopias, like powdered eggs, will be future realities. In the past, institutions—church, school, government, business, public groups—preached the Dream, and prohibited all suggestions of nightmare; even so, an insidious "Machia-

vellianism of the millions" kept the dynamic yea-nay ambiguity going. Yet in a future world without heroes and vil-
lains, we may all create together, and become caught in, one
undifferentiated Catch-22.

The agnostic's double vision informs most of the works of
Henry James and of Mark Twain. Among recent novelists,
Saul Bellow is an agnostic priest many years in the making.
As one looks at each of his novels in order, one perceives a
twenty-year struggle toward qualified affirmation. Norman
Mailer, when he functions best, screams advertisements for
himself. Though his latest works—*The Armies of the Night*
(1968) and his reports on the Miami and Chicago conventions of 1968—show him to be a prophet of the nightmare,
he strives to achieve the oldest American Dream of all: to be
rich, famous, and great. And to this agnostic hero, Norman
Podhoretz is a creative witness. "The only man . . . capable
of perfect honesty on the subject of success is Norman
Mailer." (*Making It*, said Podhoretz, is a "frank, Mailer-like
bid for literary distinction, fame, and money all in one
package.") In his essay on *Why Are We in Vietnam?*
(1967) Ihab Hassan employs an experimental form of criticism to evoke a sense of Mailer's dream-nightmare obsession.

The innocent American Adam must confront the machine
in the Garden and the serpent in the bosom and learn a sad
wisdom and the irony of experience. The agnostic priest
proclaims the *possibility* of redemption, resurrection, re-
creation out of the mature wisdom gained in Adam's fall
from noble savagehood. America may yet come of age.
F. Scott Fitzgerald, speaking in *The Crack-Up*, has the *word*:
"The test of a first-rate intelligence is the ability to hold two
opposed ideas in the mind at the same time and still retain
the ability to function." He failed that test in his life, but
passed it in one novel, *The Great Gatsby* (1925). Faulkner
passed it in "The Bear" (1942). Robert Penn Warren passed
it in his epic *All the King's Men* (1946), a synthesis of the
main strands of Dream and nightmare in *Gatsby* and "The
Bear." In his work generally, Wright Morris, more consistently than any other American writer, has passed this test.
And it is in Morris' novels that the dialectic of the hero-
witness relationship is most lucidly worked out. In sixteen
novels and three works of nonfiction, Wright Morris has developed a many-faceted, seriocomic vision of the American
Dream, landscape, and character.

One of the best ways to see the interaction of yes and no, true believer and atheist, is in the hero-witness relationship in two classic mythic expressions of the American Dream, *The Great Gatsby* and "The Bear." Wright Morris, in his commentary on classic American writers, *The Territory Ahead* (1956), says: "In Fitzgerald's *The Great Gatsby*, and I think only in *Gatsby*, the mythic vastness of this continent, the huge raw-material banquet that Wolfe bolted, received its baptismal blessing and its imaginative processing." Richard Lehan sees Gatsby as "The Nowhere Hero." Frank Kinahan examines Fitzgerald's *Tender Is the Night* (1934) as a "savage post-mortem" on the Dream. In his famous Nobel Prize speech two decades ago, Faulkner, in speaking against the atheist vision, revealed himself an agnostic. James B. Meriwether, in his preface to Faulkner's *Essays, Speeches, and Public Letters* (1965), says that "at one time William Faulkner planned a book of five or six related essays, to be called *The American Dream*. But he wrote only two chapters of it, 'On Privacy' and 'On Fear,' in 1955 and 1956." Frederic I. Carpenter declares that "in 'The Bear,' perhaps, the American myth has received its most conscious fictional embodiment. . . . the myth appears in all its ambiguity" (*American Literature and the Dream*, 1955). In his essay, Richard P. Adams sees Faulkner's "The Bear" as an allegory of "Moses and the Wilderness."

Writers such as Bellow, Mailer (at times), Fitzgerald, Faulkner, Warren, and Morris recognize the difference between what we dream and what we can expect to achieve. In the dynamic tensions between true believers, profound and shallow, and atheists, virile and anemic, functions the agnostic priest, who says: "To be given an outline, upon which you are free to improvise as your talents permit, is all the gift any man can expect of life." The American experiment has produced *both* Dreams and nightmares, and what we achieve or fail to achieve happens within the tensions, conflicts, and contraries between these polar conceptions of our experience.

DAVID MADDEN

Baton Rouge, Louisiana
July 25, 1969

The Dream Metaphor
Some Ramifications

The proposal to investigate "American Dream" and "American nightmare"—the initiating act for the present volume—is a stimulus in several directions. At the outset it makes us check our metaphors. These two look rather like bed-borne old campaigners, whom we embrace almost as often as we begin to pant with thoughts on culture. Do we know what we are up to when we use them? What do we take a dream to be? A cryptogram for reality or truth? A symbolic breakthrough into the half-light of dark closets of being? A predictive act ("prophetic soul / . . . dreaming on things to come")? The frail substance of things hoped for? An expectation sitting in the air? An aspiration? An imaging of deserts, with nothing unrewarded? A telic formula? A private assurance of things to come? A remolding of crass circumstance to heart's desire? The self actualized in the public arena? The will coercing history? A purified memory? These possibilities overlap, of course, but it is worth some redundancy to get into view a full spectrum of the possible connotations of *dream*. *Nightmare* is narrower. It may imply a gratuitous horror, a distortion of actuality, an irrational disordering where order may be expected, an unforeseen revelation of hideous truth, a truth perverted but as powerful as the real thing. In general, it is clear, a dream means something agreeable that may happen, a nightmare something disagreeable that does happen. Perhaps the worst that can be said of the figures, as carriers of thought, is that they are a little too easily picked up, walking the streets where ideas pass, and standing in doorways invitingly. We might say that they are uprooted. *Dream*, it is true, does retain something of the "joy" and "music" that belong to its past, but *nightmare*, surely, nothing of the demonic, of the incubus whose evil sport renders one hagridden.

Such glancing at the literal bases of the metaphorical structure may help us in making distinctions. Though dream and nightmare are both events of sleep, they are independent; neither has to precede or follow the other.[1] Hence nightmare does not imply a dream gone wrong; if we arbitrarily impose the meaning, we are simplifying experience. I find myself shying away from nightmare as metaphor because it implies a random, crazy, unearned affliction, and above all a transitory one. When we call painful experience a nightmare, we stress only its ability to terrify or horrify, dropping it into the vast storehouse of the oppressive and frightening without looking for significance or distinctiveness. It is a mysterious victimizing, not an understandable consequence or a symbolic enactment of the way things are. It makes us seek pity, as victims must, or unconsciously confer it on ourselves. We get a little credit for having a nightmare, some kind of purple heart. But still we don't have to live with it forever; it will pass, suddenly letting us resume ordinary living. Hence the metaphor may be self-indulgent, a way of not coming to terms with broad-daylight problems. So if we use it, we have to provide many specifications. Easier, perhaps, to find another metaphor for the sense of interrupted well-being, of a shocking intrusion by a harsh force, forgotten or unforeseen. One thinks of reveille, of the alarm clock, of the awakening. The trouble with the first is that it is too spic-and-span and scheduled, with the second that it is too ad-worn and domestic, with the third that it has been a standby of gloomy prophecy. Yet such images are on the right track. For they propose what nightmare does not: a painful beating upon consciousness of harsh realities somehow not included in our standard operating sense of what the world is like.

Take, for instance, the Black disturbances, accusations, threats, attacks, and even terrors that have emerged in the 1960's. We hardly take them in, not to mention moving from understanding into appropriate styles of behavior, if we imagine them, however unconsciously, as spontaneous tribulations that we only wish would go away and let us resume whatever quietude we seemed to have before. In a sense we cannot stop wishing them away; our problem is to prevent the wish from influencing our sense of the facts or of our deserts. We can best maintain a new wakefulness by keeping in mind the divine pronouncement to Moses on Mount Sinai, that the iniquity of the fathers shall be visited upon the children even to the third and fourth generation. Yet we are more likely, because it is easier, to fall in with the prominent American mayor who said he was tired of hearing people blamed for the ill deeds of their great-grandparents, or with Thomas Hardy, who, in one of those sentimental moments brought on by brief lapses from storytelling into polemics, said of the Mount Sinai doctrine that though it "may be a morality good enough for divinities, it is scorned by average human nature." [2] Unfortunately one cannot quite dispose of slavery and post-slavery slavery by blaming it all on the old folks; and Hardy's view—that the moral repercussions of sin beyond the lifetime of the sinner is only a theological dish nauseous to wiser palates—is out of touch with organic moral sequences not subject to a reassuring statute of limitations. The longer the wrong and the more widespread the practice of it, the more extensive and painful the righting process; the psychic marks made by wrongs endure long beyond the life of the wrongdoer; in the victims a somatic memory, so to speak, presses for the repayment, however long delayed, of the moral debt. The point is that whatever happens in the repercussions of an old evil, however fear-inspiring or incredible on the surface, makes sense as the operation of moral order and is not to be understood as an incomprehensible nocturnal mystery. But we who must pay need not fall into a paralytic total guiltiness that reduces us to passive accepters of retaliation or blinds us to the fact that some collectors of moral debt become racketeers or crave disorder for ends unrelated to justice. In the end, we can hope, they will be outnumbered by the Blacks who can forgive. The Blacks have a lot of forgiving to do, and the role of whites must be helping to make forgiveness possible. One step toward that end is the creation of a Black strength without which forgiveness cannot exist.

But if the metaphorical utility of nightmare is, as this longish example argues, questionable, the dream image has possibilities that somehow survive its long life as a cliché. Because the word has many meanings, it retains a vitality that would not survive if the word were tied only to a single popular meaning. Even in popular usage, indeed, it can point in two directions. The dream may be an end in itself or may define an end which determines the direction of a life. As an end in itself, it is the passive entertainment of gratifying visions as implied in "reverie" and "fantasy"; this appears in the secret life of Walter Mitty and in "dreams of glory" cartoons. There are several possibilities here: the dream may be a harmless indulgence, without side effects—a rest period or temporary escape; it may substitute for action in the world, regrettably or fortunately (suppose Hitler had been "only a dreamer"); it may become addictive, with the imaginary voyage replaced by the drug-borne trip. As the definition of an end, the dream embodies images of achievement that require action. Here again there is at least a twofold possibility—of the aspiration or hope which can be realized, or the image or desire which has not been or cannot be realized. "It's his dream": it is the goal which he hopes to reach. "He's dreaming": he's laboring under an illusion. Further, the dream that is out of line with reality may be cherished with naïve ignorance or with knowingness. Compare "He's dreaming" with Lamb's "Dream Children": in one, the dreamer is unaware of the irony, in the other he makes the most of it, softening it up into pathos. (See D. G. Mitchell's *Reveries of a Bachelor; or, A Book of the Heart*, 1850.) Again, the dream may take us from the psychological to the philosophical orbit: man may be, not dreaming, but dreamt. Calderón's *Life Is a Dream* (1635) embodies the familiar questioning of reality as ordinarily perceived: to construe it as a dream is a version of idealism, to which I will return later. One other preliminary distinction: the dream which images a goal may win assent or dissent from critical observers; they may find, say, "a vulgar dream of affluence" or "a vision of a juster world." In other words, in "the dream" there is qualitative as well as semantic ambiguity.

If the dream is in some sense a streetwalker, at least it is not one thing to all men, but different, if not all, things to all men. Hence its metaphorical serviceability. Even in its most precise use it will invariably carry some shadow of other meanings; thus it automatically calls on the ambiguities inherent in imaginative experience, or, in other words, the doubleness and contradictions that are needed for an adequate view of reality. Since we are never quite comfortable with dual potentialities, of course, we tend to try always for singleness. Delmore Schwartz entitles a volume *In Dreams*

Begin Responsibilities: vision does not conjure up an object for erotic fondling, but confers an obligation. But it doesn't work that way for Boyd, the hero with "imagination" in Wright's Morris' *The Field of Vision* (1956) and *Ceremony in Lone Tree* (1960): "In the dream, that is, began the irresponsibility." Morris catches the other side of the case; vision may lure and satisfy as well as obligate. Hence the dream image brings into play a set of alternative responses that compete, with no certainty about the outcome, for the psyche directing action.

It introduces, also, another set of responses—a choice between kinds of activity: the dream as guide and the dream as dictator. Here the word *idea* is sometimes used interchangeably with the word *dream* (the basic element in both is "vision," a seeing as opposed to an experiencing in the world). Robert Penn Warren touches on this problem when, in his introduction to *Nostromo*, he speaks of the "idea" as redemptive and thus an essential for everyman, who "must find sanctions outside himself" (Warren quotes Gustav Kahn's term for Conrad: *"puissant rêveur"*). The idea is beneficent in providing, as standard and spur, the possible perfection (the "ideal") which does not concede the finality of purely impulsive, random, unformed raw events in a haphazard mingling of the tumultuous and makeshift. Drawn by the idea, crude aimless movement in time seeks form and value; mere living is shaped into a life. (The concept becomes an imperative in Tennyson's "Follow the gleam.") On the other hand, the idea may rigidify and tyrannize, make facts conform to doctrine, force history into a pattern; become, for the individual, an obsession, and, for society, an ideology. We are reasonably familiar, in the twentieth century, with systems in which the socio-political idea becomes infallible dogma, literally dictating conduct in the present, and symbolically dictating conduct in the past by rewriting history. The idea that assumes power over the individual, however, and either coerces him or makes him try to coerce others and the facts, has naturally been more of a stimulus to the literary imagination. When the hopeful coercing of results by the idea is tripped up by wry or unruly circumstances, we have the comic life of Sterne's Walter Shandy. But when Ibsen's Gregers Werle keeps enforcing "the claims of the ideal" upon others, the ensuing ironies are hardly comic. When the claims of the idea inflexibly dictate a life, the end is disaster or even tragedy, as in *The Scarlet Letter* (Chillingworth and Dimmesdale), in Warren's *World Enough and Time* (1950), and of course most brilliantly in *Moby Dick* (and almost equally so in Trollope's less well-known *He Knew He Was Right*, 1869).

So, to the dualities in which the dream participates or to which it points, we add the force that draws man, and that which drives him; the molding of life, and the compelling of life; and the realism by which things out there are not modifiable, and the idealism by which they are but what we make them. As I have remarked, however, we do not always maintain the dual perspective that is called for; singleness is equally the wont of the realist turned cynic, and the idealist turned prescriber. For an example of the double vision held to very subtly we can turn to Conrad's *Lord Jim* (chap. 20): Stein, talking to Marlow about "how to be," declares that "there is only one way. . . . To follow the dream, and again to follow the dream—and so—*ewig—usque ad finem*." Let man pursue the aspiration, yes—"to be a saint, . . . to be a devil—[to be] a very fine fellow—so fine as he can never be." In the phrase "as he can never be" is one hint of the actuality always kept in sight: the double vision. But more important: the man who enters a dream "falls" into it; thus he is "like a man who falls into the sea." He is, then, in danger from the start; he is in "the destructive element." Leaving it unsaid that if man is merely passive, he is done for, Conrad stresses the fact that if man is active in the wrong way—"if he tries to climb out into the air"—he is done for. Hence the rule for survival: "The way is to the destructive element submit yourself, and with the exertions of your hands and feet in the water make the deep, deep sea keep you up." Conrad describes an experience that is danger-ous, strenuous, and inconclusive; if the struggle encompasses triumph, it is a maintenance of self rather than the imprint-ing of oneself on a page visible to others. The dream makes no presents; having it, indeed, is scarcely a distinction. For who is it who "falls into a dream"? "A man that is born falls into a dream. . . ." Being born is falling into life, and that is falling into a dream; one goes with the other; the "destruc-tive element," where one may struggle for survival, is life and the dream; the dream and the destruction are twins. These prosaic restatements hardly do justice to a very complex image. But if we cannot rephrase it satisfactorily, at least we can see Conrad maintaining a duality that often eludes dreamers, theorists of the dream, oneiromancers. Perhaps we can look in these terms at dreams having an American content.

Dreams about America are an import from Europe, where they were an old habit dating from the Renaissance. Vespucci, after all, provided some of the stimulus for More's *Utopia*. The New World led Montaigne to reflect on social and political betterment, and his thoughts are echoed in Gonzalo's picture of an ideal commonwealth in *The Tempest* (II, i, 147 ff.); and some of the ideality of *The Tempest* generally may reflect a sense of possibilities opened by America ("O brave new world"). The Bermudas were idyllically represented in poems by Waller and Marvell. Chapman envisioned a "golden world" in America, Drayton a "golden age"; Herbert saw religion moving from a decadent to a healthy land; Cowley and Davenant both thought of America as a refuge from a gross world. Swift placed the land of the Brobdingnags, in which the utopian is dominant, in northwest America. Primitivism and the cult of the noble savage, principally nourished by America, flowered in the eighteenth century, again under French auspices. Rousseau framed the dream, and Chateaubriand localized it in America (where it appeared a little later in Cooper's fiction and *Hiawatha*). Gilbert Chinard, studying this aspect of European thought, used the relevant term *"le rêve exotique."* There is a good deal of this exotic dreaming in the popular fiction of the eighteenth century, especially that which favored the French Revolution. Blake, preaching freedom, could use America as a symbol, and Coleridge could dream of Pantisocracy by the Susquehanna; the edenic America survives as late as Kafka's *Amerika* (1938) and the Swedish novelist Vilhelm Moberg's *The Emigrants* (1949). But Moberg's emigrants had to learn the facts of life, and John Barth, with the benefit of hindsight, could present equally Ebenezer Cooke's dream of seventeenth-century Maryland and his awakening.

But if such duality is more often retrospective, it is not entirely so. Shakespeare could derive the utopian from America, but he could also imagine Caliban. Eighteenth-century popular novelists could portray an assortment of transatlantic Edens and Utopias, but they could likewise satirize visions of a perfection to be secured simply by travel and without travail. If Romantic poets could repeat or recast traditional idealizations, Victorian novelists took a new look. Mrs. Trollope and Dickens traveled, and returned to report sourly on what they found. *Martin Chuzzlewit* (1843–44) debunks an American "Valley of Eden." In *The Warden* (1855) Trollope, listing the wielders of power in the world, includes "the mob in America." The phrase suggests some of the sentiments in Arnold's *Discourses in America* (1885). James's Americans were not all innocent.

The passage of time tended to restore the duality of awareness which first fresh dreams would exclude; passing time diminishes space, and the reduction of distance makes the simplistic vision less tenable. The point is that by the time of the big migrations to America, the air of Europe supplied not only a variety of dreams but also countering doubts, skepticisms, judgments, antipathies. It was historically possible for every emigrant to be of two minds. If he was not, it was simply that under the two-way pressure of the situation to be escaped from (political, social, economic, emotional), and the sense of opportunity generated by the incompletely known ahead, he could not resist the temptation of the simplistic dream—of material or political or spiritual good things to be possessed. We have not altogether broken that habit of our forebears, and our problem has been to relocate the dream in a context of adequately perceived life. We need a kind of European wariness of the unfettered dream—a wariness which in the Old World began fairly early in the New World game. We come to it with difficulty. There are various problems here.

The indispensable redemptive dream is capable of some duplicity. What it can redeem us from is gross and formless experience, an uncentered and unordered wandering, a mere mechanical responsiveness to whatever stimuli existence irrationally puts where we happen to be. It may seem, however, to redeem us from accidents, malfunctioning or malfeasance by men, the shortcomings of systems, hostility and malice, challenges and upsets, the various evildoings or failures that afflict men, whether these spring from the cosmos (Beckett), society (Brecht), or personal choice (Sartre). The yearning for salvation from the liabilities that always dog man may stimulate the vision of an eternal spiritual existence, or of a New Life here and now, or at least across the river and pretty soon. Eric Voegelin has written brilliantly of mass movements based on the theory that "the world is intrinsically poorly organized" rather than that "human beings in general . . . are inadequate," and that "salvation from the evil of the world is possible." [3]

There is a less inclusive dream of intramundane security—that of the limited Utopia for a chosen few: Pantisocracy, Brook Farm, New Harmony, the North American Phalanx, the Oneida Community. This elitist dream predicates withdrawal; the existent world is corrupt; the new place, the untouched scene promise a fresh constructive effort and a freedom from contamination. Weakness and flaws are construed to be outside in circumstances, not within; in the world around, in other people, not in the human nature that one shares. Distance and the unknown shore up the dream; but then proximity sets in, and all becomes known; and what is primarily known is a more troublesomely complex human reality than was envisaged in the original anticipations. Someone has said that we must always utopianize—in order to have, I assume, a counterbalance to a purely despairing view of reality. In that function the dream is redemptive. But here I am noting that the needed dream may incorporate an escapism that is as trouble-producing as dreamlessness—an escapism that goes beyond a natural flight from say oppression (e.g., the Nazis) to an unconscious flight from the way things are. This may carry within it an obscure flight from human nature; or, still more subtly, from oneself, or the part of oneself that appears more abundantly in others. Elsewhere, in a new community, it will be different. In another town, as Oedipus, extending his parents' attitude, thought, the curse will not hold, and only the nobility in the soul will exert power.

I hope I am keeping the concept of the dream delicately poised between the rectifying role (a source of order amid the chaotic flux) and the falsifying role (a promise of security against imperfections in the natural and social realms—a life-preserver against the destructive element). In its latter role it may assure a freedom *from* things or a dominance *of* things. In other words, the dream is like a drug that is essential to health but may become an addiction, may be taken in an overdose, or may have disastrous side effects. In the light of these diverse possibilities in the dream we can see the delicate filaments connecting the quest of religious and political freedom in America, the push on into special private utopias, the monomania of Captain Ahab, narcotic films (the sentimentality of making a valid ideal too easy), the record of ideals inadequately tempered to stubborn facts in Hawthorne's *The Blithedale Romance* (1852) and Melville's *Pierre* (1852).[4]

In American history the dream in action has repeatedly been emigration: from Europe to America, from society-at-large to utopian communities, and from the east coast to various receding wests. The distant and the unknown, as I have said, have been an important nutrient of the dream; where nothing is, all is possible, and where no man has been, human corruption may be thought to be an invention of society. Hence the lure of the frontier, which was once the Atlantic seaboard, and successively the Midwest, the mountains, and the west coast; and since then the frontier spirit has sporadically sought further, to achieve realization in Alaska and the Pacific. Pacific dreams, however, seem to be mainly escapist and self-indulgent: Utopias of passivity rather than activity. Be that as it may, the frontier has now disappeared after being available to the Western world for half a millennium—a chief spur to the millennial imagination, the vision of setting up one or another kingdom of heaven upon earth. The vanishing of the frontier throws us back on ourselves in a number of ways. Some of our tensions may be related to the final disappearance of the dream-grounds that since the sixteenth century have invited all freedoms of feeling.

When a constantly receding horizon at last becomes stationary, the dream energies that once pushed off into non-finite distance undergo drastic redirection (they do not simply disappear). Some of the utopian excitement attached to the new scene is moving to it; mobility itself seems accomplishment. When horizontal mobility is cut off because there is only more of the same thing to move to, it becomes vertical mobility: instead of going to a new world of higher quality, one goes higher in the world as it is—"success." Instead of moving away—escaping, perhaps—into a new security against the ills that flesh is heir to, one strives for the security here and now, in the current terms that are assumed to provide it—money, property, things, pleasures. We secularize the New Jerusalem: the gold and precious stones become literal elements in a short-term eschatology. The community enforced by the rigors of the frontier, or envisaged as a spiritual endowment in a Land of Promise, becomes the mechanical affiliations of club and party and job, the routine pieties of family and locality.

These are some of the expectable phenomena of the dream forced back on itself by the loss of its traditional scene or arena. Obviously they do not exhaust the dream potential, although for some dreamers they are apparently all there is to it; and to some observers we all seem tied within such closed-border dreams. Hence the talk about "the American Dream," as if there were only one, and as if it meant only rising, succeeding, getting rich, having pleasures, or exchanging clichés of value and feeling.[5] When Albee uses *The American Dream* as title of a play (1961), he exemplifies the process of showing disgust with the restricted and conventionalized dream,[6] and he uses the customary satirical method of ignoring the complexities of meaning possible to "dream" and of attributing the inadequate dream to everybody. Thus he has a target instead of a problem, and the shooting can go on forever. Norman Mailer often plays the same sort of game, but in *An American Dream* (1965) he both gets away from "the" and, with his own wild fantasy as a medium, elaborates a vision that is much more satirical; he reacts against the callow self-congratulation of the deicide and envisages an "existential conflict between God and the Devil." [7]

Albee, it seems to me, gives a clue to a good deal of current criticism of American society: it comes out of a sense of being let down or treated unfairly by the realm of dreams. People have dreams that cannot be fulfilled because things are the way they are; or dreams are fulfilled, and the dreamers remain unfulfilled; or people rely on dreams that ought not to be fulfilled because they are unfulfilling. Out of disappointment comes the impulse to blame—often broadly and indiscriminately; out of follies comes the impulse to blame those who are foolish. The result is a great cry about the false, the corrupt, the hypocritical; the abuse of American society is acrimonious, savage, unrelenting, and it seems in our day to have reached new heights of virulence.

The trouble with systematic and high-pitched abuse is that it gratifies the abuser rather than sheds true light on the situation; indignation at the others and at the world, rather than sharpening the eyes of others and the world, keeps the indignant man comfortably blind about himself. Men who keep screaming polemics against society tend to become intolerably self-righteous; such abuse is only private complacency given public existence. They fight the heartwarming melodrama of the good and true abuser against the evil world. The role of the hero is so pleasing that it becomes intellectually chic: one acquires status by denouncing civilization as a cesspool, and exchanges a secret grip with others in the fraternity. It becomes smart to damn the culture, and just as the smart always generates its own clichés, so the clichés of the with-it abuser of society are readily available to neophytes in accusation. A writer on another subject can speak casually of "expiation for belonging at all to our civilization, from which at times we must all want to find a way out." Only the "at times" qualifies a standardized gesture of repudiation.

I am not alluding to criticism by Blacks, a subject which I discussed earlier, nor to the inevitable and necessary criticism of policy, value, and tone, but to a peculiarly violent, unqualified, hostile denigration of society as a whole which is practiced by certain intellectuals, mainly professors and journalists. On the other hand, as the 1968 nominating conventions made clear, politicians make an opposite kind of good thing of various American dreams—trumpeting them, glorifying them, and envisaging fulfillment pretty soon after the election if it goes right. It is too bad to have the fundamental problem of the dream lost in this kind of melodrama, that is, an uncritical conflict between those who happily affirm and those who brutally scorn, between the view that the world is wonderful at least in hope, and the view that it is hopelessly awful. Whoever wants to think at all about the problem, and to approach an understanding of it, needs a little more assistance than he can get from automatic, self-congratulatory abuse of the civilization by intellectuals, and automatic self-serving praise of it by candidates for office. One party wants to triumph over the squares, and the other with the squares. What both ignore is the difficulties in the problem of the dream—of the kinds of dreams that may crossbreed without our knowing it, and of the relation of the dream, whatever its timbre, to the actualities in which men live.

Whether because the dream is rigid or because life is recalcitrant, there will always be a discrepancy between dream and actuality. The political response is to ignore the discrepancy or declare it easily removable; the intellectualist-critic whom I have described simply castigates and condemns, translating, it seems to me, the inevitable discrepancy into a gross evil for which the civilization ought to be punished or even wiped out. We are somewhat protected against the political extreme by the spontaneous skepticism that is always partly active as we view political phenomena; we do not have a comparable built-in corrective against indiscriminate intellectuals, whose facile denunciations—giving the denouncers easy kicks, an easy sense of righteousness, an easy triumph over others—are likely to be mistaken for the detached thoughts of disinterested students in a traditional philosophic or scientific mode. Their style, of course, betrays them to anyone who can read style, but a sense of style is not widespread. On the other hand, the denunciatory has a rather subtle charm as a side effect: it suggests, not an imperfect world that is to be borne, but a state of affairs that is not up to our deserts. It tempts us to feel sorry for ourselves. What I am getting at is the ironic ties between indignation and blame, on the one hand, and self-pity on the other. Hence one has especially to value a writer like Saul Bellow, with his regular opposition to the dual tactic of condemning others and feeling sorry for oneself.

The vanishing of a frontier—which just by existing seemed to legitimatize all dreams—has perhaps contributed to several other phenomena. A frontier means space, space implies time, and time a future in which dreams may be realized. On the other hand: no frontier, no space; no space, no time, no future: now or never. This may have something to do with the "impatience of youth" of which we hear much: the apparent intention, in the public domain, to "smite the world good" (as Dorothy Sayers put it) without delay, and, in personal and professional life, to refuse to wait for what is ordinarily earned by the revealing of merit during the passage of time—influence and power. Again, it may take something

like the end of the frontier, with its impact on long-estab-
lished patterns of dreaming, to create the climate for the
dramas of disaster that have been having strong appeal—
Death of a Salesman (1949); much of the O'Neill canon,
but especially the plays such as *Long Day's Journey into
Night* (1956) that come out of dark family history; a great
deal of Tennessee Williams—*Glass Menagerie* (1945), *Or-
pheus Descending* (1957), *Cat on a Hot Tin Roof* (1955);
Albee's *Zoo Story* (1960), and *Who's Afraid of Virginia
Woolf?* (1962). In such plays there is something claustro-
phobic; the microcosm of the theater may reflect a macro-
cosm in which borders are for the first time closed. What
comes through is the painfulness of *No Exit* (1944).

Finally, the exit that stayed open for five hundred years—
the distant frontiers that could translate every dream into a
sound vision of intramundane possibility—may, by lasting
for so long a time, have contributed to an incomplete understanding of ourselves. It has always been possible, while
envisaging a different and better life elsewhere, to siphon off
something of ourselves; or while fleeing from an external
trouble, to take an internal troublesomeness, most likely
unrecognized, into an environment somehow sensed as better for a catharsis. What frontiers provided, I suspect, was an
opportunity not only for creation but for destruction, or,
alternatively, for the seizing and holding of power that inevitably had a destructive side. The establishing of a new order,
be it theocracy or tobacco plutocracy, meant getting rid of
other claimants to the scene—that is (to maintain an
Anglo-American perspective), Spanish, French, and above all
Indians, who lasted as the enemy almost up until our time.
Someone had always to be conquered, put out of business, or
destroyed, or, as with the Africans, put under the yoke. If not
people, it was things that had to be conquered—distances,
heat and cold, rivers, mountains. In any case, one was not
only making a better world but getting the better of something or someone. We may hazard the guess that small elitist
utopias fail in part because they do not provide an arena for
destructiveness: the participants are left only with the task of
conquering themselves, a bleak prospect that seems not to
evoke a very warm or enduring commitment.

If there is virtue in the hypothesis of the dual promise [8] of
the frontier—the presumptive physical guarantor of the

dream—then the end of the frontier means not only a re-orientation of the dream but a catching up with us of elements in ourselves that have been less apparent, such as the "destructive element" within. In our day the two sides of frontier activity are, it appears, significantly split. On the one hand the creative dream of the better republic has been institutionalized—in the New Deal, Fair Deal, New Frontier. On the other hand the destructive impulse is aimed at institutions, including those that seem most hospitable to the affirmative dream. The total situation is confused; what does seem clear, however, is the spread of a destructiveness that we have not known before. "We will destroy this university," which has been heard on more than one campus, is in this country an unprecedented way of looking ahead. We might almost think that destruction has become the dream. Some practitioners of destruction seem to regard it as a value in itself, others to think of it as a prologue to a better world. But observers can rarely discover an image of anything that is to follow. Again, destructiveness may be attributed, by practitioners or observers, to causes: here we are pretty like to have the monotonous chorus of "rotten" and "corrupt." But without being a counter polemist or a defender of the status quo, one may believe that the supposed cause is simply inadequate, and that the imperfections of our life function less as a cause (which can be removed) than an occasion (which can be seized). If destructiveness is, as I am hypothesizing, inherent in human makeup, we can easily understand its finding an occasion when it seeks a catharsis. We have long thought of self-destructiveness as a tendency of human nature (in fact, it has become a cliché of analysis in both popular and literary contexts); destructiveness outward bound should be equally imaginable.

We may say that the disappearance of the frontier, which permitted the exercise of a great deal of destructiveness, is bringing this urgency home to us in a new way. We might also describe some current events as an effort to make our whole civilization into a frontier where a simpler exercise of all instincts is possible. We should note one other historical factor at work here. Destructiveness is a logical extreme of rebelliousness, and rebelliousness, we need hardly be told, is standard in youth. However, the rebellious phase in the young of our era coincides with two other phenomena in a historical nexus which is both unprecedented and of unpredictable outcome. For the first time, at least in the West, that which is being rebelled against appears to be undergoing a final loss of authority—that is, the mores and supporting beliefs which constituted a centuries-old tradition of values and conduct. This gives rebellious forces an enormous sense of power, and, more perilously, of immunity. And perhaps for the first time ever, the people in the age group to which rebellion is natural constitute a majority of the population. Put all these phenomena together, and you have a situation in which the human destructive force is very great. Add to it the destructiveness implicit in certain criticisms of society by intellectuals—for instance, the insatiate abuse of symbolic figures in public life—and the destructive drive is, as we have learned to say, escalated still further. Apparent justifications may be paraded, but hyperbole, self-righteousness, and intransigence betray motives quite distant from the righting of wrongs. The absence of any sound reason for destruction—the kind that would spontaneously attract a wide following—is revealed in the efforts of leaders in violence to latch on to the Black cause.

We have to assume, of course, that the postulated destructive instinct is of lesser strength, finally, than the constructive and creative instinct. We may suppose, therefore, that it will not be a final determinant of our history. But we do not know how much and how many it will destroy before it has achieved a catharsis. Ideally what we need is a somewhat paradoxical commitment in which a destruction that seems essential or inescapable at the moment (we tend, long after the fact, to do penance for destructiveness in the past—for ravaged nature or natives) is a lesser accompaniment of a creative effort. For five hundred years the frontiers made possible such a commitment. They are gone, and we are learning new things.

"Commitment," of course, means a direction-giving dream. If it is to work, it needs to be complex enough. But my interest is not in prescribing or prophesying, rather in examining the notion of the dream and calling attention to the multiplicity of its contents and the ambiguity of its role. Hence, though there is a history of dreams about America, and of dreams in America, there is no such thing as "*the* American Dream." Americans may dream about a range of fulfillments from conventionalized self-magnifications to morally more magnificent worlds; and if the former are more frequent, this should surprise no one who has observed the distribution of human talents (oddly enough, the talented man, to think well of himself, often uses a disproportionate amount of energy thinking ill of the less talented man). More interesting, however, is the wide spectrum of diverse and contradictory relationships between the dream and the actuality upon which it impinges. If there is no dream at all, life remains amorphous and accidental. If the dream is tailored too closely to a sense of actuality, to the way things go, life becomes a cynical acquiescence in, or a profiting from, a lowest-common-denominator existence. If the dream simply ignores reality, the dreamer becomes an eccentric, perhaps partly noble in a quixotic way, or innocuous, or even dangerous in the power to mislead. If the dream compels life instead of guiding it, the result is madness for the private dreamer, and the oppression of those compelled by the political or social dreamer (the experience of those compelled may range from minor oppressions by doctrinaire concepts in limited areas, to the general tyranny of a political dream supposed to have universal applicability).[9]

Perhaps the most representative situation is the discrepancy between dream and actuality, between the ideal that we can visualize and the instinctive and habitual ways of life that yield only partly to the idea. Here we must live with the paradox that the dream is essential and yet will never make a complete imprint on actual life, that we do not dare surrender the dream and yet are unable to surrender to it. But because it says one thing, and what we do very often says something else—the difference may be rather small or painfully large—the situation is a difficult one for the minds of all of us, because we eternally crave simplicity. The gap between what we dream and what we do tests rigorously our ability to get on without the simplicities that facilitate attitudes and actions. Too few people abjure simplicities. Many like to cry "hypocrisy" and play at *j'accuse*. Truly evil people, a destructive instinct joined with the cool calculation of the methods to power, harp on discrepancies to weaken defenses against their own predations. The immature practice only indignation and denunciation. Those on whom the maintenance of a bearable life depends—one must hope that there are enough of them—neither give up the dream nor become intolerant of actuality, neither expect the dream to dictate nor accept the total intransigence of actuality, but try to retain that precarious tension between what is and what ought to be without which we fall into total disorder or total imposition of order.

The Dream of the New

LESLIE A. FIEDLER

"What's new?" one American says to another by way of greeting; and the assumption is that among us there always is something new—or at least that there used to be, and, therefore, *ought* to be forever. And why not? since the land we inhabit, between Old Mexico and the Old Dominion of Canada, was dreamed as New from an older Old World, i.e., from a world longing to be old, needing us to be sure it was old, long before we were invented, or, even, discovered. To be sure, all of the Americas were imagined as New in that magical moment just before and after the discovery; but only the United States has accepted and glorified the notion of newness as its essential character, its fate, its vocation. To be new, to make it new, to get a new start: this has become a program on which an American can be elected to public office or launch a poetic career. It is not so much a program of revolution (such ideas belong to the Old World) as of renewal, self-renewal: not a scheme for changing things by cutting off the head of a king to make way for another regime, but of chopping the old man into pieces and boiling him up in a pot in hopes of making him young again: the method not of Karl Marx, but of Medea. And if the old man dies just as surely one way as the other, at least no one is to blame. We wanted him young, not dead, didn't we? And everyone knows (at least everyone who came to America searching for the fountain of youth) that being young is as unquestionably good, as being dead is unquestionably bad.

But in America everyone *is* young, just as everything is new—not in fact, perhaps, but mythologically, by definition, which is all that finally counts in a new world. Ponce de Leon was right: America is the Fountain of Youth, just as surely as it is El Dorado and the Passage to India. Indeed, none of the early explorers was wrong in his expectations and dreams, as long as they were mad enough: America is the place where youth is indefinitely extended, where wealth beyond measure or belief lies just over the mountains, where the man who turns his back on Europe can find Asia—the sound of sitars and the teachings of Yoga—by looking in exactly the wrong direction. *This* is what is new about America—not temporarily new, but being out of time, new forever. It is dreamland; and in dreams, time does not exist. The European landing in America confirmed two things he thought he knew but did not really, *really* believe: first, that the world was round, and second, that dreams actually exist, i.e., can be inhabited waking as well as sleeping. The new world, the *other* world, the world beyond death and the ultimate West indicated by the pillars of Hercules, had been penetrated by Europeans for two thousand years in fantasies and dreams and fables and old wives' tales—sleeping they had gone, and waking they had told their story from Plato to Dante. But at last there it was! A fact for mapmakers and explorers and even settlers. To render the almost irrecoverable shock of that realization has been the task of our writers —and to do it they have had to invent a new language, a new vocabulary of symbols and myths, able to convey the doctrine that dreaming is living, the dream is reality.

At almost the same moment that we began, Europeans were formulating an opposite doctrine: that living is dreaming, that reality is a dream; but we must not confuse the vision which moved Shakespeare and Cervantes and Calderón with the one that strove for two centuries after their time to be born in the United States; though, to be sure, the two notions complement each other. Yet finally that doctrine that life is a dream is linked to the conviction that there is nothing new under the sun; while its complement is tied to the belief that not merely east of the sun and west of the moon, but somewhere, *else*where *under* the sun, there is a place where everything is new. The great books which embody this belief, those lovely dreamy shapeless works which seem to have neither boundaries nor centers, *Moby Dick, The Adventures of A. Gordon Pym, Huckleberry Finn, Absalom, Absalom!*—works which span a hundred years but being out of time seem contemporary only with each other —are not my subject here; though I cannot resist mentioning them. Considered alone, however, they give finally a false notion of what our tradition is—for there is in all of them something left over from the old world, an aspiration to greatness perhaps, which suggests that they are belles lettres, literature in the classical sense (of the same company, say, as *Hamlet* or *Paradise Lost* or even the *Idylls of the King*); and this is misleading, since the American tradition, the tradition of the new, is precisely antiliterary, subversive—from the start what we have only lately learned to call Pop Art, products of technology rather than aesthetic objects.

The discovery of the New World made necessary and the development of a new technology in that New World made possible for the first time the manufacture, the mass production, and mass distribution of dreams. Indeed, there is only a single industry in the United States, which its bewilderingly and misleadingly various subdivisions tend to disguise even from its managers—though not from the consumers it serves who really determine the nature of its production. What that industry produces are not things—for things are old and do not interest the young of all ages who control the market —but dreams disguised as things: poor vulgar dreams they seem sometimes, but what can one expect of a population descended from the culturally dispossessed of all nations of the world? Nonetheless, the refrigerators, outsize cars, color television sets, and bathtubs with gold faucets which move from machine to home with unparalleled speed are not goods but toys, which is to say, dreams disguised as goods: the products of an unnoticed second industrial revolution, an *anti*-industrial revolution which has enlisted machines in the service of play rather than work.

To be sure, our machines are still busy (vestigially busy, I am tempted to say) with making necessities: food, clothing, shelter—but even the houses to which we aspire are play houses, the clothes play clothes, and the food play food— that Coca-Cola and bubble gum which so vex an old world that scarcely realizes how puritanical it has come to seem beside the presumed homeland of puritanism. Puritanism, after all, is a code appropriate only to the grimnesses of the first industrial revolution, which we have outgrown. A nation of magicians and magicians' apprentices no longer finds it viable; and this is precisely what we have become, unleashing (for good or for ill, but always with a terrifying innocence) that super-science and super-technology which turn out to be the old magic out of which science and technology originally emerged. This time around, however, it all really *works*, perhaps in part because we have given up the old formulas and ceremonies, the ancient pattern of mystification, in favor of a modern attempt at convincing ourselves that the instantaneous transformation of wishes into things is a triumph of rationality.

Nonetheless, one has only to behold the workings of the Ford plant or General Electric or the organization of a supermarket to be convinced that assembly line production and mass distribution constitute a ritual quite as compulsively mad as that dreamed up by any medieval sorcerer. And if simple observation is not enough to carry conviction, there exists on film the great scene on the assembly line in Charlie Chaplin's *Modern Times*, in which it is hard to tell whether he is enchanter or enchanted, but it is clear that witchcraft is somehow involved. But the film itself—all movies in fact—are products of the same dream technology which gives us vacuum cleaners and washing machines and identical cans of identical soup guaranteed to contain eleven lovely ingredients. Indeed, the movies—along with radio, and most perfectly of all television—are the supreme, the final product of that technological magic; for hard goods, old-fashioned commodities, no matter how carefully obsolescence is built into them, tend to last too long to be satisfactory as dream representations. Only what flickers for a moment in the eye, in the ear and is gone, leaving us still laughing or with the tears we need still not dry on our cheeks—only what destroys itself even as it is experienced—will do. The dream whose business is with time (the cheating of time and the consequent mitigation of boredom which is a function of time too consciously lived) is rather embarrassed by space; the twenty-one inches of a TV screen is about as much as it can comfortably use.

But a book is even smaller, fitting easily into the hand and therefore truly portable, capable of being carried even into that last place of dreams in the modern dream-house, the toilet. TV sets make it only as far as the bedroom. And books are, to be sure (the novel in particular, being the first mass-produced commodity in the modern world), a part of the ritual magic of that world, as well as one of its products. But the book, especially the fat, well-bound novel of the last couple of centuries, made to last and to be stored and inventoried on the shelves of libraries—though it came into existence at the same moment as America, and belongs essentially, as the very name *novel* declares, to the tradition of the new—represents a double and divided ambition on the part of its makers. In part they have aspired to produce entertainment for the marketplace; in part, longed to leave behind works of art; in part, tried to cheat time, and in part, striven to triumph over it. Only the best seller, the frank and flagrant best seller, represents what is truly novel about the novel, its rejection of any life longer than the dream instant. And in this sense, hard covers were doomed soon to start to disappear.

The mass-produced, mass-distributed paperback pocket book is the ideal form, or the condensed version for the *Reader's Digest*, or the comic book retelling in pictures, or perhaps best of all, the total abandonment of the printed page in favor of tape—thus putting the novel where it belongs, side by side with pop music rather than with verse epics or tragedies. Some writers these days, ranging from established figures like John Barth to young unknowns huddling over their recording devices, have become aware of this trend, and are composing directly on tape; just as earlier, some of their opposite numbers (the thirties for one reason or another was the peak period for this), coming to think of books as merely the embryonic form of films, moved off to Hollywood to compose directly for the screen. One thinks especially of Nathanael West and Daniel Fuchs. But Americans have always been especially aware of the relationship between the novel and the more popular, which is to say the newer, arts—in the beginning, of the relationship between the art novel, "serious" fiction, as we used to say, and the best seller. This awareness is scarcely avoidable in a country in which international best sellers were being produced (Susannah Rowson's *Charlotte Temple*, which appeared before the end of the eighteenth century and continued to be reprinted down into the twenties will do as an example) several decades before the emergence of any self-conscious literary artist.

Edgar Allan Poe is a key figure in the whole process; for despite the appalling seriousness with which he took himself, he was the inventor of at least two pop forms: the detective story and science fiction. In aspiration, he longed to be up-to-date; in fact, he was too provincial to do anything more than limp along behind the German experimenters who had preceded him, except when he turned to Pop Art. But this was his blessing, and has remained a lesson to us all; for the up-to-date, what is still called in some quarters the avant-garde, is quite different from the truly New. It is merely the latest form of the old, or rather a desperate bid for acceptance and the possibility of turning at last into an Old Master. One has only to think, to be convinced, of the chilling academicism of such contemporary avant-gardists (the French have a special talent for producing and over-praising them) as the unreadable Robbe-Grillet. But the instinct of Americans has always been to avoid the avant-garde, to mock its pretensions, or at least to find an antidote to it in popular culture. Nathanael West is, once more, an illustrative case, beginning in *The Dream Life of Balso Snell* with the emulation of European surrealism, but turning in *A Cool Million* to a tongue-in-cheek emulation of Horatio Alger. So, too, even earlier, Hemingway had recovered from the influence of the circle around Gertrude Stein in Paris, and Faulkner from that of a similarly pretentious though notably less talented one around Sherwood Anderson in New Orleans.

Our writers have, to be sure, profited by their exposure to the avant-garde, just as they have by their awareness of the classical past—but their relationship to both has been essentially that of mockery, their chief connection the utterly ambivalent one of parody. Not *all* American writers by any means have disengaged from the classical heritage or the experimentalist false cult of the New. One thinks, on the one hand, of Henry James and T. S. Eliot, worshipers at the shrines of the Culture Religion, or of Vladimir Nabokov, faithful (except for the blessed accident of *Lolita*) to the modes of irony fashionable in the Paris of his youth; but the writers who occur to us first in this context, typically go to Europe to die—acting out in their lives the meanings implicit in their works.

No, the real, the continuing, the fruitful relationship of the American writer to the past, all the way from Edgar Allan Poe to Ken Kesey and John Barth, the only relationship compatible with the tradition of the New is that of parody, which simultaneously connects and rejects. And it is

therefore fitting that the very first American poem, written
by a poet himself not American but attempting to imagine
in seventeenth-century England an authentic native of the
New World, be a parody-before-the-fact, as it were, a parody
of still unwritten poems to come, which, quite like our
novels, were themselves to be parodies of almost all that
Europe had thought of as being the very essence of literature. The lines were composed by Shakespeare and put in the
mouth of Caliban drunk; but listening to them one thinks of
Walt Whitman and Allen Ginsberg, who have emulated
them perhaps without knowing it, as well as of D. H. Lawrence, who thought them the key to the American character
in the early twentieth century:

> No more dams I'le make for fish,
> Nor fetch in firing, at requiring,
> Nor scrape trenchering, nor wash dish,
> Ban' ban', Cacalyban
> Has a new Master, get a new Man,
> Freedome, high day, high-day freedome, highday freedome.

"O brave Monster," says Stephano when the song is done,
"lead the way." And so he has ever since.

But Shakespeare himself—and indeed the very play in
which these lines occur—becomes the subject of parody in
The Waste Land, throughout which the songs from *The
Tempest* echo and are travestied ("O O O O that Shake-
speherian Rag— / It's so elegant / So intelligent") along with
scraps of almost everything else out of the tradition from
Spenser to Goldsmith, from Webster to Baudelaire. This is,
to be sure, "serious" parody, and Eliot may well have believed it was not the Old Masters he was mocking, so much
as the modern world in which their music tended to be
unconsciously and inevitably burlesqued; but we remember
that *The Waste Land* is a poem he conceived in madness
but could not finish in sanity; that its final shape—and
perhaps tone as well—was imposed on it by that old mocker,
Ezra Pound, who himself found his true voice when he
learned to mock "ancient music" by writing: "Winter is
icommen in, / Lhude sing Goddamm, / . . . Skiddeth bus
and sloppeth us, / An ague hath my ham." And, in any case,
Eliot's poem comes to us fifty years later in a total context of
parody which determines its meanings whatever his irrecover-

able intention. Such conscious parody is one of the chief modes of our books, in any case, and everything is fair game to our parodists: not only the great figures of the past like Shakespeare and the medieval lyricists and Sir Walter Scott, to whose travesty Twain dedicated a large part of his career; but trivial or scarcely known pop writers as well—like the unknown lady novelist so much admired by his wife, whom Fenimore Cooper travestied in his own first effort at fiction; or the writer of the first *Sot-Weed Factor* burlesqued by John Barth. Or Horatio Alger, whom many more aspiring novelists besides Nathanael West recognized as the inventor of a non-style congenial to all modern ironies.

But the process once begun is self-propagating, in theory endless—and tends finally to become confused, either by blurring away into unconscious parody (a second favored American mode) or Camp, which is to say, a parody of parody itself (a third, now immensely popular one). Mark Twain, for instance, will begin by quite consciously parodying Sir Walter Scott; then will himself be inadvertently parodied by Ernest Hemingway in an intended act of emulation; and Hemingway, in turn, even more grossly parodied by Norman Mailer, eager to establish himself at last in a great line of authentic American writing. In general, it can be said that when Americans try self-consciously to imitate a master, they end by unconsciously burlesquing him; for it is not in the American grain to be a worshipful disciple, even of a master deserving worship. Melville, for instance, using Shakespeare as a model in the dramatic Ahab chapters at the center of *Moby Dick* creates, willy-nilly, a burlesque of Elizabethan tragedy—grotesque, bloody, and tortured, to be sure, but essentially comic, quite like Shakespeare himself, in fact, trying to emulate earlier English emulators of Seneca in, say, *Titus Andronicus*.

More satisfactory by far are those *deliberate* travesties of their immediate masters by American writers knowing that to be free to "make it new" they must destroy the most recent old man, however dearly loved. Fascinatingly, the two greatest novelists of the American twenties, Faulkner and Hemingway, began their careers with mockeries of the same father-figure, Sherwood Anderson. And though Faulkner's *Mosquitoes* is finally too uncharacteristic to work, Hemingway's *The Torrents of Spring*, so long ignored, begins to seem to us perhaps the liveliest of all his books—certainly one which will be read with pleasure long after the monstrously solemn and dull late novels from *To Have and Have Not* down to *Across the River and into the Trees* have been mercifully remanded to the dust of libraries.

But to speak of Hemingway is to remember the fourth form of parody essential to American literature: *self*-parody; since, like so many of his predecessors, contemporaries, and successors (one thinks of the more notable instances, Henry James and Faulkner and Norman Mailer, but the list is almost inexhaustible), Hemingway ended by travestying his own style and themes, ended by mocking himself. I used to think of this special American fate as accidental, a function of weariness or failure of character or the nature of the American marketplace, and all these factors are, of course, important; but it seems to me now that something more essential is involved: a kind of *necessary* final act of destroying the past, required of all who belong to the tradition of the New. The American writer must be delivered of all possible pasts—not only of the great books in the canon, but of the best sellers as well, of his immediate teachers, and finally of his old selves. From his own first book and his second, the American writer can only be freed by burlesquing them—and therefore his last book is inevitably a travesty —a failure or falling off, we critics are tempted foolishly to say. But by the act of self-destruction the American novelist makes his fiction dream rather than art, what passes rather than endures, an experience almost as satisfactorily transient as television itself. The Art of the New is totally nihilistic, but it is joyously so; which may explain why our most authentic books, however tragic the lives of their authors, are if not quite blithe, funny at least.

Machiavelli for the Millions
Some Notes on Power Structures

The problem of power can never be as urgent as the reality of power. The first is philosophical—I am tempted to say, merely philosophical—while the other affects our workday. Still, the two, the problem of power and the reality of power, are curiously opposed and also related. We have had eras in our own history which seemed to be dominated by moral factors, as during the so-called Reform Era of pre-Civil War decades, which featured Horace Mann, Wendell Phillips, and similar notables. There have been other eras which appeared to be in the hands of unscrupulous agents. The Reconstruction period is notorious. Mark Twain's phrase for it, "The Gilded Age," hints that it was society's affluence which created the alleged evil.

But clearly affluence by itself does not explain anything. There were economic depressions and there were notable reformers during this affluent Age of Grant. Good times and infamous frauds flourished in earlier decades, while the Horace Manns and Wendell Phillipses nobly orated. Such characters are not quite so actively admired as one might think. Lip service and pious endorsement they receive in abundance. But it is also smart, as in history circles, to think of them as sanctimonious, shortsighted, and consciously or unconsciously serving reactionary forces, as compared, for example, to the "realistic" Jacksonians whom they opposed.

True, we term one age progressive and another age some permutation of nonprogressive. But these are only labels. Whatever may give a shade of idealism or of cynicism to a given period, certain moral and social constants persist in both, and are related.

The problem of understanding them is complicated by changing interpretations, and by shifting evaluations. That is

28

always true, and for the past as in the present. Alexander Hamilton rates now as a heartless aristocrat, and then as a farsighted statesman. It may be no surprise that the works of John C. Calhoun are being reverently collected in the South; but it may be of interest that they are also offered in excellent and respectful editions in the North, where, also, the once-admired William Lloyd Garrison is made the subject of big books, one of which was honored with a prize, which scorn and upbraid the abolitionist.

Ivan the Terrible is kindly treated and justified as a great leader and as a progressive, and a laudatory film about him is sympathetically viewed in the United States as well as in Stalin's Russia. And so with Genghis Khan, Oliver Cromwell, Louis XIV, Robespierre, and as many more symbolic figures as one wishes to name. Some of them might seem, at a quick glance, to lack a future in human sympathy. This would, perhaps, seem the case with such a character as Adolf Hitler. But not necessarily. Forgetfulness and discrimination with details work wonders with history. Other historic figures have, like this one, cut down their foes, and often with fire and sword, and emerged with vigorous and controversial reputations. Take one Bogdan Chmielnicki, a seventeenth-century Cossack who did remarkably well as a scourge, considering his more limited technological resources for curbing population growth. Yet he is considered a patriot by his people, a statue commemorates him in Kiev, Chmielnicki-grad and Chmielnicki Province memorialize him, and Ukrainian heroes can hope to win the Order of Chmielnicki. I deliberately avoid detailing his and his Cossacks' services in nationalism, notably with respect to the Jews, in order to illustrate how time can blur and obliterate disturbing details, and leave only such residue as may serve one or another contemporary purpose. It would be the purest naïveté to think of anyone at all as without hope of attracting loyalty and defense.

Not only is ruthlessness excused in human affairs. Moral and noble attitudes are often criticized or derided, and even by moralists and hero-worshipers. Numerous self-righteous people think the world needs conciliation, needs compromise, needs shallow friendship and cooperation. This seems better to them than the kind of dignity and "firmness in the right," as Lincoln put it, which could, for instance, lead to international showdowns, and so to catastrophic wars. This point of view puts a premium on intellectual fuzziness, and is resentful of history. Of what use to remember United States operations in the Philippines at the turn of the century, or Russian strategy in the Katyn Forest during World War II? Or Dominican atrocities in Haiti, or Mexican oppression in Yucatan? None of these memories serve peace today. So better forgive. Or still better forget.

Considering such a disorderly series of situations, one finds oneself inevitably back in the era of the Borgias and the Medici, and with a need for coping with their most famous, if unsolicited, spokesman. Machiavelli haunts our lives with phrases which plainly deny God, virtue, and humanity, yet which also seem to speak of things as they truly are. The evidence is not in Machiavelli's more notorious epigrams, which, if untrue, could simply be forgotten. The evidence is in his commentators, who feel compelled to revive them, if only to explain them away. But always in terms which bring out in brighter and darker hues their immortal challenge.

One editor protests that Machiavelli was personally kindly and of good ethics, but that he was driven by adversity to bitter statements—as though this somehow made their import less real. Another takes Machiavelli's *The Prince* to be a satire on tyrants, but he does not explain what social forces permitted the tyrants to flourish. Still another satisfies himself by viewing Machiavelli as confused and self-contradictory, with truth and logic triumphant over his shortsighted and crude ideas. There have been famous "anti-Machiavelli" tracts, notably by Frederick, known as the Great. Shortly after Frederick published his virtuous diatribe, following absurd wranglings with Voltaire over its wording, he himself broke treaties to undertake the swift conquest of Silesia. Frederick in the years following made his bloody mark as a warrior, a double-dealer, a disciplinarian: everything Machiavelli had urged upon his Prince.

It is obvious that it was the letter of Machiavelli's discourse which had annoyed Frederick, rather than its practice. In other words, Machiavelli gave the game away. If Frederick's good repute is merited, if he served Germany and perhaps the larger world with arts and organization, then his life justifies the Italian prophet. One can turn a famous epigram around, and observe of Frederick that hypocrisy is the tribute which virtue pays to vice.

Machiavelli himself was obviously a divided man. At one time he advises a friend to do anything he pleases without consideration for the opinions of others. At another time he praises faith and constancy at the expense of cunning and chicanery. It is the world, it is life itself, it is Machiavelli's readers century after century who choose to remember not his civic pieties and heavenly hopes—almost nobody troubles to read them—but his harsh, disillusioned, brutal conclusions.

It is always worthwhile refreshing oneself on the bare originals. Life is immoral, says Machiavelli. Nature shocks, conciliates, forgets, obliterates. Christianity is possible only in private life, since it leads us to depreciate the love of mundane things, and it makes us soft. It is better to be feared than loved, Machiavelli insists, better to be hated than despised. Life requires discipline, and discipline requires harshness. "All armed prophets have conquered, and"—he adds, remembering Savonarola—"all unarmed have been destroyed." The mass of people are fickle, shallow, ungrateful, greedy, cowardly. They always judge by appearances, and they appreciate nothing but success. Therefore, they need to be molded, rather than respected. Machiavelli adorns his terrible logic with the very robes of Christendom: "[Pope] Alexander VI never did anything else but deceive, nor ever thought of anything but deceiving, and always found dupes, yet he succeeded, for he knew this side of the world."

Machiavelli contributes his own quota of rationalizations to those of his more sympathetic readers. Nobody admits to admiring cruelty, and Machiavelli's defenders have included some of the most respectable voices of our civilization. So it grieves Machiavelli that Italy is broken up and in the hands of barbarians, as he terms the French and the Spanish. Italy needs a master. The true Prince seeks glory as well as empire. So he will not employ "harshness" for its own sake, but for the ultimate good of all Italians. Caesar Borgia was cruel, but he united Romagna; Machiavelli's own Florentines had been more humane, and as a result had permitted factions to destroy Pistoia. So mercy can harm the patriot. Liberality may be inefficient, destructive. It is better that one have a reputation for meanness, since those who are not hurt are many, and the hurt are few. The crucial quality to be sought is moral flexibility: "One should never sacrifice evil to good, when evil can easily get the better of good."

Self-preservation is the heart of Machiavelli's creed. As one commentator summed it up: "The spirit of Caesar [Borgia] was indestructible; it was the spirit of nature. His only sin was that he failed. . . . Nature was lawless, all men obeyed but one force—Necessity. And that was the truth." Such are some of the thoughts which have vibrated through more than four hundred years of experience. No doubt they have profited from the weaknesses and uncertainties of those who have found them unpleasant. The challenge of Machiavelli's best-known principles survived the turbulent events of his era, and reach directly into our own times and affect our own judgments.

Anyone observing events over the past years must note the inconstant state of glory and significance, and wonder how they affect our routine operations. In the thirties, we are severely divided on the issue of communism, some holding the U.S.S.R. to be the "Worker's Fatherland," and others not only that it stands for a cruel and murderous dictatorship in Russia, but that it threatens freedom everywhere else. Russia attacks Poland, the Spanish Republic collapses, and numerous American intellectuals announce themselves as disillusioned and cease being aware of the *Daily Worker*. World War II gets underway, and Russia, from having been an infamous partner in the Nazi-Soviet Pact, becomes a bastion of freedom, resisting Nazi barbarism.

A popular motion picture of the time, taking off from a popular nonfiction work, depicts Marshal Stalin as a shrewd, good-humored Russian equivalent of a Bronx politician, and his countrymen as just human beings. The Cold War begins, and we remember the Katyn Forest, the cruel betrayal of Warsaw, and Stalin's own cowardice and confusion during the eastward Nazi blitz. We lose monopoly of the A-bomb. U.S.-U.S.S.R. antagonism deepens. And now Stalin is dead, and there is a "thaw" in Russia. Khrushchev denounces him to the world as a tyrant, a boorish manipulator and worse. Stalin is removed from Lenin's tomb, and only anonymous donors leave flowers at his narrow grave beside the Kremlin wall.

Since then, his reputation pulses like a fever. He was responsible for defeats. He was the organizer of victory. He was a mass-murderer. Roughly but effectively, he led Russia to world leadership. He was brutal and mean. He was elemental and great. The Five Year Plans. The Moscow Trials.

Is it possible to make sense of such unrelated choices and commitments? The absolutist says no. And he is right to the extent that he clings to a particular vision of reality. He can be admired for his courage, steadiness of purpose, intelligence, even by those opposed to his principles. The Nazi Rommel was admired as "the Desert Fox" by people presumed to be anti-Nazis. But the relativist need not suffer confusion either. He can see history as giving him choices. He can, for example, accept what seems to him a great program—communist idealism, or bourgeois free enterprise—and he can also take an individual on his own terms and weigh his particular personality or career without regard to his larger social commitment.

In practice, the two approaches—the personal and the social—bear on one another, and create various currents of sympathy and distaste. Historians interpret and reinterpret the past in order to create comforting supports for the present. A John Dos Passos justifies his long career from socialism to antisocialism by emphasizing that his theme had always been freedom. Others are less conscientious about retracing their intellectual steps. They satisfy their consciences with such details as are effective for particular purposes.

The temptation is to say that might makes right, but this does not always seem to follow. Juan Perón certainly made right in Argentina during his years of power. But he was overthrown, and his career officially blackened. Despite all this, he and his prostitute wife continue to be revered and made political powers in Argentina. Evidently, the masses find little to inspire them in the present Argentinian leadership and prospects. So they cherish their memories of dashing Juan and beautiful Evita. A comparison with Adam Clayton Powell is relatively trifling and absurd, but it does give some sense of the process of social identification involved.

In the United States the social equation is complicated by the power of the masses directly to affect leadership, and to be affected by it. Not all men can become President, but enough of them can to give meaning to the old quip that since Chet Arthur could succeed Garfield to that office, no one was safe from it. Below—and in some cases above—the

Chief Executive are numerous other executives in every line of endeavor who must contrive to build their power within the structure that supports them, and to reduce the power of their competitors.

The very looseness of our social structure—or fluidity, as we prefer to say—gives reason and necessity to the least idealistic gambits of our social and political leaders. They are called many names: tycoons, bosses, czars, dictators, masters, and others suggesting unbridled power. They are satirized, exposed, and deplored. But there is evidence that they serve social purposes and are directly or indirectly supported by their rank and file. Lincoln Steffens, who probed to get to the bottom of the social process in his time, was as oddly read as Machiavelli himself. We have yet to confront the meaning of certain passages in Steffens' immortal *Autobiography*. He tells how Judge James B. Dill became a favorite target of journalists, who exposed him as a major figure in the creation of trusts. It was Dill who circumvented the laws. It was he who subverted New Jersey legislators to such effect that the state became notorious as "the mother of trusts." Steffens was astonished to learn that Judge Dill had himself passed on to reporters some of the choice examples of his skulduggery. Laughing, Dill explained that, unwittingly, the newspapermen had been providing him with free advertising. For what sounded so evil to them and to their casual and unthinking readers, sounded fine to the industrialists who clamored for Dill's professional services. They achieved, as a result, larger and larger business consolidations. The public obtained acts of Congress outlawing trusts.

The novelist David Graham Phillips wrote bitterly that to fathom the ethics of the great entrepreneurs one had to cut through the social classes until he reached the man who worked with the tools of a professional thief. The great industrial battles of his time, like the railroad wars between J. J. Hill and E. H. Harriman, seemed to bear him out. J. P. Morgan put it that he didn't pay a lawyer to tell him what he couldn't do, but what he could do. The rough plots of financiers and "captains" of business rang through the press during the eras of exposure, and presumably pilloried them for eternity.

Yet, as between the Populists and Progressives, on the one hand, and the symbols of monopoly, on the other, who enjoy the living monuments? The last Progressives supported Henry A. Wallace long ago in 1948: a dying and quixotic effort. But the names of Rockefeller, Lodge, Harriman, and Aldrich flourish today. The Huntington Library and Stanford University are meccas for intellectuals, the Guggenheim and Ford and Carnegie foundations their fountains of inspiration. Morgan survives as the hero who curbed the 1907 money panic, rather than as the buccaneer who started it. The Lamont Library houses scholars who do not seem to ponder the connection between freedom of the press and Morgan partners concerned for public relations.

Our time produces scholarly essays justifying Secretary of the Interior Albert A. Fall of Teapot Dome fame, as an individualist ruled by Western and neighborly ideals. And lest this seem a mere peccadillo in scholarship, Secretary of the Interior Stewart L. Udall had Fall's official portrait taken out of storage and restored to its place on the Interior Department's walls. Another scholar all but hails "Boss" Tweed of New York fame as an innovator in city administration. Still other scholars praise the old United States Senate, once sternly deplored as having been "the rich man's club," for having modernized and streamlined a once too individualistic and cumbersome body. There is no substantial countermovement to such social analyses. Our intellectuals are trying to tell us something. It behooves us to listen.

Several years ago, Lyle Stuart's nonconformist *Independent* printed a series of Machiavellian-style observations by a disillusioned and embittered radical. He advised readers to cheat, lie, and practice two-facedness in order to get ahead. The general effect of his essays was not to expose allegedly corrupt leaders of society. His strictures made no impression, and did not even attempt to explain the secret of their power. The essays were a total failure. They no more than revealed a soured and frustrated critic.

For he could not face up to the fact that social control of one sort or another there had to be. A democratic society is a rope of sand—a congeries of disparate personalities. They must have, or appear to have in common feelings, wants, and goals. They precipitate to the surface strategic individuals who offer tone and direction, praise and blame, emoluments and reprimands to the mass of their elite and to those beneath them. And they solicit public and private support for their establishment by means of myths, slogans, and promises.

A certain amount of this process is understood and accepted. Strong arms of defeated or retired administrations know they are ripe for firing, and they resign. They know that some of their aides will probably be replaced as well. Also, a certain amount of social skulduggery is routine and causes no excitement. Thus, the public appreciates that political promises will not be kept in all instances. But the inner workings of any administration, in and out of politics, and its relationship to its direct constituency, as well as its outside foes and friends, is more intricate. Nor is it entirely rational in the ordinary sense. People do not pause continually, as we have seen, to make past and present agree, and they often resent having this done for them. "Forget it!" is a standard American expression. It suggests that we can learn to manipulate our very subconscious so that it will not embarrass us with revelations.

Herbert Hoover's changing reputation is interesting in this respect because it shows dramatically how the public can agree to see things in varying and contradictory lights. It is well known that the campaign to identify him with so-called "Hoovervilles" was deliberately organized and projected by the publicity arm of the Democratic Party. Its aim was to undermine the good repute of one who had been world-famous as "the great humanitarian." The project was a sweeping success. Republicans who complained of the "unfairness" of the attack were at a loss to explain why they were unable to combat it. They had no understanding of why a general public which had been raised and nourished on publicity about Hoover's services in Belgium, Russia, and the Balkans, as well as in America, where "Hooverize" in the twenties entered the dictionary as meaning "saving," "public-spirited," "philanthropic"—why such a public was quick to turn against Hoover, and to accept the Democratic Party judgment of him.

Nevertheless, Hoover went on to accrete honors among the conservative elements of American society, and also among the larger population, and even among the Democrats. President Truman sent him abroad as chairman of the Famine Emergency Committee. Congress set up the Hoover Commission on Organization of the Executive Branch of the

Government, and "little Hoover commissions" followed elsewhere. When he died in 1964, there was scarcely a single
individual voice to endorse its old sincerity by publicly declaring: "Good riddance!" The President of the United
States himself, a veteran New Dealer, was at Hoover's funeral and subscribed various honors for him. It was, again, a
sign of Republican weakness that it proved wholly impotent
that year to use the universal praise and mourning for Hoover to any practical purpose.

Republican ineptitude that year, indeed, merits a small
footnote of its own. Goldwater was later to complain at
length about what seemed to him the unfairness of liberals
who interpreted his program with more imagination than
precision. For that matter, it was instructive that he would
have thought it wise to equate the Democratic Party with
liberalism. It did not occur to him or his junta to determine
why his opponents had succeeded in foisting their interpretations upon the general public. Nor did Goldwater display
more insight into his own presentations—into his own failure, for example, to win the public to joining him in his
effort to ridicule one of his antagonists for having been
named at birth "Hubert Horatio."

It is clear that the weakness and strength of factions are
less evidence of some individual's cunning and ability to
deceive than of the support or nonsupport of his followers or
electorate. A hungry and fearful depression generation was
willing to believe Hoover cold-hearted and malicious and
stupid. Later it buried him with honors. It also agreed to
perceive Goldwater as trigger-happy and impossible.
Whether right or wrong in these or other cases, the public's
judgments were *facts*. They affected events. The wise student
will handle such facts with care. He will try to understand
the needs which motivate them, and avoid the easy and
foolish pretense that they are accidents.

And, as in politics, so elsewhere. Attitudes, sympathies,
stakes in particular institutions and ideas are complicated by
the irregularity of democratic social controls—using "democratic" now with the small "d" of American life. The American is not always sure how he ought to feel and react. It is
not always clear to him who is boss, or what his party line
involves. Hence, such a book as A *Theory of Social Control*,
by Richard T. LaPiere (1954), is weakened by its assump-

tions of group uniformity. Uniformity there is to a significant extent. But the social correctives to individual deviation, such as he associates with such words as "reproach," "disdain," "derision," "taunt," "jeer," "shame," and "slight" work often in America with only moderate effectiveness. They probably require of leadership and management more variations and more effort than those correctives employed by a better organized society. For the latter can better appeal to traditions, laws, formal authority. And its directors can do so more efficiently than can the democratic opportunists who must make their own law in order to deal with the particular demands upon them created by democratic multiplicity.

Rod Serling's character Ramsey is an industrial Machiavelli in the television and screen play *Patterns*. But Ramsey is anything but alone in his cruel, egotistic, unfeeling, bullying methods. Serling's book-explication of his play tells us that half of the several hundred letters he received after the initial presentation of *Patterns* "pointedly asked if this wasn't really the story of so-and-so company with Mr. A. and Mr. B." It is impressive that the numerous executives everywhere to whom Serling points, with no school for scoundrels at which to learn their lessons, with nothing but their native wit and observations to guide them, should come up with similar techniques for social control. It suggests a combined conscious and unconscious transmission of ideas, gimmicks, and established conventions which can be used to unite social units for particular purposes.

Serling notes a substantial number of techniques by executives bent on elevating supporters and diminishing the persons they cannot use. They cut down their office facilities. They parcel out company credit and bonbons as it seems to suit them. There is the needling process, intended to shake the individual's concentration and sense of involvement. There is the malicious laughter, often senseless and without rational point, but intended to give directions to understrappers with respect to in-and-out personnel. There is the stealing of ideas. All this can be accomplished with greater or lesser vulgarity, with more or less intelligence, depending on the quality of the specific institution. Andy Sloane, Serling's protagonist, spells it out for his own: "On our level you don't get fired. You resign. . . . They create a situation you can't work in and finally can't live in—tension, abuse, mostly

subtle and sometimes violent. Chip away at your pride, your
security, until you begin to doubt, then fear. . . . Ramsey
wants me to resign. . . . He thinks he can make me miserable enough to do that." *Patterns* is not a good play. But, as
Serling notes, it quite evidently touched the nerves of many
people who felt it said something about themselves. The
most interesting fact about the play is that although it was
about integrity, it was itself twisted and mauled by its author, directors, and producers to suit various commercial
purposes. Thus, it appears that the people who made it
famous, and whom the managers sought to serve, wished to
know something about the Machiavellian threads by which
they danced, but that they could not endure seeing them too
clearly. Also, that they had no intention of doing anything
which would minimize the role of Machiavellianism in social
control. *Patterns* thus becomes itself part of the pattern it is
describing, siphoning off such discontent as it might arouse
with false aesthetic catharsis.

Such, then, are some of the details of a major facet of
social life which can take one as far afield as the remote
stretches of history, and as near as the latest newspaper
controversies. All this is not, of course, to say that there are
no alternatives to aggressive involvement in affairs. Numerous non-competitors help give warmth and variety and meaning to life. A Colonel Cook deserves his own niche in history
because, in 1827, he entered the race for United States
Representative for the Ninth Congressional District, cam-
paigning against David Crockett. It is not well known that
this district represented the second largest constituency in
the country at that time. Colonel Cook, we are told, "with-
drew from the canvass in righteous indignation over the
irrationality of the electorate, saying that he would not con-
sent to represent people who would applaud an acknowledged liar," such as Crockett certainly was, in his own entertaining way.

Randolph Bourne was touched, in the early stages of
World War I, by the story of the German woman, long a
resident in a French town, who, when German troops entered it, went around chalking on the doors of friends and
neighbors the words "Gute Leute" (good folks). Needless to
say, there are good folks everywhere, and there is good in
most people. There are people who resist opportunities to get

rich. There are individuals who give up status and emoluments for love or drink. There are, in short, impractical
people. Thoreau said he cared nothing about the history of
the Pharaohs, but would give much to know about an obscure Egyptian of the time when the pyramids were being
built. It is unlikely, however, that he would have found this
one's frame of reference to have varied markedly from that
of Pharaoh. And he would have found every social engine in
operation to persuade him to accept Pharaoh's values.

For, let it be emphasized, social control there must be,
and, essentially, this fact is accepted. A few malcontents
resist the inevitable. Extremists are upset because our government dispenses foreign aid or refuses to atom-bomb Red
China. Other extremists see a creeping conspiracy of Birch-
ites which threatens our allegedly traditional freedoms.
But most Americans are not out to overturn anything, but
only to secure and advance themselves. And to accomplish
this end, they find ways and means to move as individuals
and as groups along particular social lines.

There seem, for example, to be large and awesomely clear
divisions of prerogative unconsciously created by self-interest
and tradition. Superpatriots denounce Communist subversion and money poured out to support foreign incendiaries.
But they do not perceive the disloyalty in highway and
building contractors who in effect steal public funds and
harm American resources. And though they may be vague on
foreign policy, they are precise about who can be allowed at
the community pork barrel. No Communists need apply.

Within such natural divisions of authority, there is the
fight for status and control which varies with conditions. The
key fact, to repeat, is not the crafty expertise of the individual, but the will of his constituents. It is all a matter of social
strength. The hero of this particular complex, has been, by
far, John F. Kennedy. His effect is too immediately impressive to permit extended comment. Some individuals have put
it that they simply cannot endure disinterested examination
of his life and its meaning. There seem elements of what can
only be called reverence in some of their attitudes. An interesting complication is provided by the remarkable effort, in
December 1962, of some of his faction to undermine the
prestige of Adlai E. Stevenson, in connection with the
Cuban missile crisis. Stevenson himself had the admiration

of a substantial percentage of the people dedicated to the more successful Kennedy. They seem to have resolved their dilemmas in this particular case by voting, so to speak, to forget distasteful and confusing aspects of this embarrassing incident.

The great storms raised by the subsequent assassination and the continuing controversies deriving from it—including particularly disgusting slurs upon President Johnson—are evidence of how far we are from the kind of elite society to which Machiavelli appealed. His Prince was expected to manipulate peers, for the most part. Our own society has given every person, however competent or incompetent, an opportunity to enter into the decision-making process. Here is Machiavelli for the millions. The voice of the people has not only been heard. It has been given parity. It has been solicited, flattered, polled, geared into the highest policy.

The course of assassination shows this. Charles J. Guiteau was a disappointed office seeker, and his irresponsible shooting of President Garfield helped bring on the civil service list. Leon Czolgosz, McKinley's assassin, was a young man much like Lee Harvey Oswald: malcontent, vaguely leftish, churlish, and with a crude envy of others. But there has been no one before quite like Jack Ruby, with his impudent sense of identification with Mrs. Kennedy's alleged feelings, and his empty impulse to shoot himself a place in history. Con men, pushers, thieves, and guntoters have previously been satisfied to scratch their shallow satisfactions out of the fabric of society. They have usually harbored a naïve reverence for their betters. They have not presumed to hold the kind of social-political attitudes and ideas Ruby grotesquely assumed.

He attained instant fame, in the modern manner, but he was not accorded its ordinary concomitant: instant oblivion. For a moment, he all but appeared to have become part of the permanent scene, and, as a result, President Johnson in 1965 took the oath of office behind bulletproof glass. We hope that the threat of a proliferation of Rubys will recede, but Machiavellianism will doubtless continue to probe Ruby's place in our affairs in coming years.

Machiavelli is here to stay. We must continue to ponder the strange and wonderful turns of the public mind, so that they can be better anticipated and used to social and individual purpose. It causes the late Senator Joseph McCarthy to be remembered, though he is dead, and former Representative Martin Dies to be forgotten, though he is still alive. The public still, at this writing, makes it more or less à la mode in the North to be upset about Negro injustices, but not bad taste to make jokes about Indians, and few urge reforms in their behalf. The government does its best to keep up with the public and to control it. It fights a war, while trying to avoid an all-out war. It blunders on between cutbacks and giveaways in domestic affairs. Given the kind of society we have, it can do little better. No government can be superior to the public which has elected it. And many good people cannot see that they have much choice beyond working as best they can within the establishment, and unpacking their hearts with words when they find conditions drab and unfruitful.

This sense of fatalism is, indeed, one of the less promising aspects of our present human condition. It was widely observed, at the time George Orwell's *Nineteen Eighty-four* was published, that not only did the world he conjured up seem possible; many commentators declared that in large measure it seemed to have arrived. Such fatalistic acceptance of the logic of Orwell's novel hinted how uncreative Machiavellianism had become. It was no longer a spur to social change. It symbolized how unrealistic it seemed for any mere individual to imagine that he could be himself: unbending, self-respecting.

However, and for the last time, it was not Orwell who had persuaded his readers that human dignity was no longer feasible. It was the public which persuaded Orwell. He was convinced that for every person there was a Room Number 101, which contained the worst thing in the world: the thing to persuade him to betray himself, and his beloved, and all hope for himself and the future. For Orwell's protagonist Winston it was large, bushy, ferocious rats which would eat his face if he did not repudiate his nearest and dearest, and sincerely love Big Brother. Everyone could be bought or broken. The concept of the human spirit was absurd, archaic, dead.

It was the reading public which failed to see the flaw, the challenge in Orwell's tale. The monster O'Brien himself tells Winston that he (Winston) had not been deceived. Deep in his subconscious he had known that O'Brien was not his friend, was not his comrade, but his worst enemy. His subconscious had not prepared for the revelation. It had betrayed Winston into unpreparedness, and consequent inability to resist O'Brien's tortures. The traitor to humanity was only incidentally the devil O'Brien. Mainly, it was Winston himself.

For it is not true that the choice is between fanatical martyrdom and abasement. *Nineteen Eighty-four* is real only if one believes it. Otherwise, it is a paper tiger, and the O'Briens are powerless. For though they can indeed force human beings to concede their humanity through fiendish torments, the resourceful human being prepares against their terrors. There were a dozen occasions when and many more ways by which Winston could have died, and robbed the devil of his soul. Winston did not foresee, and he could not forearm. He implicated himself in his own moral destruction.

A civilization which does not teach its citizens how to die is no civilization at all, but, as Wendell Phillips put it, a gang of slaves. It has no philosophy, no ethics, no humanities, no social sciences. None of these amounts to anything, if it does not teach the victorious defense of principles. A wise Machiavellianism prepares for emergencies. The wise American will be prepared when he has been blackguarded or deprived. He will have another job in readiness, and good humor as he recalls the transient nature of fame and vogues. If necessary, he will be ready to die, rather than to suffer degradation.

But a program which honors humanity will not concentrate on so negative a policy as dying. The buccaneers of society like nothing so much as to bury the idealist and heap flowers at his graveside. The idealist will do his best to deprive them of their occasion. He needs to endure, if only to encourage others of his sort to remember that they are precious to humanity and need to be preserved. For the worst of a shoddy Machiavellianism might be not that it is untidy in its moral premises, not that it sponsors what the nineteenth century termed "practical atheism," but that it could be efficient without being successful. We could, in the last bunkers, be contriving to supersede each other while bombs fell which were erasing us all.

It is not the wheeler-dealer, then, on whom the spotlight needs to play. The wheeler-dealer is at best but a symbol of the trends and purposes which society has evolved. In those trends, in those purposes, the individual, whether Machiavellian or otherwise, can read his fate.

The Shifting Illusion
Dream and Fact

MAXWELL GEISMAR

The American Dream has been our ruling myth, as a culture and in the literature which both reveals and helps to shape our culture, from the days of the Founding Fathers, the Declaration of Revolution, and the Constitution itself. Those were great days indeed, heroic personages, the birth of that democratic faith and works which would change the face of the world, and alter, for the better, what had been up to then, history's sinister record of monarchy, despotism, intolerance, injustice.

This dream was bodied forth in all our major statements and documents, political, cultural, and literary, for almost two hundred years. It still persists as a cultural ideal in our mass media and in the popular notion of the American democracy; even now no American president could rise to office without a public acknowledgment of, a formal obeisance to, the American Dream. Among our major writers it has persisted in one form or another—often, most vitally, in our literary tradition of social criticism and social justice— through such figures as William Dean Howells and Mark Twain to Sherwood Anderson, Ellen Glasgow, and Theodore Dreiser. Right there was perhaps its peak and decline. This period, and what preceded it and what followed it, I intend to discuss in the present essay.

Almost from the start, too, this beautiful and touching vision of a democratic society and culture which was to redo and redeem all of history's evil chronicle contained within itself the darker element of the American nightmare; perhaps too high a hope led too suddenly to a sense of cynicism and despair. (Our own period, as I shall describe later, saw a whole series of writers from H. L. Mencken and Hemingway to Henry Miller and Richard Wright, obsessed with the nightmarish aspects of our culture.) Even the first great flowering of New England Transcendentalism, which, in such pure voices as those of Emerson and Thoreau and the early Melville along with the early Whitman, expressed the American Dream at its purest, lyrical prime, was followed directly by the crushing and bloody epoch of the Civil War.

In those pre-Civil War years of belief and beauty and innocence which marked the Old Republic, moreover, there was the strange case of Nathaniel Hawthorne brooding over Puritanical sin and guilt; and already, as D. H. Lawrence pointed out later, the shadow of the Indian tribal culture, so shamefully "liquidated" (in what is today called genocide), lay over the national and literary consciousness. In the case of Melville himself, what prophetic instinct made his epic drama of the white whale also an indictment, as he well knew when writing it, not merely of the Puritan God-Father, but of New England's religion and culture alike? And what elements of cultural fear and repression made the New England critics and censors, artists and divines alike, ministers of God and of state, conspire to strike Melville's great book off the record so completely that for almost seventy-five years his name was unheard of in our literary annals? In sober truth, the greatest artist of that period wandered to the brink of nervous collapse and insanity during those years of ostracism, when he wrote, nevertheless, what are to my mind the greatest short stories in our literature: the *Piazza Tales* (1856) and "Benito Cereno" (really a novella).

The case of Herman Melville is an instructive parable of the Artist in America. Perhaps it is not so commonly known that the later Walt Whitman, the lyrical bard of America's promises and the bright new brotherhood of man, also had his doubts about the democracy's future. Buoyed up, as were the abolitionists, by the moral splendor of the Civil War's cause and by Lincoln's heroic stature, Whitman recorded, in both his diary and his later poetry, the impact of finance-capitalism upon the Old Republic, the dawning age of the tycoons and the oligarchy, the moral corruption rampant in the post-Civil War exploitation of what was in effect an internal empire. Yet the final image of Whitman is still that of America's Orphic Bard; and Melville himself recovering from the depths of his own despair, left us, from his death-bed, the matchless parable of "Billy Budd" (1891).

But in this story, Melville's final vision of life was not that of evil lying at the center of nature, or of an evil nature controlling man's fate: nature *as* evil. In "Billy Budd" is rendered the classical concept of modern literature, the base of the tragic vision: the concept of good and evil as balanced in life, struggling with each other, and indifferent to man himself. (Later, Dreiser remarked that God meant well, but that *He* was always in trouble, and therefore constantly needed our help.) And this concept still leaves room for man's control of his own society and culture, of his own destiny. The American Dream had survived its first ordeal in the middle and latter half of the nineteenth century; but in such subsequent figures as William Dean Howells and Mark Twain it was to be tested even more sharply.

For Howells and Twain were living at the peak of nine-teenth-century finance-capitalism, the ascendancy of the in-dustrial and scientific complex, and (not to mention the closing of the frontier) the actual beginnings of the modern American empire. Both these writers grew up in the days of the Old Republic, a rural, small-town, agrarian-merchant-artisan nation which still prized individual character—virtue, honor, and independence—and both writers were confronted with the enormous social corruption of the great fortunes in the Gilded Age.

Intimate and lifelong friends as Howells and Twain were, they were of very unlike temperaments, and they reacted to their historical situation in very different ways. Howells was a fashionable and graceful novelist rather than a major talent; but as an editor and critic of great distinction he had worked his way up to a position of influence in the New England hierarchy which still controlled our literature in the latter half of the nineteenth century. When Howells made his decision to leave Boston, to surrender all his hard-won pres-tige, to come to New York and join all the forces of social unrest and social criticism of the time—this was an act of such moral courage as to make him the true dean of Ameri-can literature. From this decision also came some of his best novels and chronicles: *A Hazard of New Fortunes* in 1890, *The World of Chance* in 1893, *A Traveler from Altruria* in 1894. But Howells' "radicalism"—though he was hounded and denounced for his support of the Haymarket anarchists —extended only so far as the rather sweet and romantic doctrines of Utopian or Christian Socialism. But it was, perhaps, an unacknowledged influence on the thinking of his famous friend.

Mark Twain—who here as elsewhere was admittedly two selves, the public celebrity, the private dissenter—was by nature and temperament far more rebellious, bolder, shrewder, angrier, funnier, more penetrating and eloquent in his social commentary. As early as *Tom Sawyer* (1876) and *Huckleberry Finn* (1884), he showed his native proclivity for "nature's womb," the outlaw and pagan life as against all the famous Freudian discontents (and repressions) of civilization as it existed even in raw frontier river towns like Hannibal, Missouri. In fact it was Sam Clemens' self-education about the true nature of slavery as a social and moral evil which laid the whole basis for his blunt criticism of every other social injustice. And the series of disasters, the financial bankruptcy, the domestic tragedies, which cut his career in half, did not, in my own view, diminish his talent—as some Mark Twain scholars have proclaimed—so much as they enriched it. It was on that celebrated world lecture tour in the mid-1890's which was designed to pay back his debts—as it did—that ironically enough Mark Twain first observed the results of imperialism in Europe, Asia, and Africa.

Mark Twain was indeed the first American writer to understand the crucial nature of imperialism from the late nineteenth century to the present time: as the *method* through which a tiny segment of the world called Western white civilization attempted to control and exploit all the other huge land masses of so-called "primitive" and darker-skinned people. From this source stemmed his brilliant series of polemical satires on our missionaries in China, on the Belgian Congo, on the Russian Czar and serfdom, and—as this relentless spirit turned his gaze nearer home—on the United States of Lyncherdom, on our conquest of the Philippines, and finally, on what Mark Twain considered to be the start of a new "monarchy" in the United States, and the creation of an American empire of wealth, power, and world conquest which had swiftly encompassed the Old Republic.

Thus the world-famous figure (and the only other talent in our nineteenth-century culture to compare with the stricken Melville)—whose career had best epitomized all the glowing virtues of the American Dream—ended up as the historian of its demise and as the author of dark and night-marish parables. In another celebrated novella which is in the top brackets of our literature, "The Mysterious Stranger" (1916), Mark Twain proclaimed that the race of man was just another mistake of God's, and an object of disdainful scorn to Satan, the true ruler of the world.

I have sketched the background of contemporary American fiction. The central myth of the American Dream had two periods of revival and rebirth in our own time. Ironically, the first two decades of the twentieth century—the epoch of the muckrakers, the populist movements, of a native radicalism in our politics which culminated in the New Freedom of President Wilson and the New Deal of Roosevelt—were spearheaded by a group of talented writers who inaugurated the second great renascence in our literature. Starting as far back in the 1890's as Stephen Crane and Frank Norris, working up through such figures as Jack London, Ellen Glasgow, and Edith Wharton, to Sherwood Anderson and Theodore Dreiser, this group of mainly social realists and radical critics of American society formed the first peak of modern American fiction.

They not only "opened the road" to contemporary masters like Hemingway, Faulkner, and F. Scott Fitzgerald; they earned their own claims to distinction. To know their work (which has been curiously underestimated in recent years) is to experience the flavor of American literature at its best, and to understand much more clearly what has happened to it since then.

In this group of writers also, the American Dream and / or nightmare went through its third cycle of development since the Civil War, though of course the form of the myth varied with different writers. Jack London started his fabulously successful career as a popular fiction writer who embraced the cause of revolutionary socialism, only to end up as a disenchanted hack writer, a paranoid alcoholic, an early advocate of fascism and the superman. His prophetic novel *The Iron Heel* (1907) anticipated George Orwell's *Nineteen Eighty-four* (1949); it was from London's anti-utopian work that Orwell got his title. Willa Cather deliberately returned to the romance of frontier days in her disdain for modern commercial society; joining the church, she worked ever backwards in her fiction to regain some lost glory. Similarly, the middle-western storyteller, Sherwood Anderson, horrified by the poverty and degradation of urban life in Chicago, disenchanted by the artistic bohemias of New York and Paris, returned to the small southern town of Marion, Virginia, to preserve his faith in old-fashioned American democracy.

But it was Theodore Dreiser (in my view the greatest modern American realist, just as Melville was the greatest novelist of the nineteenth century) whose work most clearly showed the twisting and turnings of the American Dream concept. So often attacked for his later radical phase, Dreiser opened his career as a conservative, even a Darwin-and-Spencer conservative, and a realist who by virtue of his newspaper training was hard-bitten and cynical. He loved to observe the blind forces of power struggling against each other in the American scene of the 1900's; he felt equally at home with the great titans of finance (the Cowperwood trilogy) and the struggling and violent labor unions of the period. He envisioned this whole cultural scene as "the American century," in which he foresaw another blooming of our native culture and art. He was right, of course, except that the blooming took another turn toward the darker side of the American Dream. By 1925 Dreiser's most famous book, *An American Tragedy*, described his whole society as a monstrous trap, which corrupted such average souls as Clyde Griffiths through its visions of instant cash and hot culture.

A year later, in 1926, H. L. Mencken published his *Notes on Democracy*, perhaps the blackest and most nightmarish book on this subject ever written. Mencken lacked the roots and ties of a Dreiser, and Dreiser's humanity; the American scene was a farce to him from the beginning. And such were the origins of the famous "Lost Generation" of American artists who, in the twenties, brought our literature to another peak of fame and glory. I am sure that all the figures in this group—from Ezra Pound and T. S. Eliot, for example, to Ring Lardner, Ernest Hemingway, F. Scott Fitzgerald, John Dos Passos, and Sinclair Lewis—not to mention a host of critics, essayists, and other poets belonging to the same movement—are well known to the readers of this book, and I need not describe their achievement in detail.

I myself grew up in all the blazing splendor of their work. But as time has passed, and as the whole tradition of American literature before them and after them has emerged more clearly, I confess that their achievement has seemed more limited to me. In one sense they were far more "lost" than they believed they were. They were twice lost, not merely as alienated expatriates from World War I, a condition they recognized, but as alienated expatriates from their own American culture, one they did not quite realize. That famous "Coming of Age" which the literary historian Van Wyck Brooks proclaimed in the twenties, that glorious sense of being all new, all modern, all emancipated, which this whole group shared, also implied a lack of knowledge about previous American literature and the heritage of American culture (which the same literary historian, Brooks, spent the rest of his life discovering and describing). And this lack of cultural ties and tradition—acknowledging that great art is always international in effect, but specific, even provincial in *origins*—showed up clearly in the later careers of these writers.

While Pound became a Fascist, Eliot turned to the Church of England: how the Founding Fathers of the Republic would have groaned! A Melville, a Whitman, a Mark Twain, despite elements of nightmare, could never have understood *that*. Ernest Hemingway, after the great dark stories of the thirties, produced very little of consequence; and very little of his work was concerned with the United States. Like Scott Fitzgerald, Hemingway was essentially a poet of youth and physical virtue; and since both these writers lacked any sense of a cultural framework, or any true social concern, there was little left to nourish and develop their art in their maturity. Like many other figures in this group who had cut off their cultural roots, they really had no true maturity, and the whole literary renascence of the twenties, so brilliant, so glittering, so exciting at its birth, came to a tragic ending. John Dos Passos, after the great achievement of the trilogy called *U.S.A.*—still one of the key works of that period—also went into a rapid decline.

Was it really their own fault, as Bernard DeVoto said, in being so "defeatist," so alienated indeed, or in some cases so addicted to "foreign" philosophies of socialism, communism, anarchism—and did they deserve what they got? Or was something wrong with the prosperous "normalcy" of the twenties, a rich, luxurious, self-centered, and materialistic epoch which marked indeed another triumph of that "American empire" which Mark Twain had first scented, and which a decade later Mr. DeVoto himself would come to recognize? With the advent of the Great Depression, many of the expatriates returned home, and a fresh hope was born in our literature; the American Dream itself found a new expression. (This Dream always drifting into nightmare, and yet always being reborn at the critical moment!) That old-fashioned democrat, Sherwood Anderson, himself discovering a new spirit in the national consciousness, gave us perhaps the best documentary account of the depression years in such books as *Puzzled America* and his *Memoirs*.

Thomas Wolfe, among the younger writers—Thomas Wolfe, far more than John Steinbeck—best exemplified the revived hope, the promises, the vision of a restructured democracy in the United States. The beautiful and lyrical passages in *The Web and the Rock* (1939) told of the "promises" in the rustling leaves across the American continent. "And everywhere, through the immortal dark, something moving in the night, and something stirring in the hearts of men, and something crying in their wild, unuttered blood, the wild unuttered tongues of its huge prophecies—so soon the morning, soon the morning: O America." And there are those farewell lines to his editor, Maxwell Perkins of Scribners, the "Fox" of *You Can't Go Home Again* (1940): "Man was born to live, to suffer, and to die, and what befalls him is a tragic lot. There is no denying this in the final end. *But we must, dear Fox, deny it all along the way.*" And the final statement which merged this highly individualistic genius with his own people: "And the essence of all faith, it seems to me, for such a man as I, the essence of all religion for people of my belief, is that man's life can be, and will be, better."

With the early death of Thomas Wolfe, and the steady decline of John Steinbeck after *The Grapes of Wrath* (1939), American literature suffered a great loss. For a while in the forties and fifties it seemed that William Faulkner was the only high talent at work in our midst, and even then, Faulkner's work after *Absalom, Absalom!* in 1936 would never reach the peak of his early novels. Meanwhile, during the same contemporary period, our literature went through a development altogether different from anything which had occurred before.

This period is still so close to us that it seems ambiguous

and intricate, and perhaps not yet subject to definitive analysis. But from the vantage point of the later sixties, certain elements have emerged more clearly; and part of this period, at least, can be written down as history.

What has been revealed seems clear indeed. Since 1945, when all signs pointed to a literary revival comparable to that after World War I, our literature has actually been in a state of decline. Most, if not all, of the writers celebrated in John Aldridge's *After the Lost Generation* (1958) have simply disappeared from the literary scene. (Whether it is *their* fault, as he has said recently, or his as a matter of critical taste, is a moot question.) Among the real talents of the early fifties, in my own view, Norman Mailer has in effect stopped writing serious fiction. James Jones, with two big war novels to his credit, has remained stationary, and unable to deal with anything but war. And despite all the critical acclaim for William Styron's *Confessions of Nat Turner*, in 1967, this very talented artist has descended to the level of a commercial best-seller writer and a romantic pseudo-historian. Among them all, as of this writing, it is only the gifted Texas writer John Howard Griffin, author of *The Devil Rides Outside* (1952), the dark fable *Nuni* (1956), and the remarkable documentary *Black Like Me* (1961), who has continued to develop in his vision and his art alike.

I should also remember to mention the contemporary New England novelist Truman Nelson, author of two notable transcendental-abolitionist novels, *The Sin of the Prophet* (1952) and *The Surveyor* (1960), a study of John Brown in Kansas. Nelson's work was largely neglected in the fifties because of his unpopular historical position. And here we reach another key element in contemporary literature. If, during the earlier period between the world wars, many leading American intellectuals had been involved too deeply in leftist politics, now in a kind of group revulsion they moved away from *all* concern with society, culture, and history. The so-called New Criticism of our period declared its central concern to be only the work of art, naked and alone, viewed on a purely technical level which was to be devoid of psychology, society, history, and autobiography. (While this school added some valuable tools to literary criticism, its aim, on the face of it, was too narrow in scope, if not impossible to achieve.) The age of artistic withdrawal from American society in the forties was capped by the age of political suppression, censorship, and conformity known as the McCarthy period and the Cold War.

What was left in the fifties? A dominant school of *personal* sensibility and of superior entertainment best embodied in the *New Yorker* school of writers; writers who are always leading up to something that never happens, and never can happen. I am thinking of such a writer as J. D. Salinger, whose ineffable Glass family has moved further and further into Zen mysticism, total alienation, abstractedness, and pathology. (One thinks of the score of doctoral dissertations, just about ten years ago, which gave to Salinger a primary position in contemporary fiction.) And this typical writer of our period was followed by a group of similar figures who all had an accomplished technique, a highly developed sensibility, and—? I am thinking of John Updike and Philip Roth, both touching and witty in short stories, but unable to write anything of consequence in a larger fictional form.

The trouble with Philip Roth's novel *Letting Go* (1962), a purported tale of spiritual emancipation, was that there was nothing to let go *from*. I am including in this category writers of larger talent, such as John Hersey, who, starting with the excellent documentary *Hiroshima* (1946) and the solid documentary novel *The Wall* (1950), has apparently retreated into another garden of polite emotional entanglements. Yes, and even the gifted Saul Bellow, whose vision and values could belong to a larger tradition, has been so affected by our prevailing literary climate as to come to an absolute impasse, if not debacle, in the much-heralded *Herzog* (1964). The true victim of the prevailing cultural climate in the fifties was American literature itself. No wonder the cult of Henry James flourished during the same period, since James represented everything that the period craved: gentility, manners, conformity, parlor comedy, technical dexterity at the cost of content, at the cost even of his own characters, a prevailing sense of the "vulgar world," from which the superior, if not snobbish, artist qua artist could escape into a form of complex artifice which complacently labeled itself as high art.

In this view, Henry Miller and Richard Wright were the last of the giants in modern American fiction, and giants partly maimed by the conditions of what amounted to an underground existence. It was only with the recent American publication of his famous early trilogy, including *Tropic of Cancer* (1934) and *Tropic of Capricorn* (1939) – Miller's "trilogies" are both two books and a half, the last half never being written – that, at long last, Miller received the recognition in his own country that has for a long time been accorded to him in Europe and among modern artists in general.

His second trilogy, again incomplete, like the Indian blankets that left an unfinished corner so as to be deliberately "open," providing a way to infinity, *The Rosy Crucifixion* (1949–53), seems to me an even more effective work. As early as the thirties, Miller decided for himself that either American society was through or he was through with it. He jumped off the bandwagon of "success" (depicted in those great scenes in which he was a personnel manager for Western Union in New York City), went underground to live a bum's life, and to write. Sexual pleasure became both an opiate and a way of protest for him. He is the true ancestor of all the beatniks and hippies, except that he is a most immensely learned, intensely cultivated writer of major stature. To read him, after recognizing all his quirks, traps, and entanglements, is to breathe the air of great literature again. Literally hundreds of ordinary people (his old friends and acquaintances), people from the middle and lower depths of American urban society, caper, throng, prance, and stumble through the pages of his two major works of fiction.

But Miller's view not merely of the American scene but of all modern, progressive, scientific, and industrial life, is basically hopeless if not desperate. As a writer he lives, as it were, on his biological energy and his devotion to thought and art; and it is logical that his scenes of warmth and love and affection center around "old-fashioned" American life, such as the beautiful eulogy to New York's East Side in the first decades of the century.

It is curious too that Richard Wright stands at almost the opposite end of the literary spectrum, since while Miller resigned from modern society, Wright is almost the best symbol of social concern and social protest being molded into literary masterworks. This huge, raw, powerful, thrusting talent (but not as naïve or unsophisticated or craftless as it seems) first came to light in *Native Son* (1940). But earlier than that Wright had done a book of beautiful short stories called *Uncle Tom's Children* (1938), and afterwards he wrote the impressive autobiography *Black Boy* (1945).

Wright was the first to describe the agonized, tormented, and violent emotional depths of the American Negro which have since been revealed in the black protest and liberation movements of our own day. And to one degree or another we may trace the two most effective moments of the sixties as descending from either Henry Miller or Richard Wright. From Miller descended, as I've said, the beatnik and hippie traditions which, whatever their obvious limitations, provided a liberating force in our literature from the sterile conformity of the fifties. Such writers as Jack Kerouac, Allen Ginsberg, Lawrence Ferlinghetti, to mention only a few, brought our literature out of the bowers of academe back to the streets of life, a life distorted and malformed and "sick" with the modern sickness which the early existentialists first proclaimed.

From Wright descended the other contemporary tradition (which may be the more important one, since there is only one Henry Miller) that included, among many other figures (and there are many still to come) Ralph Ellison, James Baldwin, and most recently Eldridge Cleaver. Now the reason that Cleaver's talent seems to me the largest of the three, at the moment, is partly the fact that he does not have the similarity to the Richard Wright whom he admires, but also because his talent appeared in a later, bolder, and freer time in history. Ralph Ellison has almost fatally imprisoned himself in the contemporary "Genteel Tradition" of the Cold War period; and even though Baldwin turned full circle in mid-career, after denouncing both Wright and the novel of social protest, to become another revolutionary spokesman for his people, he still retains many traces of his former purely "aesthetic" training. I use aesthetics in quotes because I do not believe that any great art has come from a purely aesthetic point of view. Aesthetics is indeed the art of *transforming* experience into permanency, and the material of aesthetics must be personal, psychological, social, cultural, and historical. Aesthetics feeding merely upon aesthetics can never lead to an aesthetic achievement.

It was fortunate for Eldridge Cleaver that he appeared upon our literary scene after the civil rights struggles in the South and the protest against the foolish and immoral war in

Vietnam have loosened up our whole cultural environment. It was no coincidence that his book *Soul on Ice* (1968), written in prison by a self-taught convict serving out a nine-year term, should become within weeks of publication a national best seller of the highest quality and national importance. Like Richard Wright, like Malcolm X (Cleaver was one of his disciples) this was a new voice concerned with important matters. Nor, despite the turbulence of the black scene today, and despite all the alarums and excursions, should it surprise us that Cleaver's book is full of hope, belief, and excitement about the future destiny of his own people, and the American Dream to which they now aspire. It is Black America today that is repudiating, however rashly or unreasonably at times, just that black side of the American Dream which we have called the American nightmare.

It has always been an informed *minority*, from the Founding Fathers to the New England abolitionists, which has fostered the vision of the American Dream and finally made it prevail throughout the nation. Similarly, in the age of the great industrial fortunes after the Civil War, when it seemed that American democracy had been altogether corrupted financially and politically, it was mainly the European immigrant groups who carried and developed the ideals of social justice which animated the populists and the so-called muckrakers in our history; which led ultimately to the social reforms of Wilson's New Freedom and Roosevelt's New Deal—ideals of social justice and social reform which have now become permanently imbedded in the social structure of American democracy. One might say it is always the enlightened minority—for which men have died, been sent to prison, called traitors and the like, just as Franklin D. Roosevelt was called a traitor to "his class"—and what class could that be but the whole people of the nation?—it is always that "saving remnant" in our culture which has the clearest vision of the American Dream. It will be an evil day for the nation and for the cause of democracy itself when such minorities cease to exist, such dissensions are dispensed with, such valuable and inspiring differences of opinion—or such unpopular causes—are all compromised or forced into one monolithic mass opinion, or "consensus." That would be the end of the American Dream, from which a beneficent history, we must say, has so far preserved us.

The Compulsive Design

IRVING MALIN

Although Richard Chase, Kenneth Lynn, Frederic I. Carpenter, Leslie A. Fiedler, Walter Allen, and Harry Levin have discussed the importance of dreams in American fiction, they have not looked closely at "the compulsive design"—a recurring nightmare.

Many American heroes find that they cannot adjust to anxieties, especially to those involving cruel "authoritarians." They try to construct a design—a pattern to master their environment—but it becomes an inflexible measure which eventually destroys the self. The design, formed without knowledge or "health," dominates them and becomes their sole, godlike authority.

Our important writers frequently explore this design in relation to their own art. In such works as "The Artist of the Beautiful," "The Bell-Tower," and "The Beast in the Jungle" they maintain that the artist who creates his world in rigid ways lacks greatness—let alone humanity: he becomes a mere mechanician. But their concern with the design is not limited to neurotic daydreamers or inflexible craftsmen; when we read their fiction, we see that our average life-patterns, our rage for order, often neglect to perceive things as they are, forcing us to adopt distorted routines.

In this essay I shall follow the compulsive design as a link in many fictions which are not usually brought together and, by doing so, trace one American nightmare.

Washington Irving and James Fenimore Cooper stand apart from later nightmares in believing that life is *basically* ordered. The decorous norm—the life of reason—is always visible to them. "Man is known to exist in no part of the world, without certain rules for the regulation of his intercourse with those around him," said Cooper in *The American Democrat* (1838). "It is a first necessity of his weakness, that laws, founded on the immutable principles of natural justice, should be framed, in order to protect the feeble against the violence of the strong; the honest from the schemes of the dishonest; the temperate and industrious from the waste and indolence of the dissolute and idle." Such beliefs influence characterization in Cooper's fiction and in Irving's. Because they believe that all laws "possess a common character, being formed on that consciousness of right, which God has bestowed . . ." they judge actions in terms of the decorum supplied by God's plan. The "great chain of being" cannot give way to horror, unless the self fights it. But Irving and Cooper do not permit any savagery against the rules. In his introduction to *The Last of the Mohicans* (Houghton Mifflin, 1958), William Charvat defines Cooper's belief in decorum, and makes us see that such belief is arid ground for nightmare: "Civilization to him was a kind of decorum in which all the parts of a presumably static order have due respect for the integrity of other parts. In his fiction, each unit within this order, whether large (nation or race) or small (the family), has stable characteristics by which individuals within it are understood and can understand each other" (xii–xiii). Despite the fact that Irving and Cooper are intent upon describing such stability, they give us glimpses of "odd" characters. They believe oddness results from certain ruling passions or "compulsive" actions. Their characters do not get out of hand; they are saved from destroying themselves and world order by means of comedy or social reform.

In Book 4 of Irving's *A History of New York* (1809), William the Testy imposes his will upon the citizens of New Amsterdam. His fretful, repetitive projects—stupidly fighting the Yankees by proclamation, replacing money with beads, and outlawing tobacco—arise out of his nonawareness of reality. Although Irving delights in describing the ruler's consistent foolishness, he does not explore its psychological causes. He does not see, for example, that William is an inflexible designer, whose unsuccessful projects result from feelings of inferiority. One motive, however, is stated: "Wilhelmus the Testy, though one of the most potent little men that ever breathed, yet submitted at home to a species of government, neither laid down in Aristotle nor Plato, in short, it partook of the nature of a pure, unmixed tyranny, and is familiarly denominated *petticoat government.*" But the motive is used for easy comedy. Irving's world-view does not permit him to see that William's design—an irrational attempt to overcompensate for his own failings—attempts to displace anxiety. The ruler's problems are less significant to his creator than satire of Yankee ingenuity or henpecked husbands; William the Testy is sacrificed to decorum.

There is subdued horror in Cooper's *The Prairie* (1827) also. Ishmael Bush is "odd" because he resents the "unfair" stratifications of society; the only way he can define—and protect—himself is through continual hostility. Cooper is attracted to these vital complexities, these hints of compulsive design: however, he must demonstrate Ishmael's "evil" because the squatter's tensions are capable of destroying the "world's body." The characterization becomes ironic, almost brutal: Ishmael shoots at Ellen and Inez; he is ready to kill the trapper; he lashes out verbally at his son; and he expects such people as Doctor Bat to respect covenants which he personally disobeys.

The Prairie is flawed by Cooper's attempt to reform Ishmael Bush. Implausible to modern readers, the "reformation" of the villain is a characteristic of eighteenth-century prose and drama. This transformation is very sudden; we know, of course, that he cannot bless Ellen and Inez with as much fervor as he seems to do. Can we not say that Cooper startles us by his portrayal of Ishmael's compulsions, until— as described by Mr. Charvat—his social and religious ideals save him from a complete, lifelike description of the squatter? Nevertheless, *The Prairie*, flawed as it is, generates power because of the battle between Cooper and Bush, a battle which Bush appears to be winning, but which is won at last by the writer.

In these examples from Irving and Cooper the compulsive design is not destructive, for William the Testy and Ishmael Bush do not disturb the order in which their creators believe. William is ridiculed; Ishmael is reformed.

The psychological situation changes when we turn to Edgar Allan Poe. His fiction demonstrates that he has no faith in decorum: he allies himself sympathetically with his anxious heroes who express their tensions toward all authority in extreme ways. In some of his stories, we are confronted by monomania, the compulsive design to grasp the *thing*, whatever it may be. The designer believes that by doing so, he can gain unlimited control over his environment, neglecting that anxiety which forces him to act compulsively.

Our first designer is found in "The Black Cat" (1843). He is tender toward pets, especially his black cat, and this affection is so important to him that he tells us there "is something in the unselfish and self-sacrificing love of a brute, which goes directly to the heart of him who has had frequent occasion to test the paltry friendship and gossamer fidelity of mere *Man*." The extreme affection is an attempt to escape from human conflicts. He needs to flee from "authoritarianism," as does Bush, but unlike the squatter, he is aware of his reasons for adopting this inflexible pattern. He and Poe see nothing "odd" in his behavior.

Unsure about the reasons for his rigid affection, the hero cannot really understand why he has "intemperance." He begins to express hostility, his need to impose his will upon others because of his great anxiety, which has not been relieved by affection. Consequently, his tenderness turns to violence as he cuts out the eye of Pluto, the cat. The horror of the situation is that the hero is aware that his cat, lacking authority, cannot strike back. Or so he thinks. Then he rationalizes his wild actions—or compulsive hostility?—by referring to perverseness: "Have we not a perpetual inclination, in the teeth of our best judgment, to violate that which is *Law*, merely because we understand it to be such? This spirit of perverseness, I say, came to my final overthrow. It was this unfathomable longing of the soul *to vex itself*—to offer violence to its own nature—to do wrong for the wrong's sake only—that urged me to continue and finally to consummate the injury." But he omits the authoritarian images which he combats. He does have an underlying motive: he cuts out the eye of Pluto, and later hangs the cat, because he realizes that the animal, in loving him, *inhibits his unconscious desire to impose his will upon the environment*.

We are confronted by further irony. The hero recognizes his present lack of strength after he destroys the animal; he must discover a cat which resembles Pluto. The new cat, however, *seems* to have powerful authority, and it torments him (symbolizing that part of the psyche we call conscience?). He cannot allow things to remain the same; he attacks the cat compulsively to prove his strength. But he kills his wife when she tries to stop him, and the cat escapes.

Having expressed his furious attempt to kill anxiety, he sleeps peacefully, although before, he had nightmares of the animal, the *thing* "incumbent eternally" on his heart.

The end of "The Black Cat" resolves the problem of authority. When the police call, the hero, acting as a "temperate" man, imposes his crafty intellect upon them in much the same way he forced his will upon Pluto. His success is assured until he taps on the wall; then the cat responds, and he swoons. The cat has won: its authority is "limitless" and defeats the monomaniacal design of the owner.

The problem of authority also disturbs the hero of "Berenice." He finds that his cousin Berenice is completely different from him: he is "ill of health" and "buried in gloom"; she is "overflowing with energy." Although he tries to retreat from the world of health, half-recognizing his limitations, he submits to the superior energy of Berenice. He idealizes her. He cannot thoroughly enjoy this worship and when disease strikes her, changing her personality, he is pleased. After being inhibited for such a long time, his dream—and need—of imposing his will upon her comes to the foreground. He constructs his compulsive design when he considers Berenice a *thing*. The irony of the psychological situation is that his attempt to rule the environment, to dominate Berenice as a thing, has been responsible, in a sense, for his final defeat. Unconscious expression of power has become authoritarian; he has yielded to his own rigid design and become an automaton.

Similar psychological conditions are evident in "Ligeia" (1838). The matter is complicated by the fact that there are two heroines as there were two cats in "The Black Cat." The hero tells us that he yields to the majesty of Ligeia, his bride; she has an enormous amount of learning, a *strong* will, and intense black eyes. He regards her as his complete spiritual and intellectual authority. His submission to Ligeia will help him, he rationalizes, to reach his Faustian goal of mastering all human knowledge. But his wife grows ill; her eyes become less intense. The center of his design, her eyes help to define his dreamlike submission. Unfortunately, Ligeia's will, which had been so vibrant, becomes weaker and weaker, until she dies. The hero, left alone without any guide to command him, experiences anxiety. A "curious" thing happens. He finds that he has to direct his previously passive will to another being; the *inhibition* of will has become the *imposition* of will. He marries the "fair-haired and blue-eyed Lady Rowena" and torments her to express power. "I loathed her with a hatred belonging more to demon than to man." The "fierce moodiness" exhibited here indicates that he cannot find true happiness in domination—he must yield to a stronger force. His mind returns to Ligeia, "the beloved, the august," because she represents his true love, his compulsive need to obey authoritarianism.

Waiting for Rowena to die, he hears strange rustlings in the chamber. He feels "some palpable although invisible object" pass by his person. (We can take the object to be a ghost or an apparition arising from his own psyche. The latter accords with our present interpretation.) He also notes "three or four large drops of a brilliant and ruby-colored fluid" fall into Rowena's goblet as, in all probability, he poisons her. Finally he sees the transformation of the corpse into Lady Ligeia, with her "wild eyes" blazing. The beloved authoritarian image has returned.

Poe made a metaphysical system out of a neurosis. He was overly concerned with compulsive design and, at times, he did take "philosophical" advantage of his concern—in such stories as "The Masque of the Red Death" and "The Facts in the Case of M. Valdemar" he pushes the design to its limits, by making it the "will to power" in the face of death. Poe has taken the compulsive, private design of "Berenice" and reshaped it in extreme ways. Obsessively involved with his heroes, to the point of defending them, he is nevertheless able to make their designs grow into "divinity." His world is vertical, encompassing the heights to which anxiety drives the psyche. "It is by no means an irrational fancy that, in a future existence," says Poe, "we shall look upon our present existence, as a dream." The stories discussed show us life as compulsive dream.

That Nathaniel Hawthorne also recognizes the importance of such dreams is evident in *Passages from the American Notebooks*. "A sketch to be given of a modern reformer—a type of the extreme doctrines on the subjects of slaves, cold water, and other such topics. He goes about the streets haranguing most eloquently, and is on the point of making many converts, when his labors are suddenly interrupted by the appearance of the keeper of a madhouse, whence he has escaped" (1835 entry). The reformer has almost projected his compulsions upon sane people as did William the Testy. Also in 1835: "A person to consider himself as the prime mover of certain remarkable events, but to discover that his actions have not contributed in the least thereto." One entry in 1836 anticipates Henry James: "Two persons to be expecting some occurrence, and watching for the two principal actors in it, and to find that the occurrence is even then passing, and that they themselves are two actors." Like John Marcher and May Bartram in "The Beast in the Jungle" (1903), they live compulsively, but their lives are perfected, without their knowledge and authority, in the present. In most of his fiction, Hawthorne describes people who live by mechanized and self-destructive designs.

But "The Artist of the Beautiful" (1846) is an exception. Owen Warland attempts to achieve the beautiful in the midst of an alien environment. His dream is centered on artistic patterning of "things" which he tries to transform into ideal forms. Unlike Poe's heroes, he does not impose his will upon other people—he works the reverse way. He tries, that is, to breathe life into inanimate objects; the narrator of "Ligeia" tries to "objectify" his environment. Owen is said to look "with singular distaste at the stiff and regular processes of ordinary machinery." The irony and the terror of "The Artist of the Beautiful" are that he, like any artist, is close to the "automatic" departure from humanity, as he works constantly in his fictional world. What saves him is that he is aware of his tensions as he constructs his pattern, which, he continually notes, is organically related to these tensions. He masters his own anxieties and gains self-authority, creating a new world out of jumbled materials.

If we realize that Hawthorne's story deals, in part, with the artist's search for flexible authority, we can understand the psychological interplay. Owen Warland knows that he has to preserve his "force of character" as he achieves his design. He "must keep his faith in himself while the incredulous world assails him with its utter disbelief." The harsh environment's authoritarianism is represented by three figures: Annie, Robert Danforth, Peter Hovenden. (I take the child of Annie and Robert to stand for them.) Robert symbolizes brute force, hard masculinity. He is the blacksmith who can earn his bread with "bare and brawny arms." He is at ease with "hammer upon anvil"; no spiritual problems bother him. Peter Hovenden has submitted to the commands of money, of "cold, unimaginative sagacity." He congratulates Owen on his fixing the clock in the church steeple, and tries to destroy "the little chains, and wheels, and paddles" belonging to him. Owen chases away the "leaden thoughts" of the old man, his former master. Annie represents authoritarianism by the love she offers. Thinking she can comfort him as he works, he perceives later that she does not understand him; she plays with a "whirligig, so delicately wrought that it might be a plaything for Queen Mab." She also wants to fix things for him.

And Owen must contend with his own flaws. Rioting in wine and laziness, he doubts that he should (and can) fight everyone exerting power over his way of life. He loses faith in his own strength and desire to master the object he wants to spiritualize.

But he does regain his creative will, and he constructs a butterfly which he is confident is "alive" and beautiful. The butterfly, "Nature's ideal," is demonstrated to the three authoritarians (now four with the addition of the child), who appreciate some of its intricacies (craftsmanship), but not its wonder (art). Owen is a failure to them. *They do not understand that the thing—absorbing his own being into it —possesses life; the pattern has been achieved without compulsion.* Hawthorne writes: "He knew that the world, and Annie as the representative of the world, whatever praise might be bestowed, could never say the fitting word or feel the fitting sentiment which should be the perfect recompense of an artist." The butterfly flies across the room, returns to Owen, begins once more to fly, and is caught by the child, who crushes it. The child destroys merely the *symbol*; the *spirit* remains forever with Owen.

Unlike the artist, the scientist is an obsessed designer who forgets about humanity as he projects his ordered benevolence. Aylmer in "The Birthmark" is one example. His design is to achieve ultimate control, mastering that "fatal flaw of humanity," his wife's birthmark. Although love for Georgiana is evident at first, it yields to Aylmer's compulsion; she becomes a mark to her husband. Thus Owen and Aylmer part company; the scientist never recognizes his own anxieties, the roots of his power drive. His "creativity" arises out of misunderstood impotence.

Hawthorne, unlike Poe, does not try to *explore the causes*

of anxiety, except to imply a "religious" motive—the sin of pride: men dream of unlimited authority because they are sons of Adam; they rebel against established laws as did Lucifer and Adam. He does not perceive that pride compensates for feelings of impotence.

In *The Blithedale Romance* (1852) we are told that Hollingsworth has a philanthropic pattern to construct an edifice for housing criminals. We are not really informed why this particular pattern is formed, or why it should become compulsive. Hawthorne's description centers on Hollingsworth's *growing* monomania which Coverdale discovers to be caused by immense, monstrous self-love. Of course, we know now that the self-love is caused by *something*; it cannot be simply handed down to the reformer by Adam. *Once we* grant its *existence*, the compulsive design is powerfully rendered:

He was not altogether human. There was something else in Hollingsworth besides flesh and blood, and sympathies and affections and celestial spirit.

This is always true of those men who have surrendered themselves to an overwhelming purpose. It does not so much impel them from without, nor even operate as a motive power within, but grows incorporate with all that they think and feel, and finally converts them into little else save that one principle. When such begins to be the predicament, it is not cowardice, but wisdom to avoid these victims. They have no heart, no sympathy, no reason, no conscience. They will keep no friend, unless he make himself the mirror of their purpose; they will smite and slay you, and trample your dead corpse under foot, all the more readily, if you take the first step with them, and cannot take the second, and the third, and every other step of their terribly strait path. They have an idol to which they consecrate themselves high-priest, and deem it holy work to offer sacrifices of whatever is most precious; and never once seem to suspect— so cunning has the Devil been with them—that this false deity, in whose iron features, immitigable to all the rest of mankind, they see only benignity and love, is but a spectrum of the very priest himself, projected upon the surrounding darkness.

Hawthorne is allied with Poe in his use of this American nightmare. Both are interested in the need of men to dream of—and design—unlimited authority. Because Poe's characters pursue designs without any correctives to control them, they are more horrifying then Hawthorne's, who commit "sins" rather than design mad compulsions.

Herman Melville is close to his friend Hawthorne because his designers have mythic qualities, and he also deals with the "benevolent" compulsions of men—as Poe rarely does. Both Hawthorne and Melville are *ironists,* showing us that Faustian drives are found in weaklings, that reform can be compulsive. Unlike "our cousin, Mr. Poe"—to use Allen Tate's phrase—the two writers "intellectualize" horrifying situations, and make us think as we tremble. Poe, at his best, simply shakes us.

Melville's "The Bell-Tower"—an ironic inversion of "The Artist of the Beautiful"—concerns the Faustian drive in art. The "great mechanician, the unblest foundling, Bannadonna" hopes to construct a pattern which will enable him to seek "to conquer a larger liberty." He cannot be content with mere "combustions of applause" for his work. Anxiety compels him to make something which humanity will regard as supreme. Bannadonna is swayed by the public view, and he will do anything to demonstrate his "greatness" to others. His compulsive design to be supreme destroys the life of one subordinate who harms the bell. The fact that the bell is cracked, that there is a mark on it as there is on Georgiana's face, demonstrates that Bannadonna's mechanical project is simply human, not "divine" as he would have it. Nevertheless, the craftsman is powerful; he is not punished by the authorities who still respect him.

When he decides to breathe life into the "heavy object" (covered at this point) for the belfry of the tower, he appears to be imitating the example of Owen Warland. The difference is striking; Owen's attempt to give life to the butterfly never loses sight of his human qualities; the butterfly becomes a vital symbol offered by his creative tensions. Melville's hero, on the other hand, is intent upon the heavy object as thing, by which his anxieties will be relieved (an impossibility!) and his own name exalted forever. We term Owen an artist; we term Bannadonna a mechanician.

When the mechanician's promise that a new sound will be heard is not kept, the citizens who respect and fear him rush to the tower. There they find him, "prostrate and bleeding," at the base of his project. Now they see it more clearly. The bell was to be tolled by the domino given miraculous, mechanical life—a Frankenstein. We are told that the domino "had limbs, and seemed clad in a scaly mail, lustrous as a dragon beetle's. It was manacled, and its clubbed arms were uplifted, as if, with its manacles, once more to smite its already smitten victim." The irony is obvious; the domino created by its obsessive master has rebelled against authoritarianism. It exerts final command—Bannadonna has yielded brutally to his compulsive project.

As Melville muses about the symbolic value of the destruction, we discover that his ideas correspond to those of Hawthorne. Bannadonna, like other projectors, did not recognize his limits. In a proud way he tried to leap over them, never seeing his own anxieties. The compulsive design became more of an attempt to imitate and better the patterns of God: "He still bent his efforts upon the locomotive figure for the belfry, but only as a partial type of an ulterior creature, . . . adopted to further, in a degree scarcely to be imagined, universal convenience and glories of humanity, supplying nothing less than a supplement to the Six Days' Work; stocking the earth with a new serf, more useful than the ox, swifter than the dolphin, stronger than the lion, more cunning than the ape, for industry an ant, more fiery than serpents, and yet, in patience, another ass." Bannadonna, like Aylmer and Hollingsworth in Hawthorne's *The Blithedale Romance*, was a false humanitarian. His plan captured him; he "stooped to conquer. With him common sense was theurgy; machinery, miracle; Prometheus, the heroic name for machinist; man, the true God." "The Bell-Tower" emerges then as a parable. In spite of the fact that it presents a "compulsive designer," it views him as a Faust, not as an anxiety-ridden neurotic, because Melville's world-view is ultimately "religious."

Bannadonna can be seen in the great mechanician, Ahab, who also wants to leap over the limits set by immutable laws. His compulsive design regards Moby Dick as the "wall," the "mask," through which he must strike, so that he can relieve himself of feelings of inferiority, expressing his "will to power." Ahab views the environment narcissistically as a mirror of his own need—and dreams—to impose his will without discrimination. The following famous passage should be read in this light: "All visible objects, man, are but as pasteboard masks. But in each event—in the living act, the undoubted deed—there, some unknown but still reasoning thing puts forth the unreasoning mask. If man will strike,

strike through the mask! How can the prisoner reach outside except by thrusting through the wall? To me, the white whale is that wall, shoved near to me." It is wrong to sympathize completely with Ahab's design, a fundamentally obsessive gesture which neglects to view the whale as a living creature, both good and evil. The captain of the *Pequod* is as haunted as the hero of "The Black Cat"; both men read sinister meanings into the "harmless" actions of beasts.

In his introduction to the Rinehart Edition of Melville's *Selected Tales and Poems* (1950), Richard Chase accounts for the concern with art in some of Melville's stories. He believes that in these Melville is trying to explore the various sides of the personal crisis (in 1852–56) in which he finds himself. Like Poe and Hawthorne, Melville discovers that by probing the creative process, he can explore the validity of all patterns which try to shape life. He discovers that rigidity of design harms true perception—for artist and non-artist.

Henry James, more often than Melville, is concerned with the conflict of true and false form, the clash of creative will and destructive compulsion. He presents the groping "artist" (of Life as well as Art) who orders the chaos around him in flexible ways; and the mechanician who submits to the rigid order and the doom of lifelessness.

When we first meet her in *The Portrait of a Lady*, Isabel Archer is an "independent" young woman who intends to remain that way. Her speech, her way of walking, her treatment of the dog on the lawn at Gardencourt—in short, her manners—proclaim her as a novelty. She is admired that first day by three people who, lacking authority, cannot really be considered free: old Daniel Touchett, young Ralph Touchett, and Lord Warburton. The contrast is clear. The three men are all partially limited in their sense of independence: Daniel Touchett is too old to do anything but sit in his lawn chair; Ralph is plagued by sickness which has made him assert his independence verbally through irony; Lord Warburton is an English aristocrat confused about his country's and his own welfare. Not only is Isabel a charming, independent, and young woman to them—she is a symbol in their minds of the boundless freedom they would like to possess. And she understands their wishes in her proud, superficial way because she too is very conscious of her design: "She had a *fixed determination* [my italics] to regard the world as a place of brightness, of free expansion, of action: she held it must be detestable to be afraid or ashamed. She had an infinite hope that she should never do anything wrong." This pride can only become more dangerous when Isabel accepts the money left to her by Daniel Touchett. Unconsciously, in great measure, she does not feel restricted or bounded by anything, not even by the need for self-knowledge.

At first, the social institution which represents restriction of independence, at least in her eyes, is marriage. It will force her to define herself in terms of responsibilities not only to herself but to another person. Isabel refuses to marry Lord Warburton, who embodies the fineness of European culture —he is not a late European like Osmond and Madame Merle. Does she think about the marriage before she refuses? Or is her refusal an almost spontaneous assertion of her unconscious desires? These questions are crucial in the novel. Perhaps this statement will clarify the psychology at work: "What she felt was not a great responsibility, a great difficulty of choice; it appeared to her there had been no choice in the question. She couldn't marry Lord Warburton; the idea failed to support any enlightened prejudice in favor of the free exploration of life that she had hitherto entertained or was now capable of entertaining." It is evident that her "choice" comes from the core of her personality. Isabel is not consciously "enlightened"—to use James's word—because she acts quickly and irrationally. This action is part of a psychological and social pattern antecedent to choice. In *The Portrait of a Lady* James does not give us the beginnings, the reasons for the heroine's patterns of self-assertive, unthinking expression. He merely shows that they are there. We can easily become so conscious of Isabel's freedom of choice—she is so conscious of it—that we lose sight of her acting in the same way in regard to marriage not only with Lord Warburton but with Casper Goodward. Isabel is an innocent who does not understand her own need for freedom, and she, naturally, does not realize that her actions symbolize a peculiarly American mode of action: the curious compulsive manner in which we stress independence. It can be seen in Ishmael Bush, Ahab, and Thomas Sutpen. But in *The Portrait of a Lady*, it lies in the unconscious. Only now and then does Isabel sense, intuitively, that something is going to happen to her. At one point she says to Lord Warburton, "I can't escape unhappiness. . . . In marrying you I shall be trying to." She cannot marry him or the Bostonian because their openness represents severe restrictions upon her mechanized design to explore the mystery of life.

The inevitable happens: Isabel *does* marry Osmond who, unlike the Englishman, is mysteriously depraved and self-centered. To some her "choice" will seem odd. However, we must remember that her behavior is in keeping with her hidden nature which neither she nor her well-wishers understand completely. Naïveté is combined with spontaneity. Isabel Archer is fooled by the worldliness of Osmond, and, indeed, of Madame Merle because she admires their "freedom," their lack of boundaries. (Madame Merle does not seem to be bounded by the past or by the household. Nor does her former lover, Gilbert Osmond.) She disregards their personalities, concentrates upon them as *things* which are allied to her design. She is fooled by the dazzle of sophistication, secrecy, and worldly freedom.

If we realize that Isabel is surprised at her intentions to marry Osmond—even after she *is* married—we can see the undercurrent of determinism in the novel asserting itself overtly. Another plan which means denial of independence and love has been given to her, and she accepts it. Why? The only reason is that she has never consciously given shape to any way of life; she has never taken the time to face her unacknowledged psychological and social heritage. *She has exaggerated freedom to the point of excess, and this exaggeration has become an end in itself.* This psychological fact is the irony of the novel. The need for freedom becomes deterministic if carried to an extreme, or if not understood and mastered by the intellect. Trying to be free—with all of her wealth—Isabel is seduced by the "surface" of marital freedom. Perhaps she marries Osmond because she can no longer live alone, declaring the authority which she, in reality, lacks.

What does Isabel learn at the end of the novel? It is the lesson of "The Artist of the Beautiful": understand and shape creatively the tensions of life. She realizes that she must go back to Osmond's sterility and duplicity because she has to cope with the pattern which was given to her, and to shape artistically, in order to be free. The paradox is inescapable. She can express her independence and her art only through the conscious act of renouncing further attempts to gain freedom, and accepting the boundaries of life which in her case—and perhaps in all people's lives—have been rigidly set by subtle, external evil and innocent denial of *all* restrictions. Her knowledge comes late and surprises her: "Now that she was in the secret, now that she knew something that so much concerned her and the eclipse of which had made life resemble an attempt to play whist with an imperfect pack of cards, the truth of things, their mutual relations, their meaning and for the most part their horror, rose before her with a kind of architectural vastness. She remembered a thousand trifles; they started to life with the spontaneity of a shiver. She had thought them trifles at the time; now she saw that they had been weighted with lead." But Isabel is noble because she has the strength to accept the depth of her hardships. We leave the novel with the knowledge that perhaps freedom of choice only means the "freedom" to come face to face with the harshness of life which attacks us covertly when we are not even conscious of it; and to live with this harshness with humility, patience, and love. Leon Edel in an introduction to *The Portrait of a Lady* (Houghton Mifflin, 1957) says that Isabel "cannot change. To the end Isabel is a prisoner of her constituted self. She has been the helpless victim of her own intelligence, and she continues to be" (xix). I am more hopeful in regard to her recovery.

Leon Edel has traced James's early life in *Henry James: The Untried Years* (Lippincott, 1953). His treatment of the writer's relationship to the image of boundaries is particularly helpful in revealing the possible cause of determinism which Isabel Archer begins to perceive only at the end of her trials. If James resented somewhat his father's laissez faire attitude and the reversal of parental roles, then in later years he could easily approach the problem of these two characters with the mixed feeling that their designs are bad but lead to good insights. The question of Isabel's acceptance of the pattern of marriage created *for* her has important ramifications. These can be related to James's own need to appeal to absolutes for no obvious reasons (as Yvor Winters points out in *In Defense of Reason*, University of Denver Press, pp.

300–344), or to his renunciation of his revolutionary heritage for the already-ordered culture of England. James seems to believe that in intellectual mastery of an unconscious drive for compulsion freedom can be gained, that in the loss of self-glorification self can be found, and that in the powerful defeat of mechanized design true art can originate.

The compulsive design is also evident in the fiction of Ernest Hemingway and William Faulkner. Both writers stress the violent insecurity of their characters in a more extreme way than do Hawthorne, Melville, and James. Now endurance is the chief goal; staying alive is more important than glamorous designs of complete mastery. In his Nobel Prize speech Faulkner said the big question for our "age of anxiety" is "When will I be blown up?" We should remember this question when we consider the psychology underlying the Hemingway code and the Faulkner design.

I have tried to define the "theme of rigidity" in *William Faulkner: An Interpretation* (Stanford University Press, 1957). Faulkner believes that people try to escape from contemporary tensions by forming "inflexible patterns of behavior," which, enabling them to submit to their limited needs for self-preservation, offer apparent security. They refuse to look at their environment with sympathetic understanding. He analyzes the roots of compulsion in a more thorough way than do the earlier writers because he shows us childhood tensions.

In *Light in August* (1932) Hightower deliberately designs his life to parallel that of his grandfather. He marries his wife because she will help him obtain a position in Jefferson. He manipulates the environment in ghostlike ways as a result of his early relationship with his impotent, unreal parents. In *As I Lay Dying* (1930), Addie Bundren lives a compulsive, dead life after she learns early from her father that "living is terrible." She treats her family as "machines" in her massive preparation for death; as she imposes her will upon the members of the family, compelling them to bury her in Jefferson, they also become rigid. In *Sanctuary* (1931), Popeye also lives according to an unconscious childhood pattern. He discovers that the only way he can gain security is through physical violence. He must attempt to rape Temple (even though he is impotent), in the same way he cut up two lovebirds in his youth.

Perhaps we may say that Faulkner is closest to Poe because his characters (in the "great years"—Richard Chase's term) and Poe's live with faint glimmerings of insight into their existential anxieties. They have no real conception of their unwilling attractions to and repulsions from authority. They attempt to rule lovebirds, corpses, teeth, buzzards. My previous conclusion is valid for both writers: "The horror of the situation lies, for Faulkner, in the fact that people have neither the strength nor the insight necessary to relieve themselves of their burden. A person with a design cannot change because he cannot part with whatever value his design can offer. He is doomed. Occasionally he knows it" (15). Although many critics have noted Faulkner's treatment of compulsion, they have not demonstrated that it is a culmination of the interest of the nineteenth-century writers, and relates his work to Hemingway's.

Most critics of Hemingway would agree with Malcolm Cowley: "His heroes live in a world that is like a hostile forest, full of unseen dangers, not to mention the nightmares that haunt their sleep. Death spies on them from behind every tree. Their only chance of safety lies in the faithful observance of customs they invent for themselves" (The Portable Hemingway, Viking, 1944). Mr. Cowley thinks that Hemingway belongs with the "haunted and nocturnal writers, the men who dealt in images that were symbols of an inner world," but he does not explore the compulsive design as the missing link.

Anxiety is at the root of his characters. In his book Ernest Hemingway (Rinehart, 1952), Philip Young has shown that Nick Adams is disturbed by the tribal wrath inflicted upon Ole Anderson; by the ugliness and possible homosexuality exhibited by "The Battler"; by the inability of his parents to understand his emotional problems in "The Doctor and the Doctor's Wife." Mr. Young writes about the Hemingway character: he "was learning a code with which he might maneuver, though crippled, and he was practicing the rites which for him might exorcise the terrors born of the events that crippled him" (51–52). Mr. Young and I agree that the practice mentioned is somewhat "mechanical." Comparing Nick Adams and Faulkner's Darl Bundren and Quentin Compson (The Sound and the Fury, 1929), we can see that the characteristic youths of both writers are similar. They learn early that "living is terrible"; they try to cope with the authoritarian images which loom before them; they don't know about independence; and their actions are frenetic. There is, however, one important difference: Darl and Quentin rebel against their authoritarian images, even though they would like to flee from them; Nick Adams flees, and lives, as a coward.

Although Mr. Young views the Hemingway code as an attempt to fight anxiety, I see it as a *show* of physical and occasional mental endurance. The code becomes, in my terms, a compulsive dream of health. Nick Adams may be an "authority" for the grasshopper; the bullfighter may dominate the bull; the hunter may kill the elephant. Does this kind of authority rescue the protagonist from anxiety and despair? Despite the fact that Hemingway is confident such a code is "healthy," it represents a rigid and ultimately destructive image. Look at "Big, Two-Hearted River" (1925). Nick Adams lives according to a certain pattern—which he does not articulate—created to help him endure a terrifying existence. Because he cannot face his "obscure hurts" he accepts the environment as a good thing. But we see his flaw: he cannot fish the swamp. I am not sure that Nick will ever confront the swamp or his compulsive flight from it.

Richard Chase declares that American fiction contains many "flat" figures contrasted to the "rounded" individuals of European fiction. Perhaps the figures I have discussed are flat because they are obsessed with a design inhibiting their human completion. The attempts of Poe's heroes, Hollingsworth, Bannadonna, and Hemingway's Nick Adams to master the environment have robbed them of self-mastery. Their manipulation of people has made them things. And things lack "character."

Focus on Herman Melville's
"The Two Temples"
The Denigration of the American Dream

MARVIN FISHER

Between 1853 and 1856, Herman Melville wrote fifteen stories of varying length and style, most of which appeared in issues of *Putnam's Monthly* or *Harper's Magazine* and several of which were reprinted along with the new title story in *The Piazza Tales* (1856). None of these stories did much to bolster Melville's waning reputation or depleted royalty accounts. "The Two Temples" did least for Melville in any tangible way, for both the editor and publisher of *Putnam's*, while admiring the story, found it too potentially offensive to the religious sensibilities of many readers, and so it was never published in Melville's lifetime.

It interests me now not only as a story in its own terms but also for the way it fits with Melville's other stories and strengthens certain thematic relationships. While lacking the specific focus of a collection like James Joyce's *Dubliners* (1914) or Sherwood Anderson's *Winesburg, Ohio* (1919), Melville's stories have much in common with these later works. Melville, no less than Joyce, was intensely concerned with the moral and spiritual paralysis of his time and place, and his stories, like the fifteen stories of *Dubliners*, explore a series of social, intellectual, and spiritual crises. But the context and the crisis in Melville's stories, if not always distinctively American, always has an important connection to American culture; and in the depths of their disillusionment, these stories suggest that mid-nineteenth-century America had betrayed the promises and lost the dreams of its inception and fallen victim to its moral faults.

"The Two Temples" is one of several stories, such as "The Lightning-Rod Man" or "Jimmy Rose," which would have

76

offended American religious sensibilities, had they been understood. It is also like "Poor Man's Pudding and Rich Man's Crumbs" and "The Paradise of Bachelors and the Tartarus of Maids" in that it is constructed of facing panels contrasting New World and Old. And it is like Hawthorne's "The Celestial Railroad" (1843) or "The Minister's Black Veil" (1836) or Emerson's "Divinity School Address" (1838) in exposing painful perversions of religious purpose and meaning. Melville, however, was less the preacher and more the pathologist than his literary contemporaries. His intent in "The Two Temples," as in much of his short fiction, was to show by oblique and symbolic means that beneath the apparently living tissue and virtuous pronouncements of mid-nineteenth-century American society was a spiritual deadness, a startling insensitivity to the communal needs of the individual.

We do not learn until the second half of the story, the half that is set in London, that the narrator is a physician, but this is an important fact since each half of the two-part story constitutes an examination and description of a series of social symptoms culminating in a rather ironic and unexpected diagnosis. The first part of the story is set in New York and the narrator as physician is subordinate to the narrator as pilgrim who comes, prayer book in hand, to worship humbly at the "marble-buttressed, stained-glassed, spic-and-span new temple." Modeled after the recently completed, elegant, and exclusive Grace Church, Melville's first temple is guarded by a "great, fat-paunched, beadle-faced man" who denies entrance to the modestly dressed narrator. Here irony is heaped on irony and Melville begins his allegory without departing from the very tangible reality of New York's streets.

The temple is first of all a symbol of what American piety has become, and second, like the Wall Street law office in "Bartleby," a symbol of what American society has become. The dream of Christianity has been its promise of salvation for the meek and humble, and one segment of the American Dream has been liberty and equality within a system where special privileges based on class had no place. But Grace Church, as here represented, graces its ample pews with wealthy and well-dressed parishioners; it has no grace for the common man. And classless America is identified with segregation and exclusion based on superficial signs of status, the sort of inequity and iniquity which are associated in the American Dream with the sorrow and decadence of the Old World.

"Temple First" is thus a double-edged critique of hypocrisy in American piety and American society. Its meaning hinges on our recognizing the narrator as an essentially honest, if somewhat naïve, believer in the American Dream. He acts as if freedom of worship in the church of his choice extended to each individual, as if class distinctions had been canceled by the affirmations of democracy, as if church and state were duly separate, and as if the courts served to protect and extend the principle of liberty and justice for all. His brief experience at the Sunday service at Grace Church and his appearance before the judge on Monday morning dispel every comforting feature of the American Dream. In the nightmare of reality the New World acquires most of the worst features of the Old and loses its uniqueness, which is probably the essential quality of the dream.

In "Temple First" the alarm of experience is wound tighter and tighter until it literally goes off in an "appalling din" that brings down the wrath and justice of ordered society upon the innocent narrator. The first turn of the alarm screw on "this blessed Sunday morning" occurs when "the fat-paunched, beadle-faced man" rebuffs the narrator, who, as he is forced out of the nave, feels himself "excommunicated" or at least "excluded," his fault being a coat a bit too shabby to permit him to mingle with the congregation in one of "these splendid, new-fashioned Gothic Temples." The Gothic style, of course, is distinctly European; the "new-fashioned Gothic" in America hints at where the story is heading.

The second turn of the screw is provided by the narrator's notice of "glossy groups of low-voiced gossipers nearby," dressed in the gorgeous finery "of royal dukes, right honorable barons." Of course they are not what they seem, for democratic America stands against such artificial prerogative. They are not even members of this exclusive congregation, only lackeys in glittering garb whose function is to ornament the "noble string of flashing carriages drawn up along the curb." Had Melville gone on in this way, he would have sounded like Thorstein Veblen, but Melville's mode, especially in his short fiction, is to present imaginative glimpses of elusive and frequently unpopular truth rather than sober and considered reflection on troublesome matters. Still his depiction of the conspicuous display outside the church, inside it, and in the architecture itself lays the basis for his implicit charges of unchristian and antidemocratic values in the church and un-American attitudes in American society at large.

Noticing a small door outside the church and assuming that it leads to a place in the tower from which he might "in spirit, if not in place, participate in those devout exultations," the narrator decides to try this other mode of entry. His aim is still to "take part in the proceedings," to seek even at some distance the grace and communion to which the church is pledged. In a crucial moment he steals through the side door and makes his way up the stairs, asserting "I will not be defrauded of my natural rights." He reaches a small platform, the first of several stops on his way up into the bell tower, and finds himself enclosed on three sides by richly colored stained-glass windows which cast fantastic sunrises, sunsets, rainbows, falling stars, and other pyrotechnical effects into the air and onto the wall. But despite all this psychedelic splendor, he may as well have been, he says, in "a basement cell in 'the tombs,' " for he can see nothing outside his cell until he scratches a peephole in the center of one of the stained-glass windows. What he then sees is the beadle-faced man chasing three ragged little boys into the street. He doesn't dwell on the scene, but it does have iconographic significance that further turns the screw. Here, within the church, the poor inherit the wrath of the official guardian, and Christ's injunction to "suffer the little children to come unto me" becomes something like "the little children shall suffer if they dare."

Proceeding further up the tower, the narrator finds a small circular window which affords a view of the congregation about a hundred feet below. But the window, designed for purposes of ventilation, is covered with a fine screen and transmits a hellish blast of hot air, scorching the face of our unseen witness. He can hear the priest and make the proper responses, he can hear the organ and the uplifting hymns, but the screen darkens his view of all the proceedings below. Like Parson Hooper's black veil in Hawthorne's story, this screen "had the effect of casting crape upon all." In Hawthorne's story the piece of crape that darkens the minister's vision and hides his face signifies the minister's belief in the innate sinfulness of all men, and his unyielding insistence on this belief removes him from any joyful participation in human community, or as Hawthorne elsewhere phrases it, he has broken "the magnetic chain of humanity." The darkening screen in Melville's story, however, signifies a different truth—not that of the individual who has through pride and isolation broken that "magnetic chain of humanity" but of organized society and institutionalized religion that have blasted the hopes of democratic community and distorted the meaning and intent of Christian communion. However, the narrator, believing still in the benignity of things as they are (or as he thinks they are), tries to discount the dark view of circumstances through the screen. He will not admit, though the reader is supposed to recognize, the power of blackness to illuminate some of the less pleasant aspects of life in mid-nineteenth-century America.

Despite his efforts to compensate for his blackened vision of the assembly below, some disturbing alterations of reality result from his new perspective. Cynicism is not normally part of his nature; yet as he stands "in the very posture of devotion," responding with prayer book in hand, the scene below begins to seem a sumptuous theatrical spectacle. The chants proceed according to script; the priest appears a practiced actor, entering and exiting dramatically. His reappearance is marked by quick change of costume and his presence reinforced by "melodious tone and persuasive gesture." As Emerson had diagnosed in his personal journal and publicly announced to his audience at the Harvard Divinity School, the priest was playing a role, fulfilling a form. The spirit languished as the literalist went through his paces. Communion, Emerson insisted, ought to be a living experience, not a dead letter. And we all know of the personal crisis that led to his resigning his pulpit when he began to feel that he was furthering a form and serving a cold institutional purpose. Lack of integrity is the unspoken charge against the priest in Melville's story, the priest who tells his affluent congregation through his chosen text: "Ye are the salt of the earth." The irony in this choice of the minister's text is simultaneously an indictment of Christian ethics and democratic practice, and the narrator, from his Pisgah-like perch, gazes down not at the Promised Land of the American Dream but at an image of reality permeated by hypocrisy and social pretensions.

His experience has been unsettling but it will reach nightmare proportions before he is free again to walk the streets. Trying to exit by the same route as he had entered, he finds the door securely locked. He had come to the church, a source of salvation, to be part of a worshiping community, but finds himself isolated and imprisoned. He climbs again to his high perch, and looking down into the vast hall, he again experiences the strange power of blackness to alter expectation and illuminate hidden truth. His eye falls on "a Puseyitish painting of a Madonna and Child" on one of the lower windows but its iconographical impact on him makes it seem "the true Hagar and her Ishmael." As I have suggested, Melville has used a series of symbolic revelations to tighten the screw of terror and heighten the sense of alarm, and I think this sudden glimpse of hallowed Madonna and Child as social outcasts—outsiders in this magnificent temple of Christian worship—is the culmination of Melville's Epiphanic method, developed long before Joyce articulated its possibilities for short fiction.

Melville's narrator awakens to the full terror of his experience when he pulls a bell rope to call attention to his predicament. Instead of some gentle peal or gong, he sets off a thunderous reverberation, as if he had tripped some earth-shaking burglar alarm and roused the world to his irreverent intrusions. Hauled off by the beadle-faced man, he is handed over to three policemen, who recognize him "as a lawless violator, and a remorseless disturber of the Sunday peace." Like Bartleby, who also despaired of the possibility of meaningful communication and of the realization of communion in any spiritual sense or community in the social sense, the narrator of "The Two Temples" is led off to the Tombs. His fate is more comic than tragic, but it is black comedy, black as the vision that transforms the infant Christ into the outcast Ishmael. He comes before a judge the next morning, is quickly found guilty, fined, reprimanded, and released. There is as much justice in the Halls of Justice as grace in Grace Church, and "Temple First" has provided an overview of the American Dream and the hope of Christianity, but through a screen, darkly. Melville has impressed upon us that the atmosphere of our institutions is one where, as Emerson earlier insisted in his scandalous address to the fledgling ministers, what were once expressions "of admiration and love . . . are now petrified into official titles, kill[ing] all generous sympathy and liking."

If the cumulative revelations of the first half of Melville's diptych darken the dream of spiritual communion and democratic community, the iconography of the second half somewhat sentimentally restores his faith in man and the possibilities of spiritual regeneration. "Temple Second" is in London. The narrator has been unexpectedly dismissed from his position as private physician to a wealthy but ailing young American lady, and he is for the moment impoverished and in debt. Like Ishmael, he is "forlorn, outcast, without a friend," "a penniless stranger in Babylonian London" with its "fiendish gas-lights, shooting their Tartarean rays." He feels caught up and swept along in "unscrupulous human whirlpools," and expecting every man's hand to be turned against him, he has a series of encounters that reverse the sobering experiences of "Temple First."

The "blessed oasis of tranquility" in the midst of this urban pandemonium is not a church but a theater, a temple of entertainment, where a noted actor is on this Saturday night appearing as Cardinal Richelieu. The narrator does not feel a theater, even if he had the shilling for admission, could satisfy his psychological needs. Tired, depressed, abandoned, he is an alien in search of human fellowship. His need, as he explains it, is the same as what drew him to Grace Church: the "cheer" that results from "making one of many pleasing human faces," from "getting into a genial humane assembly of my kind," the satisfaction that "at its best and highest, is to be found in the unified multitude of a devout congregation." Still, he is pulled by the desire to see this performance. He is saved from the folly of pawning his overcoat "by a sudden cheery summons in a voice unmistakably benevolent." The caller, who seems a working man by his dress, extends a ticket which he is unable to use and urges the embarrassed narrator to take it and enjoy the show. In a single instant he has had cheer and charity thrust upon him, qualities he may have needed before but had never been offered "ere this blessed night." A minor miracle has taken place and an even greater one awaits him in the theater.

His entry into this second temple through a small side

entrance and his ascent up many twisting stairs repeats his experience in "Temple First," with the important exception that he is *welcomed* to the theater, which strangely embodies many of the characteristics of a church. The ticket-taker at the top of the stairs looks out of a little booth "like some saint in a shrine, [his] countenance . . . illuminated by two smoky candles." The orchestral music recalls the organ melodies of Grace Church, and as he looks from his seat high in the shilling gallery down through the hot, smoky air at the massed audience below, he feels the resemblance even more. But now he is not alone, he has "most acceptable, right welcome, cheery company . . . quiet, well-pleased working-men, and their glad wives and sisters, with here and there an aproned urchin, with all-absorbed, bright face, hovering like a painted cherub over the vast human firmament below." After a brief moment when he involuntarily sought in his pocket for the prayer book which was not there, one of the aproned urchins approaches him with a pot and pewter mug. Forced by his poverty to refuse what he assumes is coffee, he is recognized by the boy as an American. But the boy answers hospitably, "Well, dad's gone to Yankee-land, a-seekin' of his fortin; so take a penny mug of ale, do, Yankee, for poor dad's sake." With the mug of dark ale in his hand, the narrator confesses that he has no penny, to which the boy replies, "Never do you mind, Yankee; drink to honest dad." Moved by this gracious gesture in the midst of working people for whom poverty is no sin, the narrator offers a toast: "With all my heart, you generous boy; here's immortal life to him!" The boy moves away smiling and finds there are many more takers of his ale. Deeply affected by this second act of unexpected charity given so cheerfully, the narrator feels new life and new hope through this secular sacrament: "That unpurchased penny-worth of ale revived my drooping spirits strangely. Stuff was in that barley malt; a most sweet bitterness in those blessed hops. God bless the glorious boy!" Whether by accident or intent, Melville has linked in human action three words which are strongly linked etymologically—*cheer, charity, Eu-charist*, the latter unmentioned but unmistakably suggested. (*Eucharist* is still the word for "Thank you" in modern Greek, meaning literally "by your favor" or "by your grace.")

Although the most important action seems to be in this

topmost balcony, there are noteworthy things down below too. Mr. Macready's performance as Richelieu, the states-man-priest, is apparently a superb achievement, more moving and genuine than the priest's performance in "Temple First." The audience in the first instance seemed "one of buried, not living men"; in the second case "the enraptured thousands sound their responses, deafeningly, unmistakably sincere. Right from the undoubted heart." The first priest was a dissembler who deceived himself, the second a consum-mate actor who, as actor, was "the real thing." What he had accomplished, Melville suggests, was far more than "mere mimicry." He had elevated his art and his audience and converted a vast number of disparate individuals, the narra-tor among them, into a harmonious and "gladdened crowd." (The question this raises is "what is it then to act a part?" This is a question concerning the interpenetration of life and art—the kind of question we are more accustomed to find in Henry James than in Melville. But Melville's implied conclu-sion in this parable of the priest-actor and the actor-priest is very close to James's suggestion that "the real thing could be so much less precious than the unreal," that an artful ap-proach to life and an awareness of its symbolic moments can be more penetrating, revealing, and "real" than a thoroughly realistic approach. If this seems a side issue in Melville's story, it is, nevertheless, a relevant one.)

Melville developed his second sketch, like the first, through a series of cumulative revelations, reaching a climac-tic, if somewhat sentimentally ironic, epiphany in the cup of ale so freely given. This may seem a fictional device consider-ably in advance of his time, and indeed it is, but Melville did have a model, or at least a precedent, in the work of the two contemporaries I mentioned earlier. There is a ready connec-tion with the symbolic tales and tableaux of Hawthorne; there is a less obvious but no less important connection with the technical and the thematic elements of Emerson's "Di-vinity School Address," a deeper relationship than any I have yet mentioned.

Without ever instructing his listeners or readers in what he was doing, Emerson began his address by describing sacra-mental mysteries, such as baptism and the Eucharist, in terms of what takes place freely in nature and in human experience. Whether he was right or not, he undoubtedly felt that an audience schooled in religious symbolism would grasp his meaning and agree with the deritualizing of the sacraments in order to make them live. He also implored "All who hear me, feel that the language that describes Christ to Europe and America is not the style of friendship and enthusiasm to a good and noble heart, but is appropriated and formal." Melville did not hear him, but he certainly did read him. And what the narrator, when he blessed "the glorious boy" and drank "to honest dad," felt in the depths of his heart was the lesson that Emerson read in Jesus, who "saw that God incarnates himself in man, and evermore goes forth anew to take possession of his World."

My point in all this, however, is not to propose the "Divinity School Address" as a source for "The Two Temples" but to suggest a cultural connection that brings us back again to the American Dream and its implication for religion. We have perhaps no more articulate statement of the American Dream, its individual and national implications, than "The American Scholar." (It is a prescription for curing the pathological alienation and sterility of "Temple First.") I do not have to insist either that the "Divinity School Address" focuses the main ideas of "The American Scholar" on the narrower field of religion and the ministry and actually incorporates the Kingdom of God in the American Dream. And if, as I have tried to show, there are strong thematic as well as technical parallels between the "Divinity School Address" and Melville's "The Two Temples"—especially "Temple Second"—then I may be justified in suggesting that even the London half of Melville's diptych has more than a peripheral relevance to the matter of the American Dream.

To avoid being accused of guilt-by-association tactics, let me put it differently. "Temple First" clearly describes the American Dream rendered nightmare by increasingly rigid social organization and materialistically rather than humanely ordered social forces. In the America of "Temple First" the Puritan ethic, with its inevitable emphasis on the Kingdom of Goods, has taken precedence over the Christian ethic and its injunction to "love thy neighbor as thy self." The result has been an isolating and divisive kind of individualism that subverts the communal hope of both democracy and Christianity. "Temple Second" clearly abandons the American scene in finding relief from the nightmare of alienation, but it seems to me that the therapy by which our physician heals himself is more than the accidental experience of an American down and almost out in London, it is still the stuff of the American Dream. What Melville has implicitly questioned, however, is not the meaning of the dream or even its connection with the promised Kingdom of Christian thought. In his own way he seems to have affirmed these. It is, rather, the self-styled role of America as a redeemer nation (wherein there are seemingly insurmountable obstacles to redemption) and the idea of America as the necessary or unique locus for realization of the American Dream that he here challenges, just as Henry James has done more thoroughly. The symbolic strength of the dream survives, despite what has happened to its substance. Its power in London after being dispelled by the circumstances in New York seems to make Melville more American than ever in demonstrating that the dream is not dead, even though the nightmare is real.

Focus on Abraham Cahan's
The Rise of David Levinsky
Boats Against the Current

JULES CHAMETZKY

Abraham Cahan (1860–1951) lived a long and influential life that was in many respects a paradigm of the American Dream. Born in Vilna, Lithuania, he came to America in 1882 – the year the great migrations from Europe began – and within a few years had established himself as a Socialist, writer, and editor in three languages (English, Yiddish, Russian). He participated in unionizing activities, he wrote and translated novels, stories, articles; but it was as editor for fifty years of the *Jewish Daily Forward*, the largest Yiddish newspaper in America (and therefore the world), that he made his greatest mark. He decisively influenced the Americanization of the Jewish immigrant masses.

Radical, secular, enlightened before coming to America, he did not sentimentalize Old-World pietism, ignorance, poverty, backwardness. In his early radical period he thought it necessary to learn the language and customs of the new country and to take advantage of its opportunities for self-definition and improvement – to begin, in a sense, to acculturate one's self. As he became increasingly reformist this tendency was accentuated – but it would be a mistake to think the process was an uncomplicated one.

For one thing, using the Yiddish-language press as the chief vehicle for educating and Americanizing the immigrants (a job for which Cahan trained himself, learning to write "a plain Yiddish" at a time when most intellectuals despised the "jargon") had the paradoxical effect of molding the self-consciousness and inner cohesiveness of the group. This in turn forced upon an intellectual like Cahan his own ineluctable Jewishness. The Yiddish press perfectly expressed the American-Jewish duality. Secondly, Cahan brought to his task a "Russianized" literary sensibility, with Tolstoy and Chekhov as his models for evaluating life. Among other things, this meant that he placed a high value upon belles lettres—so that over the years he introduced to his readers, and furthered the careers of, most of the best Yiddish writers (those familiar to us would be Sholem Asch, Israel Joshua Singer, and Isaac Bashevis Singer). Its value, of course, lay in literature's being serious and moral, addressing itself to a grasp of life's realities and essentials. We can see why Howells warmly reviewed Cahan's first novel, *Yekl: A Tale of the Ghetto* (1896), and why Cahan translated *The Kreutzer Sonata* and *The Death of Ivan Ilyitch* into Yiddish. In short, Cahan was no propagandist for the American Dream.

Cahan's intention to accommodate America and the East European Jewish immigrant to each other must be seen in the light, therefore, of his civilized, cosmopolitan values. From *Yekl* to *The Rise of David Levinsky* (1917), his last and best imaginative work, he brought to bear a critically realistic sensibility steeped in three cultures. In *David Levinsky*, as John Higham points out in his excellent introduction to a recent reprint edition (Harper, 1960), Cahan combined the distinctively American theme of success with a Jewish subject matter and a Russian artistic sensibility.

The Rise of David Levinsky has been called "a better reflection of Jewish life in American surroundings than all American-Yiddish fiction put together," and "a momumental work, and surely the most remarkable contribution by an immigrant to the American novel" (Nathanael Buchwald, "Yiddish," CHAL, Vol. 4). It has been linked with *Sister Carrie* and *My Antonia* as one of the three best novels in English about immigrants—and it is interesting that of these, Levinsky is the only one written *by* an immigrant. *The Oxford Companion to American Literature* calls it "America's greatest Yiddish novel," which it is, except that it was not written in Yiddish but in English—originally as four pieces for serialization in *McClure's Magazine*, as "An Autobiography of an American Jew," beginning in 1913.

It has had its detractors among Jewish commentators who, misunderstanding Cahan's critical realism and his use of a dramatic persona, considered it a version of *Levinsky's Complaint* and hastened to condemn it as a libel upon Jews (doesn't Cahan *know* how repulsive Levinsky is? And that he is surely not representative of "the Jews"?). But the high estimate of the book stands and, I would argue, it still lives.

The scheme of the novel is simple and straightforward. In 1915, the narrator looks back upon his life from the vantage point of his success as a garment manufacturer "worth more than two million dollars." In the first part of the book he recalls his past in the *shtetl* of Antomir in Russia, the death of his mother during a pogrom, his life as an impoverished student of the Talmud, his migration to the United States in 1885 at the age of seventeen "with four cents in my pocket." Thereafter, for four-fifths of the book, the scene is America and the story is of his rise from peddler to rich man. In the process, one is tempted to say that just about all the conflicts, fears, aspirations, achievements, and failures of Jewish immigrant life are presented. We see the effects upon husbands and wives of their new cultural roles, new attitudes toward sex and love, the teeming streets, the sweatshops, unionizing activities, displaced and new intellectuals, the problems of language, real-estate speculations, the extraordinary story of the growth of the great New York garment industry and the attendant struggles between German and East European Jewry, the behavior of nouveaux riches at their pleasuring places. What saves *David Levinsky* from its merely sociological or historical interest, however, is Cahan's sensitivity to the poignant effects of this rise upon the character and inner life of his narrator. "Am I happy?" Levinsky asks in his final chapter—and he concludes, "My sense of triumph is coupled with a brooding sense of emptiness and insignificance, of my lack of anything like a great, deep interest. . . . No, I am not happy."

Now if this is not just self-indulgence on the rich man's part, it could still be seen only as the familiar, almost trite, rationalizing judgment of an intellectual (Levinsky's creator Cahan) upon the vulgar businessman: he may be rich, but is he happy? To so regard it would be unjust to Cahan's unsentimental, objective, critically realistic outlook. He is recording a perceptible reality and, on Levinsky's part, a deeply felt one. Levinsky's sense of isolation, loneliness, love-lessness—his inner hollowness despite the miraculous transformation from Yeshiva student to wealthy man of the world —is the novel's dominant theme. For our purposes, the question is, is he unhappy *despite* his realization of the American Dream or *because* of it?

Clearly, Levinsky—and behind him Cahan—was fascinated by America ("an American day seemed far richer in substance than an Antomir year") and by those who from humble origins became successful, i.e., rich, in America. It is a national fascination and of course permeates our literature. Usually, in our serious writers, the fascination with the pursuit of success ("the dirty little secret" as it is called by Norman Podhoretz) is coupled with an attempt to show the price such a pursuit exacts. Howells presented his businessman on the rise with a moral dilemma that he could resolve only by remaining honest and being content to go back to the farm; Dreiser's Carrie, from one point of view the archetypal rags-to-riches show-biz story, is morally untroubled, has no place to go back to, and with no clearly formulated ideals, no place to go forward to—she is neither happy nor unhappy. Cahan's immigrant differs from each of these examples. For one thing, Silas Lapham had a farm (and a family with him) to go back to—where the old values that presumably come from that life would sustain him (this seems to me to represent psychological and social nonsense, a daydream or fantasy, not reality). Like Lapham, Levinsky had a background of firm values that had to be abandoned in the marketplace—but unlike Lapham, the immigrant *knew* there was no going back. And unlike Carrie, who also knew there was no going back, his baggage from the old life also included many internalized values and ideals. Because of the old community and its values that he had to give up, the American version of success—so individualistic and justifiable only for its own sake—was bound to cause Levinsky unhappiness.

Crèvecoeur talks about "the new man" who leaves "behind him all his ancient prejudices and manners," in order to receive "new ones from the new mode of life he has embraced." In achieving the language and customs of the new land, Levinsky gives up, chiefly, his mother tongue and the older Jewish values. The mother tongue is literally that: the language in which all his mother's endearments, warmth, concern, and love are conveyed to him (so that thereafter her voice, presence, love were alive in his heart, he says, "like the Flame Everlasting in a synagogue"). Chief among the ancient values of the tribe that he gives up is contempt for wealth and the rewards of this ephemeral world. ("Only good deeds and holy learning have tangible worth. Beware of Satan, Davie.") Cahan was no filial pietist, but he was too perceptive not to see in his character an utter sense of inner loss in his new life and a total contradiction between his two lives. Levinsky's first words are "And yet when I take a look at my inner identity it impresses me as being precisely the same as it was thirty or forty years ago. My present station, power, the amount of worldly happiness at my command, and the rest of it, seem to be devoid of significance." And his last words are: "I can never forget the days of my misery. I cannot escape from my old self. My past and present do not comport well. David, the poor lad swinging over a Talmud volume at the Preacher's Synagogue, seems to have more in common with my identity than David Levinsky, the well-known cloak manufacturer."

His past and present did "not comport well"—what a persistent motif among American writers—all of them immigrants or descendants of immigrants, country boys in the city, city boys in the country, westerners in the East, easterners in the West, all embracing the conflict of cultures within them and in the society. For Levinsky the reason for the power of the success ethic is well-laid in the portrayal of his early poverty and deprivation, a fatherless child living in a basement with three other families, being beaten by his Hebrew teacher because he was a charity scholar. The portrayal of *shtetl* life is authentic—no Edenic idyll. For the immigrant, the American Dream of acceptance into mainstream society, the promise of meaningful work and material well-being was obviously desirable—and of course still is for the dispossessed inside and out of our society. Yet the dilemma persisted: how to make up for the acute and inescapable sense of loss—of the mother, of childhood, of innocence. Despite everything, one kind of paradise was lost. The rite of passage from one state to another was so much more than symbolic: the ocean crossing, the cutting off from one culture and the emergence in a new one, was absolute, complete, traumatic—a second birth.

The new world this new Adam was born into showed many unlovely sides, but in a passage of almost Jamesian astuteness, Levinsky embraces his complex new fate: for "while human nature was thus growing smaller, the human world was growing larger, more complex, more heartless, *and more interesting* [italics mine]." Levinsky says yes to the Satan the old Reb at home had warned him about ("Beware of Satan, Davie. When he assails you, just say no, turn your heart to steel and say no"). Rich in the things of this world, he finds at last that he has purchased them at the expense of his inner spirit. At the end Levinsky yearns for more spiritually satisfying fare than business and the success ethic. He envies those of his brethren who have distinguished themselves in science, music, art, and he says that if he had it to do all over again he would *not* think of a business career.

So ends *The Rise of David Levinsky*—a haunting, suggestive, and I think finally, prophetic book. Two generations from Levinsky, most thoughtful people in the Jewish community are aware of the spiritual malaise that seems to be at the heart of its present more or less affluent American existence. Certainly this awareness is discernible in the work of serious American-Jewish writers. A few years ago I tried to show how the treatment of language from Abraham Cahan to Saul Bellow reflected the increasing ease of accommodation of the American-Jewish writer to his ambivalent experience in the New World. In the Jewish renaissance, as it were, of the fifties, these writers felt free to use the materials of their lives in America—as Jews—without an awkward and crippling defensiveness or sentimentality; part of their impulse was to discover, name, and win back an important part of themselves ("Notes on the Assimilation of the American-Jewish Writer: Abraham Cahan to Saul Bellow," *Jahrbuch für Amerikastudien*, 9 [1964], 172–80). That process, which seemed to me then completed, goes on. In *Augie March* and *Herzog*, it is the early days with Grandma Lausch and on Napoleon Street in Montreal that are most alive and felt. Alfred Kazin's *Walker in the City* seems to me more compelling than *Starting Out in the Thirties*, in which the bedazzled young graduate breaks out of the ghetto into the wider world of letters only to offer us, at the end, literary gossip instead of profound experience. Paul Jacobs asks at a crucial point of his life, when he was thrown back upon himself, *Is Curly Jewish?* and discovers that inside the tough thirties radical there was a young Jewish boy all along. "So we beat on, boats against the current, borne back ceaselessly into the past."

An audacious and paradoxical exception to these observations—and perhaps the final act in the drama of David Levinsky and his descendants—is to be found in Norman Podhoretz's *Making It* (Random House, 1967). The chief revelation Podhoretz comes to is to accept his drive for success as a good thing. He has none of Levinsky's qualms about success and its pursuit, having learned, finally, and found the strength to admit to himself, that it is "better to be famous than obscure, rich than poor, a success than a failure." Doesn't the writer intend us ironically to qualify this gem of wisdom from the analyst's couch which the narrator (an intellectual) shares with us? In any case, unlike Levinsky, he experiences no malaise (except when others don't *know* how successful he is), no sense of inner loss. The two halves of Podhoretz's life are seen to comport well enough. The boy of humble origin has risen to riches and success, but not like a vulgar garment manufacturer. Podhoretz fills the void left by Levinsky precisely by "making it" in a field that embraces "science, music, art." Moreover, he has made it as editor of a magazine that celebrates ethnic identity, welding it to a secure Americanism. The hero of *Making It* seems to have resolved all ambivalence and contradiction. He *deserves* that drink at poolside on a Carib isle where his adventures culminate and he discovers how sweet success is: it turns out that *nothing* very important has been given up for the bitch goddess.

And yet. The writer is surely offering us the point of view of a created character; there must finally be a controlling irony at work. How else to regard that final image of felicity and fulfillment at poolside—so unmistakably the same as that of any latter-day garment manufacturer? If we are not to consider this with a redeeming irony, can it be taken seriously? Is that what the whole American adventure comes down to? Is that then how a man is to live in our time? One may legitimately ask such an old-fashioned, Tolstoyan question in an essay on Abraham Cahan. Cahan let us see that the unsatisfactory answer provided by his American life is what troubled David Levinsky.

Sinclair Lewis and Western Humor

JAMES C. AUSTIN

There are two contradictory sides to the work of Sinclair Lewis. He has been called a realist, a satirist, a social critic on the one hand; a romantic, a sentimentalist, and a Babbitt on the other. He lastingly branded American smugness and hypocrisy, yet defended American warmth and integrity. Some commentators have recognized his inconsistencies and have more or less succeeded in explaining them. Perhaps the most successful and the most recent critic is D. J. Dooley in *The Art of Sinclair Lewis* (1967).

Many critics have pointed out that his middle-class world was a nightmare world; at times his vision resembles that in *The Waste Land* of people walking meaninglessly around in a ring, or the Orwellian image of drawn and cowed people in an Airstrip One. But his florid, loud-mouthed representatives of the class which spins not and toils chiefly at salesmanship proved to be richly varied and full of life and gusto. Lewis was never happier than when a Marduc or a Pickerbaugh, a Windrip or a Blausser, had sprung full-blown into existence in the world of his imagination and begun to wax eloquent. These were characters to be treated with satiric humor; some of them were menaces, some of them were conspiring to destroy all freedom and all individuality, but except in his gloomier moments, Lewis never believed that they would succeed. He kept his faith in the American Dream (pp. xv–xvi).

The conflict within Sinclair Lewis was not unique. He expressed a dilemma which, as Charles L. Sanford suggested in *The Quest for Paradise* (1961), was a part of the culture of the Middle West. Further, he drew upon the humor of that region for his mode of expression. Lewis was not only a product of his region but the outstanding representative of the tradition of American humor as it developed in the Northern states west of Ohio.

In Sauk Centre, Minnesota, around the turn of the cen-

94

tury, Lewis could read George Ade, Finley Peter Dunne (Mr. Dooley), and Henry M. Hyde (One-Forty-Two) in copyrighted columns in the Minneapolis *Tribune*.[1] He could also read the witty Ralph W. Wheelock, who wrote a daily column, "Thoughts on Things: Material and Immaterial," for the same paper. He certainly read the comic filler, which sometimes made up a third of the copy, aside from advertising, in F. E. Barnum's Sauk Centre *Avalanche*, a newspaper for which young Lewis worked for at least a few days. The point is not that he was specifically influenced by any one of these writers, but that a journalistically-minded boy could not have escaped an awareness of the humor that was a lively part of Western newspapers.

The Western humor that Lewis knew as a boy derived from the old Yankee humor. Constance Rourke, in *American Humor* (1931), clearly distinguished the two main streams of native humor. Although the comic Yankee was a close relative of his Southern counterpart with the coonskin cap, he favored certain forms, techniques, and subjects that distinguished him from the Davy Crocketts and Sut Lovingoods. In brief, the Northern humorist preferred the loosely connected anecdotal essay—often in the form of a letter to the editor. He relied on wordplay for most of his comic effects, frequently employing a highbrow style to mock highbrow pretensions. He delicately avoided sex and scatology; and violence was minimized or dehumanized. His wit generally had a satiric edge; he ridiculed, however mildly, politics and society. All these traits contrast with the boasting, boisterous, sadistic, colorful humor of the Old Southwest. And they are all represented in the opening paragraph of one of the first books of Yankee humor, Seba Smith's *The Life and Writings of Major Jack Downing* (1834):

I now take my pen in hand to let you know that I am well, hoping these few lines will find you enjoying the same blessing. When I come down to Portland I didn't think o' staying more than three or four days, if I could sell my load of ax handles, and mother's cheese, and cousin Nabby's bundle of footings; but when I got here I found Uncle Nat was gone a freighting down to Quoddy, and Aunt Sally said as how I shouldn't stir a step home till he come back agin, which won't be this month. So here I am, loitering about this great town, as lazy as an ox. . . . I've been here now a whole fortnight, and if I could tell ye one half I've seen, I guess you'd stare worse than if you'd seen a catamount. I've been to meeting, and to the museum, and to both Legislaters, the one they call the House, and the one they call the Sinnet. I spose Uncle Joshua is in a great hurry to hear something about these Legislaters; for you know he's always reading newspapers, and talking politics, when he can get anybody to talk with him. I've seen him when he had five tons of hay in the field well made, and a heavy shower coming up, stand two hours disputing with Squire W. about Adams and Jackson —one calling Adams a tory and a fed, and the other saying Jackson was a murderer and a fool; so they kept it up, till the rain began to pour down, and about spoilt all his hay.

There is a similarity between that paragraph and the opening paragraphs of Sinclair Lewis' *The Man Who Knew Coolidge* (1928), which is the purest example of native American humor that Lewis composed:

And I certainly do enjoy listening to you gentlemen and getting your views. That's one of the nice things about being on a Pullman like this: you can guarantee that you'll meet a lot of regular he-Americans with sound opinions and ideas.

And now let me tell you: the way I look at these things—

I don't mean to suggest for one second that I've got any better bean than the plain ordinary average citizen, but I've given a whole lot of attention to politics and such matters and—In fact, strikes me that it's the duty of all the better-educated citizens to take an interest in the affairs of the State, for what, after all, as a fellow was saying to us at the Kiwanis Club the other day—what is the Government but the union of all of us put together for mutual advantage and protection?

And me—why say, I read the political editorials in the *Advocate*—that's the leading paper in my town—Zenith—I read 'em like most folks read the sporting page. And as a result of all this and certain personal information that I can't disclose the sources of, I've come to the firm conclusion—

Here's something maybe you gentlemen never thought of. . . .

And the monolog rambles on to Calvin Coolidge, the speaker's daughter and son, Prohibition, labor relations, and so on and on.

It is more than coincidence that both Lewis' narrator, Lowell Schmaltz, and Smith's Jack Downing are traveling peddlers with little sense of humor. Both speak in the first person and wander from subject to subject without any seeming connection. Both make the most of incongruous juxtaposition of words. Jack's reference to the meeting house, the museum, and the state legislature in one series is no accident. Nor is Schmaltz's "And me—why say, I read the political editorials in the *Advocate* . . . like most folks read the sporting page." Jack's first sentence, "I now take my pen in hand, . . ." mocks genteel epistolary style, while Schmaltz's assertion that "it's the duty of all the better-educated citizens to take an interest in the affairs of the State" mocks the pretensions of the bourgeois gentleman. As for taboos, in all their loquacity neither Jack Downing nor Lowell Schmaltz ever mentions anything more shocking than the latter's "I *have* got a lady friend in New York, simply a little darling and at least twelve years younger than Mame, too—but I don't believe in divorce, and then there's the children to think of." Finally, both Seba Smith and Sinclair Lewis satirize politics and society. While Smith leads gently into ridicule of the Maine legislature and later of the social and political implications of Andrew Jackson's administration, Lewis dryly exposes the complacency of the middle-class supporters of Calvin Coolidge.

As Yankee humor moved west with the pioneers, it did not merge with Southern humor to form a single Western humor, as has often been implied. It occasionally showed the influence of the Southern tradition, of course. Mark Twain, the greatest Southern yarn spinner, left his mark on virtually all American prose writers who succeeded him, not least of all the humorists. But just as the humor of Texas and Oklahoma is simply an extension of that of the Old Southwest, so the humor of Minnesota is basically the same as that of New England.

Still the humor of the northern West and Midwest developed a certain emphasis that gave it a new complexion. That emphasis was an ambivalence, a reaction against itself, even in the end a kind of self-torture. There was a jarring note of skepticism in some of its most cocksure assertions. There was a defensiveness in its tolerance, an uneasiness in its smugness, a neurosis in its common sense, a deviousness in its prudery, an irony in its boasting. Such contradictions can be seen in the writing of the Midwestern humorists Finley Peter Dunne and George Ade, in the witticisms of numerous Midwestern newspaper writers, in the novels of Sinclair

Lewis, and in much of the comedy in the *New Yorker*, which was influenced by Midwestern humor despite its Eastern protestations. They are an essential part of the character of the Little Man, whom Norris Yates, in *The American Humorist*, has shown to be the chief character type in twentieth-century humor, and a reflection of the American self-image.

One example of the ambivalence of the Midwestern mind was in its attitude toward moral "decency." On the whole, Northern humorists retained the prudishness of their puritan and genteel forebears. Harold Ross's strict standards of morality in the *New Yorker* are well known. The outright bawdiness in the Sut Lovingood yarns of the Southern writer George Washington Harris is nowhere to be found in the work of James Thurber, for example, or of Sinclair Lewis. But Northern "morality" had its obverse side—its contradictory reaction against its puritan background—which showed itself most often in the "dirty story." It was notably furtive and puerile. Wilford H. Fawcett, a Minnesota acquaintance of Sinclair Lewis', established a fortune with his *Captain Billy's Whiz Bang*, a humor magazine catering to that taste. The following joke from the December 1920 issue (page 17) will illustrate:

LEAD ME NOT INTO DEEP WATER

The teacher had requested that each pupil bring an original short poem to school next day. After two hours of earnest effort, little Johnny produced this one:

> Poor little Mary a-fishing for bass,
> Waded in water up to her knees
> And dried herself on the cool, green grass.

"Why, Johnny," said the teacher. "That doesn't rhyme very good, does it?"

"No," replied Johnny, "the water was too shallow for bass fishing."

The "smuttiness" of the *Whiz Bang* is implied in the characters of Lowell Schmaltz, Tub Pearson, and Clif Clawson, though Lewis correctly left it to implication.

A more attractive aspect of Western humor was its tough egalitarianism, which was closely related to regional pride, though there was a negative side to this characteristic too. The following item from the Minneapolis *Journal* for December 21, 1898 (page 4, reprinted from the Omaha *Herald*), reflects the positive aspect.

> A Boston girl, who witnessed an Indian sham battle in the west, thought she would try to talk to a young Indian brave sitting next to her. "Heap much fight," she said. Lo [?] smiled a stoical smile, drew his blanket closer about his stalwart form and replied: "Yes; this is indeed a great exposition, and we flatter ourselves that our portion of the entertainment is by no means the least attractive here. May I ask who it is that I have the honor of addressing?" The dear girl from Boston was thunderstruck. She blushed a rosy red—even Boston girls can blush when they thaw out—and hastily fled. She had been addressing one of the Carlisle Indian school graduates.

Not all Western humor was so kind to the Indian, but a disdain for class distinctions and for the superior airs of Easterners was pervasive. Another item in the same paper for December 18, 1899 (page 4), reads: "After mature deliberation the editor of *L'Autorite*, a Paris daily, has come to the conclusion that America is It and the Americans They, and he gives some figures that go to show he isn't so very far off, either. This may be news to the Paris editor's subscribers, but it is a matter of common knowledge on this side of the pond."

Examples of the same kind of boosting are lavishly abundant in Lewis' novels. The following lines, spoken by Alec Kynance in *Dodsworth* (1929), are typical: "Europe? Rats! Dead's a doornail! Place for women and long-haired artists. Dead! Only American loans that keep 'em from burying the corpse! All this art! More art in a good shiny spark-plug than in all the fat Venus de Mylos they ever turned out."

Yet social and regional pride had its obverse side. The boosting spirit was common in all Western humor; more so, in fact, in the South than in the North. Pride in fertility of the soil, the abundance of game, the healthiness of the climate, the growth of towns and of business was perhaps the outstanding trait of Texas humor. Newspaper humor was especially given to boosting, for advertising the locality was considered to be the duty of the press to its subscribers and its advertisers. But even in the newspapers and probably more often in folk humor, local pride was often a mock pride. And in the North, where the geography gets more and more inhospitable the farther west one goes, the humor often turns in upon itself. The South Dakota saying, "There will always be another year," is at least as much a grim recognition of crop failure as it is an expression of hope.

The following quip from Ralph Wheelock's Minneapolis *Tribune* column for January 18, 1902, is expressed in a light tone of mockery. It was written while Minneapolis was enjoying an unusually warm winter: "It is no longer proper to say from 'hades to breakfast,' in describing any great range of expression. According to the data furnished by the weather bureau in Eagle, Alaska, the mercury dropped to 68 below last winter, and in Phoenix, Arizona, it went to 119 above in June last. From Eagle to Phoenix is the proper expression. About midway you will find the delightfully temperate climate of Minnesota all year around." Or more directly satirical is the same columnist's comment on water pollution, a problem that was beginning to arise in the growing towns and cities of Minnesota. It refers to St. Cloud, the principal town in Sinclair Lewis' home county, lying some seventy-five miles up the Mississippi from Minneapolis. "St. Cloud is in the midst of a boil-the-water agitation," wrote Wheelock (January 14, 1902). "Can't be that our supply has taken to running up hill."

Other Western journalists were of a more sarcastic turn than Wheelock. A brief item in the Sauk Centre *Avalanche*, written while United States troops were putting down the Philippine attempt to achieve independence (February 23, 1899), is in direct contrast to the chauvinism expressed in "America is It and the Americans They": "In a recent speech Cashman K. Davis is reported as saying, 'the United States is the great and consecrated evangelist of humanity.' Certainly we are. Didn't we declare war with Spain in the name of humanity—to see Cuba free. Now, haven't we given Spain $20,000,000 to purchase the Philippines, and are we not pushing our 'evangelist of humanity' in the shape of rapid fire guns and 13 inch cannon promiscuously among the Filipinos so that they, too, may become humane, and bend to the iron will of the dominant party in this great and glorious land of liberty loving people."

Or, to choose an example from B. A. Botkin's A *Treasury of Western Folklore* (1944), there is deliberate mockery of the boosting spirit in the following account of a Western tornado: "On the 18th of May in 1916, a man near Scotland,

South Dakota, had just put the finishing touches on a garage
in preparation for a new Ford that he intended purchasing
when one of the typical midwest cyclones appeared on the
horizon. After the passage of the storm he emerged from his
cyclone cellar and was surprised to find in his garage a brand
new Buick bearing a Kansas license tag." The underlying
grimness, the even masochistic enjoyment of hardship and
failure, is perhaps the outstanding characteristic that distin-
guishes the humor of the Midwest and Northwest. It contrasts with the boasting and the sadism of Southern humor.
It is an expression of disillusionment with the boosters'
dreams. The land of milk and honey, the Beulah Land,
turned out often to be the heartbreaking and backbreaking
land of Ole Rölvaag's *Giants in the Earth* (1927) or of some
of Willa Cather's novels. It is the basic ingredient of all of
Sinclair Lewis' most effective satire. Humor was, perhaps, a
way of making life more bearable, but it was not a happy
humor.

The so-called "revolt from the village"—which was simply
an extension of the revolt from the farm—was an expression
of the same discontent, the same self-torture, that is expressed in Western humor. But Sinclair Lewis, Sherwood
Anderson, and Edgar Lee Masters vehemently denied that
they were revolting against the village. In fact, Carl Van
Doren's theory of the revolt was a half-truth. Though perhaps illogical, there was a sort of love-hate syndrome in
Western and Midwestern character. The evils of the village
and the farm were very real, but there were also values and
pleasant memories. Indeed, there was an ingrained loyalty to
the region and a kind of exasperated humility in the face of
its evils.

Walter Blair, in an article entitled "The Urbanization of
Humor," pointed out that the "crackerbox" tradition in
American humor had become citified and sophisticated in
the twentieth century.[2] By way of illustration, he cited Harold Ross's often-quoted statement that the *New Yorker* was
not written for the old lady in Dubuque. But Blair failed to
say that it was read in Dubuque. What is more, Ross himself
came from Aspen, Colorado, James Thurber from Columbus, Ohio, and Ring Lardner from Niles, Michigan. Preceding them in the urbanization of American humor were the
Chicago journalists George Ade and Finley Peter Dunne.

In *The American Humorist: Conscience of the Twentieth*

Century (1964) Norris W. Yates argues that the Little Man of Ade, Thurber, and other twentieth-century humorists was in part a result of the urbanization of the humor of the Midwest. The Little Man was overwhelmed by nature, women, and machines. In a sense, he was the opposite of the giants in the earth and the rip-roaring Davy Crocketts and Mike Finks. He was a glorification of the urban middle-class American with some education, yet he was an anti-hero. He was neurotic, but at bottom he was sane in the midst of an insane and at least partly malignant world. He was the comic symbol of the lost generation, and his more tragic or pathetic side was shown in the work of F. Scott Fitzgerald, another Minnesotan. He was a reaction against the noble frontiersman, the indomitable pioneer, and the mythical cowboy—dreams which still persist and which have their spiritual truth as the Little Man has his realistic truth. Dreams which Walter Mitty dreamed. Dreams which were vulgarized and commercialized in the mind of George F. Babbitt.

As everyone knows, Babbitt was something of a self-portrait of Sinclair Lewis. Lewis was forever torn between the dreams and the reality. His later work was often almost sentimentally nostalgic about the simplicity and morality of Midwestern small-town life. "It is twenty-nine years since I left Sauk Centre," he wrote in 1931 in "The Long Arm of the Small Town." "Yet it is as vivid to my mind as though I had left there yesterday. . . . It was a good time, a good place, and a good preparation for life" (*The Man from Main Street*, pp. 271–72). On the other hand, his exposure of the smugness, materialism, and anti-intellectualism of the small town hardly needs illustration. The irony of the opening paragraphs of *Main Street* (1920) is apparent as the book proceeds: "The days of pioneering, of lassies in sunbonnets, and bears killed with axes in piney clearings, are deader now than Camelot; and a rebellious girl is the spirit of that bewildered empire called the American Middlewest." And the prologue to the same novel is a gem of satiric exaggeration: "Main Street is the climax of civilization. That this Ford car might stand in front of the Bon Ton Store, Hannibal invaded Rome and Erasmus wrote in Oxford cloisters. What Ole Jenson the grocer says to Ezra Stowbody the banker is the law for London, Prague, and the unprofitable isles of the sea; whatsoever Ezra does not know and sanction, that thing is heresy, worthless for knowing and wicked to consider."

In ridiculing the Midwest, Lewis was ridiculing himself, and it is that masochistic twist which sometimes makes his humor painful. In his nonfiction—frequently more fictitious than his fiction—Lewis often ridiculed himself directly. In "I'm an Old Newspaperman Myself," he pictured himself in Sauk Centre as "a skinny, perpetually complaining small boy named 'Ole Doc Lewis's youngest boy, Harry,' or, more intimately, 'Claude Lewis's red-headed kid brother,' " and he deliberately exaggerated his ineptitude as a journalist (*The Man from Main Street*, p. 76). Note that even in his youth he was complaining, and his most successful work might be viewed as a long series of complaints sublimated by humor. The innocent pose had developed from the bumptious wisdom of Major Jack Downing in the 1830's to the self-torture of the Little Man in the 1920's.

Furthermore, the masochism extended to the Midwestern readers of Lewis' work, at least according to Lewis himself: "*Main Street* . . . was my first novel to rouse the embattled peasantry and, as I have already hinted, it had really a success of scandal. One of the most treasured American myths had been that all American villages were peculiarly noble and happy, and here an American had attacked that myth. Scandalous! Some hundreds of thousands read the book with the same masochistic pleasure that one has in sucking an aching tooth" ("Self-Portrait [Nobel Foundation]," *The Man from Main Street*, p. 54). And the number of readers who identified themselves with Carol Kennicott was surprising.

Lewis' early novels may be seen as an experimentation with his native humoristic elements before reaching his stride as an American humorist in *Main Street*. *Our Mr. Wrenn* (1914), for example, was a sentimental picture of what Lewis himself called "a very little Little Man" ("Breaking into Print," *The Man from Main Street*, p. 73). *Free Air* (1919), on the other hand, reverted to the Western hero type, in the person of the mechanic Milt Daggett, who melodramatically rescues and marries the sophisticated Eastern belle Claire Boltwood. Meanwhile, the author was polishing his already natural "journalistic manner," to quote Alexander Cowie in *The Rise of the American Novel* (1948), a manner that "relied in part on vivacity of tone and on the apt use of the vernacular." His unflattering depiction of Western geography is also evident in *Free Air*, where he described Minnesota mud, or gumbo, as "mud mixed with tar, flypaper, fish glue, and well-chewed, chocolate covered caramels"; and in the same novel he described sardonically the towns of "Gopher Prairie" and "Schoenstrom."

The continuing debate over Lewis' ambivalence—his savage ridicule as against his "happy endings," his deadly effects as against his protestations of sympathy—is perhaps due to the fact that Lewis was a humorist first and a satirist only secondarily. Furthermore, he was attempting to transform the brief hit-and-run method of newspaper humor into the sustained form of the novel—a feat at which no one but Mark Twain had really succeeded before him. Critics have pointed out that the latter part of *Main Street* is no longer social satire, but restricts itself to the personal relationship between Will and Carol Kennicott, and concludes with their reconciliation. The same criticism can be leveled at most of the novels that followed *Main Street*. The apparently happy ending is, of course, a convention in the comic novel. Whether this is an aesthetic flaw, a slavish bowing to tradition, is largely a matter of individual taste. The farcical ending of *Huckleberry Finn* has likewise been debated. Twain too was a humorist—though he became a straight satirist in his old age, with "The Man That Corrupted Hadleyburg" and *The Mysterious Stranger*. Actually, the endings of *Main Street* and *Huckleberry Finn* are only partly happy. Carol Kennicott achieves submission, not victory: "She looked across the silent fields to the west. She was conscious of an unbroken sweep of land to the Rockies, to Alaska; a dominion which will rise to unexampled greatness when other empires have grown senile. Before that time, she knew, a hundred generations of Carols will aspire and go down in tragedy devoid of palls and solemn chanting, the humdrum inevitable tragedy of struggle against inertia." And Huck concludes: "But I reckon I got to light out for the territory ahead of the rest, because Aunt Sally she's going to adopt me and sivilize me, and I can't stand it. I been there before."

It is not necessary to exclude other views in order to view Sinclair Lewis as a humorist. But it helps to clarify our conception of his total achievement to see him as a novelist working with the journalistic and folk materials of native American humor to arrive at a culminating expression of that humor as it had developed in the upper West. Like much of the humor of that region, Lewis' humor reflects the contradictory pulls of regional loyalty and realistic clear-sightedness, of pride and complaint, of a dream and a disillusionment with that dream.

Focus on F. Scott Fitzgerald's *The Great Gatsby*
The Nowhere Hero

RICHARD LEHAN

The American writer, torn between mutually exclusive cultural imperatives, has long suffered from a kind of schizophrenia. Over and over, he has tried to reconcile a materialism which he could not accept with an idealism that he could not realize. Henry James is a case in point. His Christopher Newman in *The American* turns his back on a greedy America and goes to Europe in search of vague cultural ideals. What he finds in Europe is that such ideals do not exist—that if America has money without tradition, Europe has tradition without the means to finance it. Honor has become meaningless—proved by the death of Valentin in a duel over a mercenary strumpet. At the end of the novel, Newman himself is caught in the same kind of meaningless situation. He can exercise his will—that all-important faculty in James's fiction—but he cannot really change his situation or the world in which he lives. With Valentin dead and Claire de Cintré in a nunnery, Newman is bereft of both friendship and love, and his burning the letter is a meaningless act, except as an act in and for itself, a gesture which is its own justification.

James himself discussed America as a kind of cultural limbo in *The American Scene*, written in 1904, after his long absence from America. The horror he expressed in the face of a growing American materialism is the same kind of horror that Henry Adams voiced in *The Education of Henry Adams*, where he symbolized the new materialism in terms of the dynamo, which for Adams represented a principle of uncontained, even destructive energy, an apocalyptic threat.

While Mark Twain was perhaps more ambiguous, he treated the same duality in *A Connecticut Yankee in King Arthur's Court*, and once more showed modern man tearing down an old world of hierarchy and principle for a new world of western "know-how." An American sense of pragmatism competed once again with a world of fixed values.

F. Scott Fitzgerald was as much concerned about these cultural dualities as were James, Adams, Twain, and the host of other American writers who have treated this theme. In many ways, the problem for Fitzgerald focused upon his father, a Southerner who embodied "the old courtesies" in a new industrial world where success demanded the kind of ruthless energy that his father lacked. Fitzgerald was both embarrassed by and proud of his father's failures—embarrassed because it revealed that the times were too much for his father; proud because conversely his father was better than the times.

Nick Carraway has these same ambivalent feelings about Gatsby. Gatsby is obviously not with it. He is no match for Tom Buchanan, who represents the kind of energy and force —the spirit of Adams' dynamo—which is necessary for success in a materialistic America. Gatsby, who is really a phony broker, has become a grotesque distortion of the successful man, a pathetic extension of what Tom Buchanan embodies. Yet Gatsby's fidelity to an ideal, to a dream, is an admirable, albeit a romantic quality of mind. Fitzgerald equated the dream with the spirit of the past, with the spirit of the Dutch sailors for whom America was a dream, a matter of possibility, a new world waiting to be formed. He also equated it with the spirit of Benjamin Franklin, who best embodies the kind of western pragmatism which finally won out as well as the rags-to-riches ideal which Gatsby accepted so completely. And lastly, he equated the ideal with a woman, with Daisy Fay, who had abandoned Gatsby for Tom Buchanan, the man who best embodied the final heritage of Benjamin Franklin.

These three "equations" are the source of Gatsby's dream and Nick Carraway's nightmare, for Gatsby never learns that the dream is dead, and Nick's discovery of this fact leaves him as hopeless, as culturally displaced, as Henry James's Christopher Newman. Indeed, such is the fate of the new man in the land discovered by Christopher; and if we look closely at these three "equations," we can clearly see what Fitzgerald was trying to tell us about America and how, as a novelist, he was saying it.

The references to America as a new world are "laid on" the novel—that is, this idea is never systematically developed but is instead implied. Nick thinks of himself as a Westerner, and here we have the suggestion of the frontier, long since gone, of course, when Fitzgerald was writing the novel. Nick also thinks of himself as a frontiersman when he gives directions to a man lost on West Egg. And lastly, Nick wonders what the Dutch sailors thought when they first saw Manhattan. All these references link Nick and Gatsby with a world that no longer exists, a world that has been lost in the back rush of time, a world that offered more in promise than has been realized in fact. While this theme is not the key one in the novel, it is important, because it sets the context within which Gatsby's story is told; it establishes the fact that, like Gatsby, all Americans live in a world of betrayed promise, a world that could never be—and "So we beat on, boats against the current, borne back ceaselessly into the past" (Scribner's paperback edition, p. 182).

Here we have the theme that links Fitzgerald so closely with writers like James, Adams, and Twain who contrast the values of modern America with those of the past. Fitzgerald's view is really as apocalyptic as Henry Adams' because it leaves no real basis for hope. We can only look nostalgically back at what could have been; we have no way to exercise the will to realize an ideal. Nick's return to the West is as meaningless a gesture as Christopher Newman's burning de Bellegarde's letter. It is an act in and for itself, not heroic as the critics insist, but antiheroic, a subliminal recognition of cultural defeat—of a world that offers no basis for an act beyond itself, no basis for meaningful commitment.

If Adams, James, and Fitzgerald share this theme among themselves, they also share it with Oswald Spengler. In a letter to Maxwell Perkins, Fitzgerald said that he read Spengler the summer he was writing *The Great Gatsby*, "and I don't think that I ever quite recovered from him." The importance of this remark has been somewhat belied by the fact that Spengler's *The Decline of the West* was not translated into English until after Fitzgerald's novel was published, and Fitzgerald did not read German. To believe, however, that he did not know Spengler because he had not read him directly is to be a victim of literal-mindedness—and does not take into consideration the use that Fitzgerald often made of secondary sources and of what friends told him. Spengler was in the air during the early part of the twenties; there were countless summaries of his ideas (which is probably what Fitzgerald had in mind when he spoke of reading Spengler); and Fitzgerald could not long have talked with friends like Edmund Wilson without being exposed to these ideas. Moreover, many of Spengler's ideas had been approximated by Brooks Adams (Henry's brother) in *The Law of Civilization and Decay*, published in 1896. (The second chapter of this book on the Middle Ages is particularly interesting in the light of Fitzgerald's later use of the Middle Ages in his abortive novel, *Count of Darkness*.)

Spengler discussed at great length two kinds of cultural periods—the Faustian and the Apollonian. The Apollonian, or classical period, was one of order and harmony with man generally self-satisfied. The Faustian or modern period is one of flux and disruption with man generally dissatisfied and longing for the unattainable. Spengler felt that there was nowhere to go after the Faustian period (that it marked the kind of cultural limbo within which Nick Carraway and Christopher Newman find themselves) and that after the rise of the big cities controlled by the monied thugs ("the new Caesars," he called them) the last Faustian man would be destroyed, to be replaced by the "colored" races—the Negroes and the Chinese—who would use Western man's technological know-how against him.

Whether or not Spengler directly influenced *The Great Gatsby* can perhaps be argued. What cannot be argued, however, is the remarkable similarity between Spengler's ideas and the design of the novel. Gatsby is the last of the Faustian men, the modern man living in the flux of the big city, longing for the unattainable, doomed in his combat with the Tom Buchanans, the new Caesars, in a world that contrasts remarkably with an older order, a world that has been covered by the ashes of time—just as the green breast of the new world has given way to the Valley of Ashes in the novel itself. That Tom's world will in time give way to another, more primitive, culture is suggested in a number of ways. Tom, for example, discusses with some fear the rise of the colored races (see pp. 13–14), and Nick and Gatsby see a white chauffeur driving two Negroes (an inversion of their roles) across the Queensboro Bridge.

When Tom is discussing these matters, he refers to God-dard's *The Rise of the Colored Empires,* a nonexistent book. Fitzgerald was obliquely referring to Lothrop Stoddard's *The Rising Tide of Color,* published by Charles Scribner's Sons in 1920. Like Spengler, Stoddard believed that the colored races would eventually control the world. He argued that the white man controlled four-fifths of the world but lived pri-marily in Europe and North America, which composed only one-fifth of the land. As a result, one-fifth of the white race, around 110 million persons, were expected to preserve the status quo in the face of a disgruntled colored population eleven times that number. The night of the big party, the owl-eyed man picks Volume 1 of Stoddard's lectures from a shelf in Gatsby's library.

Because so much of what Fitzgerald was saying about America was said obliquely, through the use of descriptive detail and allusion, the import of these matters has been lost on many of the critics. Fitzgerald placed his two principal characters, Gatsby and Nick Carraway, in a cultural limbo, where the past has been corrupted and where the idealists crash upon the hard rocks of ruthless materialism; he placed them in a world of Tom Buchanans, where the Faustian man is an intruder.

For if Gatsby cannot seal the hole in time, cannot buy back the past, he also cannot commit himself to the future. Fitzgerald inverted the rags-to-riches story and made Gatsby the victim of his Benjamin Franklin-Dan Cody (James J. Hill) dreams. One way that Fitzgerald did this was to make Gatsby an ersatz profiteer. Like a character in an inverted Horatio Alger novel, he struggles up from his bleak begin-nings to make a great deal of money and to buy a mansion overlooking Long Island Sound. Only the mansion is on West Egg, which houses the new rich, and not East Egg, which houses the established rich; and the money comes from bucket shops, bootlegging, and gambling.

Gatsby in many ways marks the logical end of the Alger tradition. He is, to put this differently, the end product of the American Dream, the grotesque embodiment of what America can offer its ambitious young. At one point in the novel, Tom Buchanan buys a dog for Myrtle Wilson from "a gray old man who bore an absurd resemblance to John D. Rockefeller" (27). Gatsby himself also has an absurd resemblance to the robber barons. To be sure, he lacks their ultimate refinement of taste and their final established status; but he shares their motives, wants what they want, and is just as unscrupulous in the way he operates. Rockefeller's dealings with Standard Oil share a quality of mind that Gatsby brought to Meyer Wolfsheim's operations. Enough money can buy respectability in America—just as today we know that the Mafia has moved into many "legitimate" businesses—and when Daisy leaves Gatsby because he lacks the proper social credentials, she is being more faithful to the letter than the spirit of the law.

As I pointed out in my *F. Scott Fitzgerald and the Craft of Fiction*, Gatsby grotesquely resembles Tom Buchanan. Both Gatsby and Tom are brokers—only Gatsby is a phony broker; but where the legitimate ends and the phony begins is a debatable point in Fitzgerald's world, where Gatsby's motives are in many ways at one with Tom's. Only Gatsby's lack of taste marks the substantial difference, and this is also a matter of degree—Gatsby with his silver suits, golden ties, and pin-striped shirts; Gatsby in his phony feudal castle built by a wealthy brewer (be it noted) who wanted to thatch the roofs of the surrounding houses; and Gatsby in his oversized yellow car embellished with chrome. Yet the grotesque qualities of Gatsby seem, at times, to extend to America itself, or at least to New York, which Nick at one point describes as a "city rising up across the river in white heaps and sugar lumps all built with a wish" (69).

Gatsby becomes the absurd incarnation of Benjamin Franklin and the Gilded Age tycoon. Mr. Gatz makes the connection when he shows Nick the copy of *Hopalong Cassidy* in which Gatsby set down Franklin's formula to success and when he remarks that if Gatsby had lived he would have become another James J. Hill (169 and 174). Gatsby did not just become another Franklin or Hill; he went beyond them and became their grotesque extension in time. He came to embody the values that Henry James turned from in terror in *The American Scene*. He came to represent the decline of cultural ideals which Henry Adams warned us about in apocalyptic terms in his autobiography.

At the end of the novel, Nick visits Gatsby's house and erases an obscene word some boy has scratched on Gatsby's steps and which stood out clearly in the moonlight. The harsh difference between the word and the moonlight marks the contrast between Gatsby's dream and the harsh reality of life which besmirched it. Nick wants to keep Gatsby's dream inviolate in the face of a world hostile to both the dream and the dreamer. Nick's act, of course, is only a gesture, as his final flight back West is only a gesture, for the dream was destined to fail, destined to be mocked and violated; and in the case of Jay Gatsby, one cannot separate the dreamer from the dream.

One also cannot separate the dreamer from the object of the dream. Daisy Fay is a symbolic object of love in a world where the promises of the past have been betrayed and the future has been grotesquely mocked. What is important is Gatsby's attitude toward Daisy, which is the same attitude that the Dutch sailors bring to America. For the aim is not to have Daisy, but to want her; and when she appears to be Gatsby's or when she is lost forever, the world changes. As long as Daisy was beyond his reach, the green light on her dock was a resplendent symbol of desire. When Gatsby meets Daisy after five years and feels her love for him return, it became once again a mere "green light on a dock. His count of enchanted objects had diminished by one" (94). Fitzgerald clearly makes Gatsby into the Faustian man, the man who must have an object of desire. Once Gatsby loses his sense of expectation—and Nick in great part shares with him this experience—there is nowhere to go, nothing to live for.

As I have explained at some length in my book on Fitzgerald, *The Great Gatsby* is a *roman à clef*. All the characters have their counterparts in Fitzgerald's own experience, and he was using the novel to work out in fiction matters that he could not work out in life. Yet Fitzgerald went beyond the actual facts of his experience, particularly when he made the novel a story of double adultery. If Daisy was naïve and innocent when Gatsby first met her, she has come a long way when Gatsby returns to her after an absence of five years. Fitzgerald's story would seem more sordid than it does if he had not projected it against a world of dreams, romance, and summer moonlight. Tom's relationship with Myrtle Wilson is as sordid as Myrtle's relationship with George Wilson is pathetic; Nick feels morally stained in his relationship with Jordan Baker; and Tom and Daisy's marriage has been a string of infidelities.

The love Gatsby has for Daisy seems to be the one pure impulse in a corrupt world—a desire that partakes of the promises of time. But this promise is eventually betrayed, just as the promises that America held out to the world were eventually betrayed. When he meets her five years later Daisy is not the girl that Gatsby knew in Louisville; time and Tom Buchanan have changed her; and this is what Gatsby cannot understand when he returns to her. " 'Oh, you want too much!' Daisy cries to him. 'I love you now—isn't that enough? I can't help what's past' " (133). But this is not enough for Gatsby, who mistakenly believes that one can buy back the past. Daisy has been corrupted by the past, a fact that emerges only too clearly when she quickly abandons Gatsby after she finds out about his underworld connections. She runs back to Tom knowing that his cruelty can offer protection. Like so many Americans, Gatsby is "borne back ceaselessly into the past" (182); only it is the corrupted past; and, as a result, he breaks "up like a glass against Tom [Buchanan's] malice" (148).

This is the point that Nick Carraway learns in telling Gatsby's story. It is the lesson, however, that leaves him morally paralyzed, desiring a world that is "in uniform and at a sort of moral attention forever" (2). The story that Nick tells begins the first week of June and ends the first week of September in 1922. It is a "summer" story—a story of betrayed hope that begins with the cool breezes of June, reaches a climax in the violence of August heat, and ends with the yellow days of September, with the leaves falling the fatal day that Gatsby goes for his first and last swim in his hitherto unused pool. The move from summer to fall reinforces the move from hope to disappointment, from romance to tragedy, and from expectation to awareness—an awareness for Nick (and the reader) that both Gatsby and America have been betrayed by unfulfilled promises.

When the dream fails them, Fitzgerald's characters look first nostalgically to the past and see it in terms of what might have been. Soon this nostalgia turns to horror as they realize how they have betrayed the promises of youth, how they have wasted their talents. Thus we move from one circle of experience to another in *The Great Gatsby*, the personal experience duplicating and reinforcing the cultural experience, Gatsby's sense of lost promise duplicating the lost promises of America itself. In *The Great Gatsby*, we move with Nick Carraway from dream to horror—from the dream of the early explorers who first saw the green breast of the new world, to the commuters who pass daily through the Valley of Ashes, which parallels our move from a young army officer named Gatsby to his grim and pathetic funeral.

When Nick leaves Gatsby the night of Myrtle Wilson's fatal accident, he says, "So I walked away and left him standing there in the moonlight—watching over nothing" (146). At the very end of the novel, as Nick looks out into the dark of Long Island Sound, he realizes that both Gatsby's dream and that of the republic lie behind us, and his last sentence catches the rhythm of his previous words, "So we beat on, boats against the current, borne back ceaselessly into the past" (182). Gatsby watches over nothing, and we beat on into the past. The two ideas merge on the level of style as well as on the level of narrative theme. We move from hope to despair, from the present to the past where the promises of a young country and a young man have given way to—"nothing."

The meaning of Gatsby's story was not unknown to Henry James, Henry Adams, and Mark Twain. Gatsby was not the first of the nowhere heroes, and he is obviously not the last; but he is perhaps the most vital, and his story reveals a quality of mind that is our legacy from the Gilded Age.

Focus on F. Scott Fitzgerald's
Tender Is the Night

FRANK KINAHAN

Our age of national innocence is over. The vague pre-Mencken suspicion that a dark wet something lurked just below the placid surface of the American Dream has been confirmed by fifty years of periodic depression and almost constant war, and the best of our authors during that same period have been critics rather than proponents of our national ethos. F. Scott Fitzgerald is no exception. The Dream dies a most savage death in the case of Jay Gatsby; and *Tender Is the Night* is a most savage postmortem. The central concern of that work is the tension between the Dream and the harsh reality underlying it; and this theme is developed primarily in terms of the personality of Dick Diver. Indeed, the contradictions inherent in his character are the same as those of the Dream as a whole; the Dream evaporates and Dick dies for much the same reasons and with the same inevitability.

The narrative thread of the novel is interwoven with certain recurrent motifs. The first of these I call the "two-worlds" motif. We sense from the novel's start that all its major characters straddle two continents, with greater or less success. Rosemary Hoyt is described as a combination of "the French manners of her early adolescence and the democratic manners of America" (8). (All references are to the Scribner edition, Fitzgerald's original arrangement of his materials, rather than to Malcolm Cowley's later "redesigning." One can question the artistic merits of the structure Fitzgerald selected; but the fact that this structure is the one he wanted is apparent, both from his *Letters*, his notebooks [*The Crack-Up*: cf. esp. pp. 180–81], and the recent study by Matthew Bruccoli [*The Composition of Tender Is the Night*: University of Pittsburgh, 1963].) The magazines she buys for her mother are *Le Temps* and the *Saturday Evening Post*. Dick's wife Nicole is "the granddaughter of a self-made American capitalist and the granddaughter of a Count of the House of Lippe Weissenfeld" (53). Dick himself is the young American psychiatrist who finishes his studies and begins his practice in Switzerland. The problems caused by this clash of two cultures will become more clear below; I want to point out here only that all the novel's major characters are expatriates, with the significant exception of Tommy Barban.

But the two-worlds motif applies in a special sense to Dick and Nicole Diver; the physical fact of their expatriation might in fact be taken as merely a symbol of their far more profound emotional isolation. Their "two worlds" are interior as well as geographic. The surface they present to society is that of the well-adjusted husband and wife; the hard fact of the matter is that they are actually doctor and patient as well, preserving their ultra-sane appearance in the face of a quite real insanity. Let me take this a step further and point out that in one sense they are not expatriates at all, since they really inhabit neither America nor Europe: "Their own party was overwhelmingly American and sometimes scarcely American at all" (52). Rather, they live in an intensely personal world that floats somewhere outside of our own notions of space, a world that Dick has created in hopes of saving Nicole: "in fantasy alone she finds rest" (*The Crack-Up*, 168). Nicole is well aware of what Dick has done; they sit, as she says, on "*Our* beach that Dick made out of a pebble pile" (20). Dick is elsewhere portrayed as "recreat[ing] the unity of his own party" (52), as having "made a quick study of the whole affair, simplifying it always until it bore a faint resemblance to one of his own parties" (59), as "resolv[ing] things into the pattern of the holiday" (85); and it is this constant sense of Dick as creator that lends to his eventual self-destruction its irony as well as its poignance.

I stated above that Dick's world seems beyond our version of space (consider, for instance, this passage: "[Their] table seemed to have risen a little toward the sky like a mechanical dancing platform, giving the people around it a sense of being alone with each other in the dark universe, nourished by its only food, warmed by its only lights" (34); and it seems to be outside the demands of time as well. The opening scene is set on the Riviera. (Identifiable as the Hotel du Cap at Antibes: cf. *The Crack-Up*, 19, 44. I want to mention here as well that I am indebted to Mr. Bill Byrom, Harvard GSAS 2, for having suggested to me the importance of the theme of mutability.) The time is, appropriately enough, "out of season," allowing the Divers to perpetuate their private world. That they do so is clear: "The Divers' day was spaced like the day of the older civilizations to yield the utmost from the materials at hand" (19). Their very lives, in short, are "out of season," outside of space and time; Rosemary sums it up best: "Beyond the inky sea and far up that high, black shadow of a hill lived the Divers. She thought of them both together, heard them still singing faintly a song like rising smoke, like a hymn, very remote in time and far away. Their children slept, their gate was shut for the night" (40). And the gate remains shut for Nicole's sake. The image is not a random one; it conveys the very real barrier that exists between the Divers and the "real" world. That barrier is but rarely removed, and Dick, caretaker as well as creator of his world, is quite conscious of removing it when he does do so: "Then, without caution, lest the first bloom of the relation wither, he opened the gate to his amusing world" (28). His children sing a song that has a subtle but substantial relationship to Nicole's sometimes desperate situation: "Ma chandelle est morte / Je n'ai plus de feu / Ouvre-moi ta porte / Pour l'amour de Dieu" (29). It is this same door that Dick has opened to Nicole and shut behind her. The world the gate protects is one in which she can survive; since time does not affect it, there is no question of mutability, no question, in fact, of movement. This immobility is not ennui; it comes closer to what T. S. Eliot describes as "the still point of the turning world": "Even in their immobility, complete as that of the morning, [Rosemary] felt a purpose, a working over something, a direction, an act of creation different from any she had known" (17). And Nicole fits happily in: "Then Nicole. Rosemary saw her suddenly in a new way and found her one of the most beautiful people she had ever known. Her face, the face of a saint, a Viking madonna, shone through the faint motes that snowed across the candlelight, drew down its flush from the wine-colored lanterns in the pine. She was still as still" (33). Rather like the rich, then, this world is different from yours and mine. Its difference consists essentially in its dreamlike qualities; the most appropriate comparison I can think of is the moment when Dorothy first opens the door to her house, which has landed in Oz, and the earlier black-and-white shots of the Kansas plains are replaced by the kaleidoscopic colors of fairyland. The first lengthy description of Nicole, for instance, finds her walking in her garden "between kaleidoscopic peonies massed in pink clouds, black and brown tulips and fragile mauve-stemmed roses, transparent like sugar flowers in a confectioner's window" (26). Later on, she goes on a shopping spree with Rosemary. The actress is very much the product of her mother's realistic attitudes; she buys two dresses, two hats, and four pairs of shoes, and buys them with her own money. Nicole, on the other hand, "bought from a great list that ran two pages, and bought the things in the windows besides"; and what she purchases is basically "dream equipment," objects that both describe and help to perpetuate her detachment from reality: "colored beads, folding beach cushions, artificial flowers, honey, a guest bed, bags, scarfs, love birds, miniatures for a doll's house and three yards of some new cloth the color of prawns. She bought a dozen bathing suits, a rubber alligator, a travelling chest set of gold and ivory, big linen handkerchiefs for Abe, two chamois leather jackets of king-fisher blue and burning bush from Hermes" (54–55). In Paris, the whole group goes for a ride in the Shah of Persia's car, commandeered somehow by Dick, and "Its wheels were of silver, so was the radiator. The inside of the body was inlaid with innumerable brilliants which would be replaced with true gems by the court jeweller when the car arrived in Teheran the following week. There was only one real seat in back, because the Shah must ride alone, so they took turns riding in it and sitting on the marten fur that covered the floor" (77). Even the most mundane of events is somehow transformed; Dick goes to a bank to cash a check and there meets the heavyweight champion of the world. Rosemary again epitomizes the situation when she sees the Divers as "hovering like people in an amusing dream" (77), for so they are. Their situation must be such, for Nicole must be allowed to continue to dream. They must and have become expatriates from the real world.

It is this sort of world that Rosemary enters. She fits in perfectly, and this is no surprise; she is an actress, after all, and thus a sort of dream merchant herself. A second recurring motif is that of the stage. Fitzgerald strikes its first note early in describing the home of the Divers, Villa Diana: "On such a stage some memorable thing was sure to happen" (29). Rosemary feels right at home; at one point she goes up to Luis Campion, a minor character, who "was weeping hard and quietly and shaking in the same parts as a weeping woman. A scene in a role she had played last year swept over her irresistibly and advancing she touched him on the shoulder. He gave a little yelp before he recognized her" (41). And afterwards, when she first tries to seduce Dick, she realizes that the moment "was one of her greatest roles and she flung herself into it more passionately" (64). The moment is of course a quite serious one, but Rosemary treats it as simply something from behind the fourth wall; she thus shares with Nicole an inability to distinguish between her life and her art or, to put it otherwise, dream and reality. Ironically enough, the only character able to make that distinction is Dick, who himself has created the dream. Rosemary fails to seduce him; Fitzgerald catches the stage quality of her dialogue superbly: " 'I knew you wouldn't,' she sobbed. 'It was just a forlorn hope'" (66). And Dick's response points up his awareness of his (and Rosemary's) world as stage: "Good night, child. This is a damn shame. Let's drop it out of the picture." His awareness stems greatly from the fact that he himself is an actor; in the bank scene, for instance, he decides to go to a teller "who was young and for whom he would have to put on only a small show. It was often easier to give a show than to watch one" (89).

The reasons behind the necessity of Dick's being as he is are clear: he must fit into the dream world he has created for Nicole, and acting is one way of doing it, is another form of dream. Thus, "He saw Nicole in the garden. Presently he must encounter her and the prospect gave him a leaden feeling. Before her he must keep up a perfect front, now and to-morrow, next week and next year" (166). It is this façade that Rosemary falls in love with, this new role that she selects; she says to Dick, for instance: "Oh, we're such *actors* —you and I" (105). And they are.

Fitzgerald, then, has set up a play situation, a personal

dream; and the central question then becomes whether or not the dream world Dick has created can survive the realities underlying it. Book 1 ends with the revelation of Nicole's insanity; and it is at this stage in the narrative that the theme takes on more universal dimensions. Book 2 is basically a rather violent denunciation of America in terms of this same dream motif; the dream in this instance is the American Dream, but the facts beneath it are no less brutal. It becomes clear, for instance, that Nicole's insanity stems from the fact that she was seduced by her father when she was a child. Fitzgerald has here combined two of the most heinous acts of man, incest and child seduction, and our reaction of disgust is instant and almost primordial; even the compassionate psychiatrist Dohmler, having heard the father tell the story, "sat back in the focal armchair of the middle class and said to himself sharply, 'Peasant!'—it was one of the few absolute worldly judgments that he had permitted himself for twenty years" (129). Yet the family is elsewhere described as "an American ducal family without a title—the very name written in a hotel register, signed to an introduction, used in a difficult situation, caused a psychological metamorphosis in people" (158). What seems on the surface to be the cream of our crop, the fulfillment of our dream, has turned amazingly sour in reality; and it seems as if none of the members of this particular "ducal family" escape corruption, not even Nicole. In the scene in which she is trying to win Dick's love, she takes him to a hillside outside the clinic and plays American songs for him on her phonograph. They sit down "behind a low wall, facing miles and miles of rolling night. They were in America now, even Franz with his conception of Dick as an irresistible Lothario would never have guessed that they had gone so far away" (135). And the scene is then described as follows: "The thin tunes, holding lost times and future hopes in liaison, twisted upon the Valais night. In the lulls of the phonograph a cricket held the scene together with a single note" (136). That the scene could be so held together is a subtle indication of how tenuous, even superficial, the situation is; yet Dick's impression of the scene is that Nicole is a "scarcely saved waif of disaster bringing him the essence of a continent" (136), as, in Fitzgerald's view, she is, though that "essence" has little to do with the type of Boy Scout oath that the Dream embodies. It is instead the type of thing that Fitzgerald later mentions in a description of American actors, who "were risen to a position of prominence in a nation that for a decade had wanted only to be entertained" (213). The last member of the Warren family, "Baby," gets no such subtle treatment; she is simply portrayed as crass and philistine, the archetype of the rich American, her car with "a hundred superfluous horses" (145), her personality devoid of any redeeming qualities of taste or sensitivity. Her name holds a hint to her nature; it obviously signifies her lack of maturity, but hints in more subtle fashion that there was something slightly gangsterish about her as well. The word "baby," that is, was argot in the twenties for what later came to be termed "moll" and has since come to be called, courtesy of Hell's Angels, "old lady." That Fitzgerald was aware of this connotation is clear from *The Crack-Up*, in which he refers to a headline: "What news from New York?" "Stocks go up. A baby murdered a gangster" (31).

As embodied in the Warren family, then, the American situation is viewed as a tension between the innocent façade of things, the Dream, and the ugliness or superficiality behind the façade. This same tension is present in Dick himself; indeed, he is explicitly equated with the American scene. He first arrives in Zurich, for instance, "on less Achilles' heels than would be required to equip a centipede, but with plenty—the illusions of eternal strength and health, and of the essential goodness of people; illusions of a nation, the lies of generations of frontier mothers who had to croon falsely, that there were no wolves outside the cabin door" (117). His education is thoroughly American; when he has finished describing his projected first book to Dr. Dohmler, the doctor comments that "You are an American. You can do this without professional harm. I do not like these generalities. Soon you will be writing little books called 'Deep Thoughts for the Layman,' so simplified that they are positively guaranteed not to cause thinking" (138). And Dohmler's remarks describe what was for Fitzgerald the essential qualities of American education; as he puts it elsewhere, "There was even a recurrent idea in America about an education that would leave out history and the past, that should be a sort of equipment for aerial adventure, weighed down by none of the stowaways of inheritance or tradition"

(*The Crack-Up*, 109). His youth is the youth of America, the "unaging American face" (119); and, finally, the seeming completeness of his personality, the factor that Rosemary most admires, is part of a peculiarly American kind of charm: "Lucky Dick can't be one of these clever men; he must be less intact, even faintly destroyed. If life won't do it for him it's not a substitute to get a disease, or a broken heart, or an inferiority complex, though it'd be nice to build out some broken side till it was better than the original structure" (116). Significantly, there lies beneath this charm, this embodiment of the American best, a certain superficiality: "In the dead white hours in Zurich staring into a stranger's pantry across the upshine of a streetlamp, [Dick] used to think that he wanted to be good, he wanted to be brave and wise, but it was all pretty difficult. He wanted to be loved, too, if he could fit it in" (133). And it does seem a bit odd that the man who wanted "to be a good psychologist— maybe to be the greatest one that ever lived" (132)—did not consider love a necessary part of his equipment.

It would of course be unfair to say that Dick is the fleshed-out persona of only the superficial and charming side of America. Though there is a certain element of superficiality in his character, he is also capable of hating the superficial: "From his father Dick had learned the somewhat conscious good manners of the young Southerner coming north after the Civil War. Often he used them and just as often he despised them because they were not a protest against how unpleasant selfishness was but against how unpleasant it looked" (164). Or, as he says elsewhere: "Good manners are an admission that everybody is so tender that they have to be handled with gloves. Now, human respect—you don't call a man a coward or a liar lightly, but if you spend your life sparing people's feelings and feeding their vanity, you get so you can't distinguish what *should* be respected in them" (178). Such statements denote Dick's self-awareness, his understanding of the realities beneath the dream he has created. The tension of the situation tires him, and he wonders whether it will break him in time, whether the dream must die. Its death begins in the middle of Book 2.

The flashback technique of the second book returns us first to where we were at the first book's end, Nicole's breakdown, and then proceeds from that point. Dick nurses

Nicole back to health over several months, but the harsh fact of her illness has begun to wear on him. He takes a vacation from the clinic in hopes of recovering his own peace of mind, and meets Tommy Barban in Munich. Barban tells him that Abe North has been beaten to death in the Harvard Club, a New York speakeasy. It was with Abe and his wife Mary that those seemingly timeless Riviera vacations had been spent. To couch Abe's death in the symbolic context of a motif I spoke of earlier, his murder at this stage of the narrative points up the real and pressing fact of time and mutability and foreshadows the inevitable destruction of the Riviera dream world. We are back in season in spite of ourselves. Dick has earlier hinted at his awareness of the inexorability of change; he is dining with Baby at Caux, and watching Nicole on the dance floor: "The orchestra was playing 'Poor Butterfly'; young Marmora was dancing with his mother. It was a tune new enough to them all. Listening, and watching Nicole's shoulders as she chattered to the elder Marmora, whose hair was dashed with white like a piano keyboard, Dick thought of the shoulders of a violin, and then he thought of the dishonor, the secret. Oh, butterfly—the moments pass into hours—" (152). The passage is Fitzgerald at his most subtle; its connotations are clear. In attempting to put across a sense of mutability, it is completely appropriate to portray a son now old enough to dance with his mother and a father whose hair is dashed with white. Moreover, both Nicole and the elder Marmora are described in terms of a musical metaphor; and the comparison thus implied between them hints as well that time and change will affect her as they did him. Lastly, the choice of song is so much in context that we could easily overlook its significance. The moments do, after all, pass into hours; Dick, aware of that fact all along, was able nonetheless to fight it; but Abe's death brings it violently back to his attention. The youthful fantasy has begun to crumble, and the larger dream of America has begun to die as well. The war has taken place, and our innocence is gone: "[Dick] slept deep and awoke to a slow mournful march passing his window. It was a long column of men in uniform, wearing the familiar helmet of 1914, thick men in frock coats and silk hats, burghers, aristocrats, plain men. It was a society of veterans going to lay wreaths on the tombs of the dead. The column marched past with a sort of swagger for a lost magnificence, a past effort, a forgotten sorrow. The faces were only formally sad but Dick's lungs burst for a moment with regret for Abe's death, and his own lost youth of ten years ago" (200). The "real" world is knocking on the gate that had been sheltered so long. Nicole is in fact insane; Abe is in fact dead; and from this point it is but a short step to the denouement. Dick's father dies; he returns to America to visit the grave, and in so doing bids goodbye to all that was solid in his American background. The Diver family graveyard is described as follows: "These dead, [Dick] knew them all, their weather-beaten faces with blue flashing eyes, the spare violent bodies, the souls made of new earth in the forest-heavy darkness of the seventeenth century." Dick's comment is brief and final: "Good-by, my father—good-by, all my fathers" (205).

Symbolically speaking, he has broken by this point with whatever in his American past was real enough to help support him. There is nothing now to prevent him from breaking with his past completely; he returns to Rome and meets and mates with Rosemary. The incident marks the end not merely of Rosemary's youth but of what remained of Dick's as well; for his success in preserving his dream world depended directly and primarily upon his extraordinary control over himself and consequent control over those whose light and dark depended upon his constant shining forth. From an artistic point of view, the next event in the narrative is inevitable; he gets drunk and into a fight with a cab driver, and the impression created is that a primordial violence, heretofore restrained, had at last thrown off the controls of its past and made itself manifest: "The passionate impatience of the week leaped up in Dick and clothed itself like a flash in violence, the honorable, the traditional resource of his land" (224). And the violence with which the police answer his attack is subtly shown to be as atavistic as the attack itself: "he was dragged along through the bloody haze, choking and sobbing, over vague irregular surfaces into some small place where he was dropped upon a stone floor" (226). Dick, the American dreamer, has fallen into what Fitzgerald considered the American dilemma: "Fifty years ago we Americans substituted . . . violence for dignity under suffering" (*The Crack-Up*, 208). And his reaction to this transformation is thoroughly American as well: he returns to the clinic and begins to drink.

Throughout the novel, alcoholism is the symbol of the flawed American. Abe North, failed composer, is constantly drunk, and Nicole's father seems to have as his one object in life the destruction of his liver. I would like to suggest that this is primarily because drunkenness is the closest one can come to dream; and all the characters who rely on alcohol have seen their own dreams die. As Fitzgerald puts it, "people display a curious respect for a man drunk, rather like the respect of simple races for the insane. . . . There is something awe-inspiring in one who has lost all inhibitions, who will do anything" (108). In any event, an incipient alcoholism marks Dick's decline; and Nicole, in rather a seesaw fashion, grows stronger as he weakens. This is perhaps the most subtle section of the narrative. The general view of the other characters is that Dick simply "can't take it"; and while there is an element of truth in this, the themes I have been dealing with would seem to indicate a deeper truth. Dick—and not a few critics have made this a point for complaint—is not destroyed by any single factor or event; and while this statement is true, it seems to me to miss the point; after all, a man does not grow old overnight. He is rather destroyed by the gradual but relentless deterioration of all things in his life, as a man grows old gradually and in many ways. I mean to say that he has arrived at a stage in his life where everything—his failure with Nicole, her insanity, Abe's death, Rosemary's maturation, his father's death, his disgrace in Rome, the insensitivity of an Englishman casually encountered in a hotel bar in Rome, a ride "along cheerless streets through a dank November night" (221), a young Spaniard's pitiable homosexuality (Dick, speaking to the boy, "talked automatically, having abandoned the case ten minutes before. . . . Dick tried to dissect . . . the courageous grace which this lost young man brought to a drab old story . . . into pieces small enough to store away—realizing that the totality of life may be different from its segments, and also that life during the forties seemed capable of being observed only in segments" (245); the thievery of their cook, the terrible secret he and Nicole have had to share so long, the sight of bodies tanning on the beach—all this, and more, undoes Dick in the end. The real world, changing, fragmented, violent, has reasserted that dreams cannot endure. The revelation is gradual, and so is the consequent decline; but it is natural; it is inevitable.

When the random drift of things finally becomes clear to Dick, he destroys the dream as surely as he created it; and, as he had created it for Nicole's sake, he destroys it for much the same motive. Nicole, herself slowly waking to reality, has some inkling of the reason for his actions: "That he no longer controlled her—did he know that? Had he willed it all?" (301). And Dick confirms her suspicion: " 'What do you get out of this?' " she demanded, and he answers: "Knowing you're stronger every day. Knowing your illness follows the law of diminishing returns" (267). And the reversal of their roles is at this point almost complete. Nicole, with the bulk of Dick's energy by this time transferred to her, completes it, finally, by marrying Tommy Barban.

Fitzgerald's incredible craftsmanship is as apparent at the end of the work as it was at the beginning. It is Tommy Barban that Nicole marries. I said at the start that all the major characters are children of two worlds, Dick and Nicole most of all and Nicole, because of her schizophrenia, far more than Dick; but Barban is the exception. All the other characters are expatriates; Barban is a European, first and only. All the other characters are fragmented in one way or another; Barban is of a single piece with himself. His actions and reactions are instinctual, almost animalistic, as opposed to the analytic and therefore fragmenting intellectuality of Dick. Dick "move[s] on through the rain, demoniac and frightened, the passions of many men inside him and nothing simple that he could see" (104). Nicole thinks, toward the novel's end, that Tommy "gave one an entire nut to crack, this man, instead of giving it in fragments to pick at for meat" (293). Tommy earlier speaks of himself in the same vein: "After all, I am a hero. . . . I have ferocious courage, usually, something like a lion, something like a drunken man" (270). I commented earlier on drunkenness as a symbolic state of integrity; and the same applies to "ferocious courage," though Fitzgerald does not explicitly say so. W. B. Yeats put it well in his "Under Ben Bulben": "You that Mitchel's prayer have heard / 'Send war in our time, O lord!' / Know that when all words are said / And a man is fighting mad, / Something drops from eyes long blind, / He completes his partial mind, / For an instant stands at ease, / Laughs aloud, his heart at peace." The description might well apply to Tommy; Dick finds him in Munich "at a table laughing his martial laugh: 'Um-buh—ha-ha! Um-buh —ha-ha!' As a rule, he drank little; courage was his game and his companions were always a little afraid of him" (196). Finally, his name. It is chosen with as much care as are the others. "Diver," for instance, is a precise description of what Dick eventually does. "Nicole Warren" neatly conveys Nicole's mixed heritage and, by implication, the double life of her dreaming mind. I have already spoken of the implications of "Baby." And "Barban": Fitzgerald probably knew its etymology; the word is so appropriate that it is hard to believe he did not, deriving as it does from *barbaros*, the Greek word for "foreigner." But even without this most basic meaning, expressive as it is of Tommy's undiluted Europeanism, the word makes its point with its connotations of "barbarian," which is what the savage and integral Tommy is. It is this quality that most attracts Nicole, and this too is natural, inevitable: that she should choose the one character in the book who does not inhabit two worlds at the time when she begins to be cured of her schizophrenia and meet the real world whole for the first time. His relationship with her at an end, Dick returns to America and, when last heard from, is practicing medicine in a place whose name is the novel's final irony: Geneva, New York.

Both Nicole, seduced in her childhood, and Dick, awakened slowly to reality, are the embodiments of lost youth, "all the lost youth in the world" (134). Children of two countries, they had no country at all but the one they themselves had created. When that dies, as it must, Dick has purchased at the price of all he loved an understanding far more profound than that of the young medical student who, wanting to be the greatest psychologist in the world, wanted to be loved, too, if he could fit it in: "On [another] occasion, back in Dohmler's clinic on the Zurichsee, realizing [his] power, he had made his choice, chosen Ophelia, chosen the sweet poison and drunk it. Wanting above all to be brave and kind, he had wanted, even more than that, to be loved. So it had been. So it would ever be" (302).

In light of the above, these lines from Keats's "Ode to a Nightingale" may seem more appropriate:

> Adieu! the fancy cannot cheat so well
> As she is fam'd to do, deceiving elf.
> Adieu! adieu! thy plaintive anthem fades

> Past the near meadows, over the still stream,
> Up the hill-side; and now 'tis buried deep
> In the next valley-glades:
> Was it a vision, or a waking dream?
> Fled is that music: —Do I wake or sleep?

Fitzgerald chose lines from the poem's fourth stanza to serve as both title and epigraph for his own work, but his familiarity with and love for the poem as a whole is made clear in a letter to his daughter Scottie. He speaks in that letter of the fact that "For awhile after you quit Keats all other poetry seems to be only whistling or humming," and refers specifically to "the *Nightingale*, which I can never read through without tears in my eyes" (*The Crack-Up*, 88). I think he must have had the poem as a whole in mind when he was writing *Tender Is the Night*, for the concerns of both the book and the poem are essentially the same. Keats too was speaking of the tension between dream and reality, the preferability of dream and its lamentable evanescence; and though Fitzgerald finally settled on lines from the fourth stanza, he might as easily have chosen the eighth, and final, verse. The fancy, after all, cannot cheat so well as she is famed to do; and in the last analysis, "Was it a vision, or a waking dream? / Fled is that music: —Do I wake or sleep?"

Focus on William Faulkner's "The Bear"
Moses and the Wilderness

RICHARD P. ADAMS

The first epigraph of Yeats's 1914 volume of poems is the statement "In dreams begins responsibility." Faulkner makes a similar statement in Go Down, Moses, and he adds that a man who dreams and who then refuses to accept responsibility has nightmares. In the fourth section of "The Bear" Ike McCaslin fancies himself as a Moses appointed by God "to set at least some of His lowly people free—" But the argument of that part of the story, in the context of the whole book, makes it clear that Ike, imprisoned in his own impotence, fails to set anyone free.

Ike's illusion of freedom, and of power, arises from his relation to the wilderness, which is said to be "his mistress and his wife." When he is initiated, at the age of eleven, by shooting his first buck, he believes that "he ceased to be a child and became a hunter and a man." He feels "consecrated and absolved . . . not from love and pity for all which lived and ran and then ceased to live in a second in the very midst of splendor and speed, but from weakness and regret."

In "Delta Autumn" this illusion is thoroughly dissipated, and Ike suffers keenly from both weakness and regret. He is nearer eighty than he will admit, and still one of the best hunters in the camp, but there is reason to doubt that he has ever been fully a man. After he has lectured the younger hunters on men's responsibility toward women and children, he is made to remember that he has failed his wife and failed to have any children of his own. He then fails Roth Edmonds' mistress and child, and the young woman devastatingly exposes his humiliation with her demand, "Old man . . . have you lived so long and forgotten so much that you dont remember anything you ever knew or felt or even heard about love?" The doubt is that Ike has ever known or felt

129

enough love to be really aware of the responsibilities that a loving man must undertake, and gladly does undertake, whether he lectures about them or not.

Ike sees one aspect of the American nightmare when he realizes that the wilderness, which according to the myth should have been the new Eden for man's regeneration, has been and is being ruthlessly exploited by a mechanistic enterprise, and that man, instead of being liberated from the corruption of the Old World, has been enslaved and further corrupted in the New. Ike maintains that God "made the earth first and peopled it with dumb creatures, and then He created man to be his overseer on the earth and to hold suzerainty over the earth and the animals on it in His name, not to hold for himself and his descendants inviolable title forever, generation after generation, to the oblongs and squares of the earth, but to hold the earth mutual and intact in the communal anonymity of brotherhood." According to Ike, the discovery of America, the dispossession of the Indians, the Civil War, and the history of his own family are phases of God's plan to regenerate the earth and fallen humanity. Yet, even before he knows the ugly details of his family history, Ike is forced to recognize that there is another side of the coin. On the plantation which his grandfather has created, the wilderness has been subdued: "Carothers McCaslin . . . tamed and ordered or believed he had tamed and ordered it for the reason that the human beings he held in bondage and in the power of life and death had removed the forest from it and in their sweat scratched the surface of it to a depth of perhaps fourteen inches in order to grow something out of it which had not been there before and which could be translated back into the money he who believed he had bought it had had to pay to get it and hold it and a reasonable profit too." Ike tries to argue that this apparent ownership is not real, and he tries to believe that the wilderness cannot be destroyed. But his cousin McCaslin Edmonds is able to bring more facts and better logic to bear in support of his contention that old Carothers "did own it. And not the first. Not alone and not the first since, as your Authority states, man was dispossessed of Eden." The wilderness is being destroyed.

Ike says that the loss of Eden, and all subsequent dispossessions, have been due to man's lust for possession, and that the discovery of America has revealed "a new world where a nation of people could be founded in humility and pity and sufferance and pride of one to another." He believes that he is helping to found such a nation by renouncing possession of the plantation. Or at least he hopes that his own innocence, which has been preserved by his naïve relation to the wilderness, will be protected against the curse which his ancestors have brought with them "from that old world's corrupt and worthless twilight as though in the sailfuls of the old world's tainted wind which drove the ships—" But, by preserving his innocence as an American Adam, Ike abdicates the role of Moses. He liberates no one from the Egyptian bondage of segregation, least of all himself. He does not even succeed as Adam; the wilderness, "that doomed wilderness whose edges were being constantly and punily gnawed at by men with plows and axes who feared it because it was wilderness," continues to recede. He does not try to emulate Christ, except in becoming a carpenter. He is Isaac, but with a difference, as he says: "an Isaac born into a later life than Abraham's and repudiating immolation: fatherless and therefore safe declining the altar because maybe this time the exasperated Hand might not supply the kid—." Like Esau, as he is forced to admit to himself when Lucas Beauchamp claims the legacy left by Carothers McCaslin to his Negro son, Ike has sold his birthright for what amounts to nothing.

Ike tries to convince himself, in "Delta Autumn," that he has achieved an ultimate peace in what still remains of the wilderness. His own life and the wilderness are "two spans running out together, not toward oblivion, nothingness, but into a dimension free of both time and space where once more the untreed land warped and wrung to mathematical squares of rank cotton for the frantic old-world people to turn into shells to shoot at one another, would find ample room for both—the names, the faces of the old men he had known and loved and for a little while outlived, moving again among the shades of tall unaxed trees and sightless brakes where the wild strong immortal game ran forever before the tireless belling immortal hounds, falling and rising phoenix-like to the soundless guns."

That is the dream at last, and it is essentially a dream of death. It has been, actually, Ike's dream all along; and all along it has had its nightmare aspects, which the events of

"Delta Autumn" quickly confirm. When Roth's mistress comes to the camp, Ike is overwhelmed with horror and outrage to learn that a new act of miscegenation has been committed. *"Maybe in a thousand or two thousand years in America*, he thought. *But not now! Not now!"* In this rejection Ike is really saying no to life, which can only be now, which loves and sins and suffers and creates always in the present moment. The contrast is imaged in the touch of his hand on that of the young woman: "he didn't grasp it, he merely touched it—the gnarled, bloodless, bone-light bone-dry old man's fingers touching for a second the smooth young flesh where the strong old blood ran after its long lost journey back to home." He is left lying, shaking, on his narrow cot, cold not so much because of the autumn rain as because of his inability to live in the life of his time. "This Delta, he thought: This Delta. *This land which man has deswamped and denuded and deriverved in two generations so that white men can own plantations and commute every night to Memphis and black men own plantations and ride in jim crow cars to Chicago to live in millionaires' mansions on Lakeshore Drive, where white men rent farms and live like niggers and niggers crop on shares and live like animals, where cotton is planted and grows man-tall in the very cracks of the sidewalks, and usury and mortgage and bankruptcy and measureless wealth, Chinese and African and Aryan and Jew, all breed and spawn together until no man has time to say which one is which nor cares. . . .* No wonder the ruined woods I used to know dont cry for retribution! he thought: The people who have destroyed it will accomplish its revenge." Ike's nightmare is his vision of the life he has repudiated. It is a vision of fertility by a sterile and impotent man, a vision of activity in the present by a man who clings to an Eden that was never really present, even in the most remote past.

In constructing this tale, Faulkner obviously had in mind a great deal of literature and legend about the American past, and particularly about the dream of innocence, the nightmare of exploitation, and the many responsibilities that have arisen in the development of the New World. Ike has much in common with Cooper's Natty Bumppo, who is also initiated by Indian tutors as a hunter in the wilderness and who laments the destruction of the wilderness by the ever-advancing settlers. Hawthorne's Young Goodman Brown offers a more complex and equivocal precedent. Brown tries to be initiated in the wilderness, not as a hunter but as a citizen of Salem Village. His failure, like that of Ike, appears to be associated with a fear of mature sexual feelings and actions, and of the responsibilities they bring. The difference is that Ike finds a vast amount of good in the forest, where Brown is able to see only danger and evil. Huckleberry Finn, on the river, in the early stages of the journey with Jim, is more nearly parallel with Ike. But Huck is considerably more effective in dealing with problems of civilized life, and his author avoids the theme of sexual maturity.

A larger parallel can be demonstrated between "The Bear" and *Moby Dick*, which was one of Faulkner's favorite books. The whale in the ocean symbolizes the pervading principle of life in the unconscious universe; the bear in the woods has a similar value. The destruction of Old Ben by Lion and Boon, by guns and a knife, is a more pessimistic outcome, from a romantic point of view, than the destruction of Ahab and the *Pequod*, but the conflict is essentially the same. Men use mechanical means to exploit the earth and its creatures, including other men; and the result is sterility. To such men the earth becomes a waste land. "The Bear" is again pessimistic in that it has no character closely resembling Ishmael either in his ability to disassociate himself from the hunt or in his ability to find a position in civilized society from which he can tell the story. Ike is not successful in doing either of those things. McCaslin Edmonds, who in some ways is more like Ishmael than Ike is, also resembles Ahab, being master of the plantation and its people in much the same way that Ahab is master of the *Pequod* and the crew. In *Moby Dick* the whale is almost a god, and Ishmael, seeking him in a proper spirit, finds a true and good relation to both nature and society. Ike seeks the bear in an even more exalted spirit, and he too receives a revelation and develops certain virtues, but he remains almost completely passive. His relation to the hunt is equivocal, and he never finds his proper relation to society.

There is perhaps a still more complex parallel between "The Bear" and Poe's *Narrative of Arthur Gordon Pym*, but it is not so clear, except in the minor instance of Dirk Peters' killing a huge bear with a knife. Less obviously, the two

stories share a preoccupation with labyrinthine imagery associated with themes of rebirth, and something of an obsession
with problems and conflicts arising between black people
and white people. These matters are more subtly handled by
Faulkner than by Poe, but the themes and many of the
images are closely related.

If there is an influence from Poe on "The Bear," it is
probably reinforced by Conrad's *Heart of Darkness*, which
expresses the theme of race relations much more clearly in
terms of exploitation of black men by white men than Poe's
narrative does. In this comparison, Ike comes out somewhere
between Kurtz, the missionary turned exploiter, and Marlow,
the spectator who learns in the heart of darkness something
that he must lie about in the false light of conventional
society.

These parallels suggest the breadth and depth of the context in which Faulkner placed "The Bear" and in which his
story needs to be understood. He recognized the conflict
between the spirit of life and mechanistic exploitation of the
earth, which had preoccupied Cooper, Thoreau, Melville,
Twain, the naturalists, and many more recent writers. In
"The Bear" he represented that theme in full force and
subtlety, in all the poignancy of the American dream of
innocence regained, and the betrayal of that dream by greed,
injustice, and lack of love.

But "The Bear" goes at least one step beyond that theme.
The central issue is the failure of Ike McCaslin to achieve
moral or sexual maturity. It is this issue which places "The
Bear" in the context of "Young Goodman Brown," many of
Henry James's stories, and a number of modern works, notably *The Great Gatsby*, in which the American dream of
innocence preserved beyond the years of actual childhood
turns inevitably into a nightmare of impotence and sterility.

The whole moral formula of "The Bear" is therefore
highly complex. It is, roughly, that an American boy who
dreams the American dream must outgrow innocence. If, like
Ike, he tries to withdraw from responsibility for what has
been done, because evil has been done, he will make himself
powerless to do any good. There can be no modern Eden,
because we bring our past with us into whatever new world
we find or try to create, and our past includes the Fall of
Man. The Adam of the new world of America is Carothers

McCaslin, ruthless, powerful, and apparently without any scruples at all. If we are to be redeemed from his sins, we must be as powerful and perhaps as relentless as he, and at least as determined to control exploitation as he is to profit by it. His grandson Ike will not save us, or free us, or relieve us of the burdens of error and of guilt that we have inherited. We must try to save ourselves and one another by being involved with one another in responsible actions that will acknowledge the errors and the guilt, and that will build something better in the present and for the future.

"History on the Side"
Henry Miller's American Dream

ALAN TRACHTENBERG

Henry Miller left America in 1930, a man close to forty, hoping to find himself as a writer in Paris. There was nothing in America to hold him; from almost every point of view he was a failure, a restless drifter between ill-assorted jobs. Money, fame, position eluded him, and the values which supported the devotion to these ends came to seem hollow and inhuman. He tried to devote himself instead to writing, to become an artist as an alternative to the unhappy bourgeois life he had tasted. His first efforts, never published, were conventionally literary. But the journey to Paris worked a transformation, and by 1940, he was internationally known, well on his way toward the fame and wealth he now enjoys. Since his return to America Miller's prestige as a spokesman for the pursuit of personal freedom has grown enormously. The legal decisions which have made his books available represent a turning point in popular culture; they opened the door to a kind of frankness in regard to sexual matters unimaginable twenty years ago. To his readers Miller offers a "wisdom of the heart" which celebrates obedience to desire and loyalty to self. The often hilarious comedy of his early work has given way to a more earnest style of exhortation to love, to enjoy, to be. Miller's criticism of American values, especially the idea of deferring pleasure for the sake of future success, has a wide currency, from hippie culture, to the New Left, to the more sophisticated of the mass media. His idea of America, then, and his exact relation to the values he criticizes, deserve closer attention and more precise judgment than they usually receive.

In his major work, the trilogy *Tropic of Cancer* (1934), *Black Spring* (1936), *Tropic of Capricorn* (1939), Miller had written of his contempt for modern America and of his attempts to purge its sickness from his system. In 1940, World War II forced him to leave Greece and return to the "home" of his earlier agonies. At first he imagined the visit would be short-lived: "unlike most prodigal sons, I was returning not with the intention of remaining in the bosom of the family but of wandering forth again, perhaps never to return." Somewhat like Henry James almost forty years earlier, Miller felt a special need to explore the American terrain, "to effect"—as he wrote in the preface to the ensuing account of his explorations, *The Air-Conditioned Nightmare* (1945)—"a reconciliation with my native land." He wanted "a last look at my country . . . to embrace it, to feel that the old wounds were really healed." The book is a chronicle of a rambling automobile trek through the Midwest, the South and Southwest, and California. "My one thought," Miller explains, "is to get out of New York, to experience something genuinely American. . . . I want to get out into the open." In a way the jaunty excursion recapitulates the westward routes of pioneers in the last century. But civilization does not recede; it pursues Miller, and although he settled a few years later at Big Sur, the California of the book (in "Soirée in Hollywood") epitomizes the nightmare of the title. "Walking along one of the Neon-lit streets. A shop window with Nylon stockings. Nothing in the window but a glass leg filled with water and a sea horse rising and falling like a feather sailing through heavy air. Thus we see how Surrealism penetrates to every nook and corner of the world." Los Angeles frightens him as a sign of the future.

In its structure as a series of separate sketches of places and persons, and more interestingly, in the way the expatriate experience in Europe tempers observation and judgment, the book bears comparison with James's *The American Scene* (1907). For both writers America had been a troubling experience; both record premonitions of disaster, of "blight," in the money-getting and the frenzy of change; both search for such cultivated amenities as parks, respect for the past and old age, and are irritated to miss them in America; both discover in themselves a surprising attraction to and sympathy for the South, where Miller, for example, finds "a different rhythm, a different attitude." "You can sit on a bench in a tiny Confederate Park or fling yourself on the banks of a levee or stand on a bluff overlooking an

Indian settlement, the air soft, still, fragrant, the world asleep seemingly, but the atmosphere is charged with magical names, epoch-making events, inventions, explorations, discoveries." As for the rest of America, except for the "boundless immensity," the sense of "the infinite *previous*" of the far West, as James put it, life is without grace, popular culture an "intellectual pablum," and "universal acquiescence" to profit-seeking and mechanization is the rule. "Nowhere," writes Miller, "have I encountered such a dull, monotonous fabric of life."

But these resemblances between the two books are superficial. In its mood of disengagement, of easy relations along the road, Miller's work is more in the spirit of Jack Kerouac's *On the Road* (1955) than of James's intense scrutiny of American society. James presents himself as a "restless analyst," whose responses, with their own special history and cultivation, play a major role in whatever he describes or relates. The drama of the book is held in the texture of each encounter, each struggle to attain a clear perspective. Miller is considerably less scrupulous about his responses. Often he is simply a passive reporter, a funnel for an indiscriminate flow of details. James worked up his material as a novelist; each detail is made to express larger patterns of feeling and idea. Details arouse associations which deepen the sense of personal history implicated in each encounter.

Miller's use of detail is more like that of a satirist than a novelist. "Everything is caricature here," he writes in a passage which demonstrates the flat, uninflected flow through which he achieves his characteristic effects:

I take a plane to see my father on his death-bed and up there in the clouds, in a raging storm, I overhear two men behind me discussing how to put over a big deal, the big deal involving paper boxes, no less. The stewardess, who has been trained to behave like a mother, a nurse, a mistress, a cook, a drudge, never to look untidy, never to lose her Marcel wave, never to show a sign of fatigue or disappointment or chagrin or loneliness, the stewardess puts her lily-white hand on the brow of one of the paper-box salesmen and in the voice of a ministering angel, says, "Do you feel tired this evening? Have you a headache? Would you like a little aspirin?" We are up in the clouds and she is going through this performance like a trained seal. When the plane lurches suddenly she falls and reveals a tempting pair of thighs. The two salesmen are now talking about buttons, where to get them cheaply, how to sell them dearly. . . . The girl falls down again—she's full of black and blue marks. But she comes up smiling, dispensing coffee and chewing gum, putting her lily-white hand on someone else's forehead, inquiring if he is a little low, a little tired perhaps. I ask her if she likes her job. For answer she says, "It's better than being a trained nurse."

Caricature is Miller's method in much of the book, and it is a method which accounts for the strength and energy of many passages. "Put the 58,956 crippled and killed this year back on the asphalt pavement and collect the insurance money. . . . Buy six Packards and an old Studebaker. . . . Dial 9675 and tune in on Bing Crosby or Dorothy Lamour. . . . Be sure to buy a slab of gum, it will sweeten the breath. Do anything, say anything that comes into your head, because it's all cuckoo and nobody will know the difference."

Like James, Dreiser, and Fitzgerald, Miller assails the American Dream of permanent wealth and happiness as the automatic reward of individual effort and excellence of character; he joins in the attack on the Dream as a hoax and a fraud. But where the others dramatize the process of belief and disenchantment, where they take account of losses and gains, analyze the social matrix of illusion and credit the desire for success as human facts worthy of compassion, Miller alternates between satire and direct assault. Less the novelist, he reveals himself as far more the moralist, which raises questions about the grounds of his moral fervor.

Since he settled in California in 1944, Miller's moral vision has become a major note in his writing. It is based on a vision of modern society as irredeemable, unchangeable, except through some form of apocalypse or shattering revelation. By "society" Miller means the way of life depicted in the caricature—the style of daily living, rather than the structure of social relations which gives that style a concrete historical setting. Any redemption must find its source outside social relations, that is, outside history. "To live beyond the pale, to work for the pleasure of working, to grow old gracefully while retaining one's faculties, one's enthusiasms, one's self-respect, one has to establish other values than those endorsed by the mob." The "mob" is Miller's indiscriminate label for American "society," the antithesis to which is the "artist." "It takes an artist to make this breach in the wall."

Miller devotes much of *The Air-Conditioned Nightmare* to portraits of artists, intensely private and often eccentric individuals who live apart from entangling relations and pursue their visions. Weeks Hall on his magnificent Southern plantation in Louisiana; Dr. Souchon, the surgeon painter; Albert Pike, the Arkansas dreamer; Dudley, the desperate, half-mad young writer of "Letter to Lafayette" (a portrait with premonitions of the Beats a decade later); Hilaire Hiler, the muralist; Edgard Varese, Alfred Stieglitz, John Marin—these are the main characters who people the book, and it is through them that Miller presents his hopes for redemption. His artists are a life-giving elite. "The world goes on because a few men in every generation believe in it utterly, accept it unquestioningly; they underwrite it with their lives. In the struggle which they have to make themselves understood they create music; taking the discordant elements of life, they weave a pattern of harmony and significance. If it weren't for this constant struggle on the part of a few creative types to expand the sense of reality in man the world *would* literally die out."

This redemptive function Miller assigns to his artists is a familiar idea with roots in nineteenth-century antibourgeois sentiment. Miller's artist is often the free bohemian, whose life on the fly is a deliberate slap at the order and routine of respectable life. But he is also something more. With all the eclecticism of Miller's thinking about art, and the important influence of European ideas, especially Surrealism, at bottom he is still attached to the idea of a particularly American function for his artist, or for personal liberation as such. To be sure, the idea does not often reach the surface of his writings, but there are enough clues to suggest that Miller hopes for a specifically *American* redemption—indeed, we discover, a return to traditional or mythic national values. How else are we to understand Miller's description of the present money-getting as a "bitter caricature" of the ideals of "our liberty-loving forefathers"? Or his mention of "a great social experiment . . . begun on this virgin continent"? "Here we are," he writes, "we the people of the United States: the greatest people on earth, so we think. We have land, water, sky and all that goes with it. We could become the great shining example of the world; we could radiate peace, joy, power, benevolence." These passages are all taken from *The Air-Conditioned Nightmare*. Later he writes in *Remember to Remember* (1947), "I would like to take this country of ours and recreate it—in the image of the hopes it once inspired"—a revealing comment and a revealing title.

The image of the "air-conditioned nightmare," in short, affirms implicitly a "dream" as a measure of judgment. In his earlier books America represented death and destruction of spirit. The American city suffocated him; he needed to escape. In *Black Spring*, the most successful of his books in evoking both the suffocation and the frenzy of release, he writes: "Swimming in the crowd, a digit with the rest. Tailored and re-tailored. The lights are twinkling—on and off, on and off. Sometimes it's a rubber tire, sometimes it's a piece of chewing gum. The tragedy of it is that nobody sees the look of desperation on my face. Thousands and thousands of us, and we're passing one another without a look of recognition." His feelings boil and verge on obscene violence: "Ought to grab a revolver and fire point-blank into the crowd." "*Smash it! Smash it!* That's all I can say." In large part his feelings arise from a sense of disillusion and defeat. "Once I thought there were marvelous things in store for me. Thought I could build a world in the air, a castle of pure white spit that would raise me above the tallest building, between the tangible and intangible, put me in a space like music where everything collapses and perishes but where I would be immune, great, godlike, holiest of the holies." Now that he has fallen and faced his reality (only a tailor's son), the dream of immunity seems an outrageous cheat. He feels lost and can find nothing in the American city to answer his needs for liberation. The solution is to destroy the old American world in himself, the world of fraud, materialism, gadgetry, the dream turned nightmare, and to die into a new, free being.

But does the new being Miller elicits from his desperate experiences really constitute a rejection of the American Dream? Or is it a translation of the values of the Dream from economic and social terms to psychological and aesthetic ones? To be "immune, great, godlike" remains the goal of his energetic assault upon the world, and in a sense he has freed himself to undertake that assault in a manner which has something in common with the fantasies of urban popular culture—fantasies of escape from conventions of family and work, of personal license in pursuit of pleasure, of "doing your own thing." If the heart of the American Dream is the image of the unfettered man "making" himself by accumulation of goods and credit, assuring a place for himself at the American banquet, Miller has detached the activity from any social end, and celebrated the act of accumulating experiences, especially sexual experiences, as an end in itself. Instead of a duty, life becomes an adventure—but still an adventure of self-aggrandizement and self-creation. By inverting the Horatio Alger style of the Dream, Miller discovers its essence, the desire to have what William James called a "moral holiday" as a permanent condition. "I have no money, no resources, no hopes. I am the happiest man alive."

The excitement in Miller's early work is its authentic emotion of release, its unhindered explorations of the suppressed fringes of middle-class fantasies, where respectability fades into criminality. It is a literature of pure disengagement and self-assertion, an act of aggression against all confining values. "For me the book is the man and my book is the man I am, the confused man, the negligent man, the reckless man, the lusty, obscene, boisterous, thoughtful, scrupulous, lying, diabolically truthful man that I am. I am thinking that in that age to come I shall not be overlooked. Then my history will become important and the scar which I leave upon the face of the world will have a significance. I can not forget that I am making history, a history on the side which, like a chancre, will eat away the other meaningless history. I regard myself not as a book, a record, a document, but as a history of our time—a history of *all* time." Exempt from convention, from personal ties, from history and politics, the self finds its realization in sheer flight. Its freedom is the escape from necessity.

The flight from history, from social ties and obligations, is the clearest mark of Miller's underlying commitment to an American Dream. The idea of a "history on the side" may have replaced the "castle of pure white spit," but the motive of immunity from time and society remains intact. Not wealth but voluntary poverty, not excellence of character but its exact reversal, become the means toward this immunity. Miller's career, as recounted in his books, can be taken as a quest for ultimate self-transcendence, for the perfect frontier where without any encumbrances the self can feed on the world without distraction.

Once we become aware of these familiar American aspirations in Miller, it is not surprising to discover other elements of the cultural pattern, especially the obsession with memory, the attempt to recapture an idealized past. While Miller rejects history as "meaningless," as a "cancer," his works are obsessed with the past. The personal past becomes a virtual alternative to world history. The pattern completes itself when we encounter passages which can only be described as "pastoral" in their yearning to recapture earlier moments of peace and harmony. To be sure, Miller's work will resist any reduction to a simple pattern. But in regard to his relationship to the American Dream, it is important to recognize what ideas and feelings he shares with his culture.

Miller is an urban pastoralist. "I was born in the street and raised in the street," he writes in "The Fourteenth Ward" (*Black Spring*). "The post-mechanical open street where the most beautiful and hallucinating iron vegetation, etc." His memory is of iron gardens. "Where others remember of their youth a beautiful garden, a fond mother, a sojourn at the seashore, I remember, with a vividness as if it were etched in acid, the grim soot-covered walls and chimneys of the tin factory opposite us." The imagery suggests an infusion of pastoral feelings into a technological landscape. "No one seemed to notice that the streets were ugly or dirty. If the sewer mains were opened you held your nose. If you blew your nose you found snot in your handkerchief and not your nose. There was more of inward peace and contentment. . . . The foam was on the lager and people stopped to chat with one another."

The significant pastoral elements are found not only in the imagery of the Fourteenth Ward, but in the spirit with which Miller recaptures the "inward peace and contentment." To be born in the street, he writes, "means to wander all your life, to be free. It means accident and incident, drama, movement. It means above all dream." The Fourteenth Ward is in effect a dream, a dream of lost youth.

In youth we were whole and the terror and pain of the world penetrated us through and through. There was no sharp separation between joy and sorrow: they were fused into one, as our waking life fuses with dream and sleep. We rose one being in the morning and at night we went down into an ocean, drowned out completely, clutching the stars and the fever of the day.

. . . .

And then comes a time when suddenly all seems to be reversed. We live in the mind, in ideas, in fragments. We no longer drink in the wild outer music of the streets—we *remember* only.

Now, after the "great change" of maturity, of loss of childhood, pastoral experience becomes the effort to recover the early moments in memory. "We walk the streets with a thousand legs and eyes, with furry antennae picking up the slightest clue and memory of the past. In the aimless to and fro we pause now and then, like long, sticky plants, and we swallow whole the live morsels of the past."

The natural imagery, the suggestion of yearnings for an organic relation with elements of the self, appear again in *Tropic of Capricorn*, where Miller describes the experiences which led to his escape from America. He roams the streets of New York with a sense of helplessness and strangeness. From Spengler he gains the conviction that the megalopolis is the last gasp of a dying civilization, and decides to purge himself, "to die as a city in order to become again a man." And the image which carries this wish is of a "natural park" —not forest or wilderness, but "park," an area made by design yet retaining its nourishing links with nature. "I shall be law and order as it exists in nature, as it is projected in dream. I shall be the wild park in the midst of the nightmare of perfection." Through such cultivated wildness Miller determines to awake from the American nightmare, the mad yearnings for money, possessions, status. Wildness will kill the nightmare, in order to release the dream.

By "wild park" Miller means in part the untamed, unformed impulses floating in his deep self. The "gob of spit in the face of Art," the "kick in the pants to God, Man, Destiny, Time, Love, Beauty . . . what you will," which introduces *Tropic of Cancer* are marks of this wildness, his rejection of conventional constraints upon expression. He will dishonor all pieties in order to honor the piety of free expression. In "Reflections on Writing" Miller connects his ideas of personal and aesthetic freedom. He is, he writes, "a man telling the story of his life," an inexhaustible process of surrender to the flow of existence. The writer needs to create an illusion of flux. Conscious technique, plotting, balancing of tone and weight, allowing patterns of words to judge and qualify each other, deliberating upon resonances—all this interferes with the pure act. Only by "the very accurate registering by my seismographic needle of the tumultuous, manifold, mysterious and incomprehensible experiences which I have lived through" is anything achieved. Of course this too is a convention, an artifice, chosen deliberately in order to render a sense of having freed oneself from all controls. "We are dealing," Miller writes, "with crystalline elements of the dispersed and shattered soul," and to convey the idea of dissolution faithfully, he will project his "self" as the *persona* of the "shattered and dispersed ego," manipulating "the flotsam and jetsam of the surrounding phenomenal world" through the *persona*.

The wild park, the park of the unconscious, which the writer both invokes as theme and employs as technique, is meant to dispel the nightmare of the city. Liberation is expressed in the act of writing, in its putative freedom from restraint. Flow takes the place of plot. The *persona* commands a range of styles—comic vernacular, high-flown prophecy and exhortation, surreal fantasy—but it does not possess any genuine plasticity. It is beyond change, beyond the ability to register experience as anything other than force, energy, impact. The effect is to make voyeurs of the readers, not participants. Self-absorption indulged on a scale of verbal magnificence is Miller's essential form of liberation. His "history on the side" is autobiography in which event and fantasy have identical status. To discriminate would be to falsify the flow, the tangled undergrowth of the "natural park" of the self.

The park image confirms Miller's attachment to Romanticism. But his version of the creed of the self is notably stripped of the social vision of Emerson, Thoreau, and Whitman. Miller's idea of freedom, of the natural and the wild, intensifies as his *persona* moves further away from society, from any relations in which history is an interference. Miller's Paris, for example, is portrayed as the perfect medium of his hero's release. It is the Paris of declassed expatriates, émigrés, failed artists. *Tropic of Cancer* conveys virtually no sense of Paris as a complex fact in the shared consciousness of people who live and work there. The book does not portray the way of life of Paris, but an idea of Paris where the raffish bohemian life seems the rule. In Miller's version, rootlessness *is* the way of life. The setting thus offers no social or historical resistance.

With all his apparent toughness and nonchalance, Miller's *persona*, unlike Céline's, has striking moments of softness. One such moment, in which the sentimental underpinning of Miller's romanticism becomes unmistakably clear, is the ending of *Tropic of Cancer*. Miller could hardly show himself as more American—one might even take a jaundiced view and say, as more of an American tourist—than in this conclusion, as he stands by the "green and glassy" Seine, thinks vaguely about New York, its crowded streets, the complications he left behind, and suddenly feels "a great peace" come over him. "Here," he writes, "where the river gently winds through the girdle of hills, lies a soil so saturated with the past that however far the mind roams one can never detach it from its human background." He feels "this river flowing through me,—its past, its ancient soil, the changing climate. The hills gently girdle it about: its course is fixed."

The tone of the passage, with its hints of portentous feeling, implies something of a discovery for the hero, a new understanding. But if we try to penetrate to the exact meaning of this feeling, if we ask what he means by "past," by "human background," we are left with a suspicion that the described moment is more a function of the inveterate Americanism of the hero than of the actual scene. His own history by now fragmented, oppressive, he is overcome with awe and reverence for the European "past"—not a specific past, but simply "the past."

In *The Colossus of Marousi* (1941) the configuration becomes even clearer. Miller left France in 1939, choosing this critical moment in European history for a pilgrimage to the sources of Western civilization. "I felt completely detached from Europe," he wrote, which, as George Orwell pointed out, meant detachment from war, fascism, and resistance. The war was a fulfillment of sorts, the necessary and expected prelude to a new apocalypse. If the *Tropics* document the disease, *Colossus* projects a hearty sense of health and new life, suffused in the bright Aegean light. It is the least troubled, the most accepting and affirmative of Miller's books.

Once again the affirmation is decidedly American, a special mixture of verve and banality. What moves Miller more than anything else in Greece is the antiquity of the land. "Things long forgotten came back with frightening clarity." With "real" history raging about him in Europe, Miller discovers for himself a more meaningful history while exploring classical ruins.

I am a native of New York, the grandest and the emptiest city in the world; I am standing now at Mycenae, trying to understand what happened here over a period of centuries. I feel like a cockroach crawling about amidst dismantled splendors. It is hard to believe that somewhere back in the leaves and branches of the great genealogical tree of my life my progenitors knew this spot, asked the same questions, fell back senseless into the void, were swallowed up and left no trace of thought save these ruins, the scattered relics in museums, a sword, an axle, a helmet, a death mask of beaten gold, a bee-hive tomb, an heraldic lion carved in stone, an exquisite drinking vase. I stand at the summit of the walled citadel and in the early morning I feel the approach of the cold breath from the shaggy gray mountain towering above us. Below, from the great Argive plain the mist is rising. It might be Pueblo, Colorado, so dislocated is it from time and boundary. Down there, in that steaming plain where the automotrice crawls like a caterpillar, is it not possible there once stood wigwams? Can I be sure there never were any Indians there?

Later, lounging on the grass near Agamemnon's tomb, he watches some people in the distance measuring a plot of land, and has a flashing insight. "What is vital here is land, just land. I roll it over on my tongue—land, land, land. Why yes, *land,* that's it—I had almost forgotten it meant such a simple, eternal thing."

Land, wigwams, the Great Plains—it is as if Miller had to get to Europe to find the American frontier. Like Mark Twain's raftsman, the Greeks are "like men ought to be—that is to say, open, frank, natural, spontaneous, warmhearted. These were the types of men I had expected to meet in my own land when I was growing up to manhood. I never found them." It becomes clear that Greece helps him discover an American tradition—a tradition, it should be noted, which has its life mainly in literary convention—in the images of frontiersmen as heroes, of endless space in "nature" as the escape route from "society," of pastoral childhood.

Wishing to make "history on the side," Miller slips into familiar American ways of evading history altogether.

In *Tropic of Cancer* he writes that he ceased to be an American when he realized that "everything American will disappear one day." This recognition, he felt, made it impossible for him to remain inside "the warm, comfortable bloodstream where, buffaloes all, we once grazed in peace." He at least is no buffalo—"not even a spiritual buffalo." He prefers "an older stream of consciousness, a race antecedent to the buffaloes, a race that will survive the buffalo." If the buffalo represents the destruction of the West, the failure of Americans to possess the land with the intimacy of Greeks and Indians, as well as the mindless herd instinct of modern Americans, then Miller's antecedent race sounds very much like the lost possibilities for purity and self-sufficiency and timelessness lamented with such monotony in American culture. As the historical possibility diminishes, the dream persists, becomes even more detached, becomes the American Dream. When Miller settled at Big Sur, one of the points farthest west on the continent, and later Los Angeles, to enjoy the fruits of a successful self-made career, he may have discovered that "reconciliation" with his native land was not such a difficult matter after all. In most essential matters he had never left home.

Focus on Thomas Wolfe's
You Can't Go Home Again
Agrarian Dream and Industrial Nightmare

C. HUGH HOLMAN

Thomas Wolfe's *You Can't Go Home Again* is a fictional record of the conflict of the American Dream with a capitalistic society and the descent of that Dream into nightmare. Early in the book, its protagonist, George Webber, says that "we are all savage, foolish, violent, and mistaken; that, full of our fear and confusion, we walk in ignorance upon the living and beautiful earth, breathing young, vital air and bathing in the light of morning, seeing it not because of the murder in our hearts." Wolfe has expressed here in miniature a controlling theme and a shaping opposition that govern the book. For almost as clearly as Steinbeck did, he contrasts the Dream and promise represented by the natural world with the nightmare that man makes for himself within it. The Dream is basically simple and rural; its betrayal is the achievement of complex urban and industrial forces.

At the core of all Thomas Wolfe's work stands a single personality—that of Wolfe himself, whether represented as Eugene Gant in the early works or George Webber in the late ones. This personality forms a record of how the world has impinged upon the author, of how he has come to know it and himself. Wolfe could speak of himself as this personality with the unembarrassed assurance that Whitman had that he was speaking of the generic American. But this concern underwent slow but important changes. In *Look Homeward, Angel*, the self-discovery of the artist was the focus, but in *You Can't Go Home Again* Wolfe had come to see that such a focus was wrong. He has George Webber say of his first novel—which was transparently also Wolfe's— "the young genius business gets in . . . the wounded faun business . . . and it twists the vision. The vision may be shrewd, subtle, piercing, within a thousand special frames accurate and Joycean—but within the larger one, false, mannered, and untrue." In the later book the focus has shifted to the outer world, and he attempts to make the central personality function in a manner he described once in a letter: "The protagonist becomes significant not as the tragic victim of circumstances, the romantic hero in conflict and revolt against his environment, but as a kind of polar instrument round which the events of life are grouped, by means of which they are touched, explained, and apprehended, by means of which they are seen and ordered."

You Can't Go Home Again cannot accurately be called a novel. It lacks a formal plot; it is a collection of incidents that happened to or are observed by the protagonist but in which that protagonist frequently plays only a minor part; it was left in a fragmentary form at Wolfe's death and was assembled by his new editor, Edward Aswell, working from an outline and having to choose among versions, write links, change names, and give the appearance of a unified work of fiction to a mass of manuscript of an incomplete novel. Yet the work has special merits that none of Wolfe's other works possess, and although it is an anthology of parts, the parts themselves are often magnificently realized. It stands at the opposite end of the spectrum from Wolfe's first novel, *Look Homeward, Angel*. That book was the lyric cry of a self-centered and introspective boy, a record of the adventures of his spirit in "the meadows of sensation." *You Can't Go Home Again* is the social testament of a maturing—if not fully mature—man.

The essential vision of this personality is that of the provincial, middle-class American. Wolfe had grown up in a small southern mountain town, close to the towering hills, responding intensely to the natural forms of beauty around him. He had absorbed from the social-political Populism which was still strong in North Carolina during his childhood and youth a democratic liberalism, and he brought to bear upon his people a criticism very much like that of Sinclair Lewis, which was both mocking and loving. This attitude is shown in the satire of *Look Homeward, Angel*, where the young artist is simply rejecting the ugliness and materialism of the environment in which he lives and dreaming of shining cities, distant people, and inevitable triumphs.

The structure of the novel and the maturing of the protagonist are consonant; between the outer view of society and the inner seeking of the soul there is a shared and constant dream, the aspiring dream of every middle-class provincial American boy who has turned his back upon home to seek triumphs in the citadels of culture and power. *Look Homeward, Angel* is structurally the most satisfying of Wolfe's novels not only because the *Bildungsroman* has a built-in pattern and wholeness but also because the American boy's dream is at its center and that dream is not yet being torn by fundamental doubts; its realization is not only possible, it seems almost within the outstretched, grasping fingers.

But Gant-Webber moves from the hill-encircled world of his childhood into a series of persistent disillusionments. The enfabled rock of Manhattan he greets with a joyous cry only to discover that it harbors cruelty, falseness, and betrayal. He seeks friendship with a limber-wristed aesthete, Francis Starwick, and only when the fact is driven home with a force so great it can no longer be resisted does he acknowledge that Starwick is a homosexual. He visits Europe seven times—indeed he spends over a fourth of his last twelve years abroad —but everywhere the promised order is denied him. He goes to Hitler's Germany and finds himself the darling of a great capital city, and it takes him a while to recognize beneath the orderliness, the beauty, the symmetry, the green faerie world of the Tiergarten and the efficiency of the city trams that there is the calamity of man's injustice and hatred, the bitter desire to emasculate and to destroy, and so he must bid farewell to "the other part of his heart's home." But it is America caught in the bitter struggle of the Depression that put his dream to its most severe test and converted it into a nightmare of poverty and suffering.

Like Whitman, whom he resembles more than any other American writer, Wolfe celebrates the beauty and the glory of his native land, the wonder and the grandeur of its towering mountains and its rolling plains. Like Whitman he makes music from the names of places and people, of streams and towns. Like Whitman he sees himself as a representative American, declaring "from the unique and single substance of this land and life of ours must we draw the power and energy of our own life . . . the substance of our art. For here . . . in hard and honest ways . . . must we who have no more than we have, who know no more than what we know, who are no more than what we are, find our America." But like the Whitman of *Democratic Vistas*, Wolfe, too, sees the cancerous growth that gnaws away at the body politic. Wherever he turns he finds hungry men, mistreated men, men weighed down by injustice. How to reconcile the two—the glorious promise of America and the injustice, cruelty, and oppression of America—became for him both a personal problem and an artistic problem.

You Can't Go Home Again is the record of the failure of that ultimate effort at reconciliation. When Wolfe moves from the focus on the individual to a focus on society, he needs something other than the coexistence of these attitudes. They need either to be reconciled or one needs to triumph over the other. Or if they are to be held in balance, they must be treated with equal force and dramatic conviction. It is not enough to have one dramatized and the other rhetorically expressed.

Wolfe's view of the American nightmare, pretty clearly grounded in his attitude toward the economic system, is the middle-class Agrarian view opposed to an industrial capitalism. George Webber says at one place in *You Can't Go Home Again*:

Sometimes it seems to me . . . that America went off the track somewhere—back around the time of the Civil War, or pretty soon afterwards. Instead of going ahead and developing along the line in which the country started out, it got shunted off in another direction—and now we look around and see we've gone places we didn't mean to go. Suddenly we realize that America has turned into something ugly—and vicious—and corroded at the heart of its power with easy wealth and graft and special privilege.

Although Wolfe did not care for the Nashville Agrarians and they were harsh critics of his books, this view of American society is one they would have endorsed. *You Can't Go Home Again* is a record of that wrong track, told in the form of almost disjointed episodes of disillusionment and failure.

It tells of George Webber's life in Brooklyn; of the real-estate boom and collapse in his hometown, Libya Hill; in a complex and carefully wrought short novel, of the world of the very rich in contrast to that of the laboring classes that serve it; of the disillusionment that follows Webber's success as a novelist; of his journey to England and of a meeting with a famous novelist Lloyd McHarg—Sinclair Lewis under very thin disguise—who shows him the emptiness of fame; in a tightly constructed short novel, of his love for Germany and his sense of its evil; and finally—in a letter to his editor—a statement of what he feels his credo to be. It is loaded with dramatic pictures of the nightmare world which Wolfe believes America in the Depression to be. And, as he usually does, Wolfe makes his statements through representative characters, through typical actions, through descriptive passages that become vignettes that express his meaning, and through direct rhetorical assertion. To a startling degree the dream in *You Can't Go Home Again* is expressed through rhetorical assertion, and the nightmare through dramatic presentation. The nightmare makes the more powerful impact, although the dream may be more quotable.

Wolfe seems to see a common—and simplistic—basis for the darkness that engulfs the American Dream, and an examination of a few of the dramatic modes in the novel points to it.

Four characters, each indicative of the failure of the promise, show a distorted way of life. Judge Rumford Bland, the syphilitic blind man, who embodies much of the best tradition of the South of his boyhood and yet is totally corrupt, appears only briefly in the novel, when Webber meets him on the train to Libya Hill. His background has to be dragged in as remembrance, yet he is certainly a powerful representative of his culture. He makes his living through the most cruel and usurious lending to Negroes. He has an office as an attorney in a disreputable building within thirty yards of the city hall, and he is a creature of the night. Though an able man, there was, Wolfe wrote, "something genuinely old and corrupt at the sources of his life and spirit." But he added, "At the very moment that [people] met him, and felt the force of death and evil working in him, they also felt—oh, call it the phantom, the radiance, the lost soul, of an enormous virtue. And with the recognition of that quality came the sudden stab of overwhelming regret."

Another figure of this nightmare evil is Adolf Hitler, "the dark messiah." Webber—and Wolfe—had felt at first in

Germany that "it was no foreign land to him," and there he had tasted the intoxication of great acclaim. It was not easy for him finally to see in *Der Führer*, who had brought such great material order to Germany, the "shipwreck of a great spirit." He wrote of Webber's experience: "The poisonous emanations of suppression, persecution, and fear permeated the air like miasmic and pestilential vapors, tainting, sickening, and blighting the lives of everyone he met. It was a plague of the spirit—invisible, but as unmistakable as death."

Another is Mr. Merrit, the representative of the Federal Weight, Scales, and Computing Company, who was all Rotarian smiles and good fellowship but who, when overheard tongue-lashing Webber's friend, Randy Shepperton, gave George the feeling that he was "in some awful nightmare when he visions someone he knows doing some perverse and abominable act." When later Randy tries to explain that Merrit has to do these things because "He—he's with the Company," Webber remembers a picture he had seen

portraying a long line of men stretching from the Great Pyramid to the very portals of great Pharaoh's house, and great Pharaoh stood with a thonged whip in his hand and applied it unmercifully to the bare back and shoulders of the man in front of him, who was great Pharaoh's chief overseer, and in the hand of the overseer was a whip of many tails which he unstintedly applied to the quivering back of the wretch before him, who was the chief overseer's chief lieutenant, and in the lieutenant's hand a whip of rawhide which he laid vigorously on the quailing body of his head sergeant, and in the sergeant's hand a wicked flail with which he belabored a whole company of groaning corporals, and in the hands of every corporal a knotted lash with which to whack a whole regiment of slaves.

Still another is Mr. Frederick Jack, Wall Street financier, living in great luxury and playing with stocks and dollars in a vast and amusing gamble. Speaking of these speculators, Wolfe said, "they bought, sold, and traded in an atmosphere fraught with frantic madness. . . . it was one of the qualities of this time that men should see and feel the madness all around them and never mention it—never admit it even to themselves." At the other end of this mad gamble of speculation is a figure absurd enough to be in a contemporary black comedy, Libya Hill's town sot, old Tim Wagner—"diseased and broken . . . his wits were always addled now with alcohol," but the word had gotten around among real-estate speculators that he had a mysterious power of financial intuition, so the men of the town "used him as men once used divining rods," and he rode in a magnificent car with a liveried chauffeur, and moved with "princely indolence."

All these men are exploiters, but Wolfe has too a large gallery of the exploited. They include Randy Shepperton, a kind and generous man; the anonymous citizens of Libya Hill who are swept under in the collapse; the servants at Jack's, upon whom the success of his personal life depends; Mr. C. Green, who commits suicide by leaping from the Admiral Drake Hotel and only in that violent moment elicits attention to the grey cipher which his life has been; Lloyd McHarg, Nobel Prize novelist for whom world fame is not enough and who constantly tastes bitter ashes on his tongue.

The two finest sections of the book were originally written as short novels—"The World That Jack Built" and "I Have a Thing to Tell You." "The World That Jack Built"—the title is a pun—is a 175-page account of a great party given by Mr. and Mrs. Frederick Jack just a week before the stock market collapse which precipitated the Depression. This novella is Wolfe's best and most objective piece of sustained narrative. It is rich in social satire, in portraits of people from all classes, and in interlinked symbols that carry a heavy freight of meaning. The party ends in a fire which empties the guests and the apartment house residents into a courtyard, where for a moment they feel a sense of community, and which also takes the lives of two gentle and kindly elevator operators, one old and one young, but both of whom believe in the economic system. Wolfe was here attempting to imprison a view of a society in a single complex social act, modeling his effort on Proust's *Sodom and Gomorrah*. At the conclusion he comes to a direct judgment of the people of this world. He sees them as gifted and personally honorable, but he condemns "their complaisance about themselves and about their life, their loss of faith in anything better." Webber is at the apex, he realizes, of one aspect of his dream —the point of success and his acceptance by the world's great—yet finds himself dismayed rather than delighted: "now to have the selfless grandeur turn to dust, and to see great night itself a reptile coiled and waiting at the heart of life! . . . To find man's faith betrayed and his betrayers throned in honor, themselves the idols of his bartered faith!"

Certainly these are not deep or profound thoughts. They express a common kind of middle-class democracy. Pamela Hansford Johnson is probably too harsh when she says, "His is a young man's socialism, based on the generous rage, the infuriated baffled pity; like the majority of young, middle-class intellectuals, he looked for 'the people' in the doss-house and upon the benches of the midnight parks," for Wolfe simply did not see the world in abstract terms. He was able to relish the fame that Germany heaped upon him without seeing the true nature of the Third Reich—although he certainly was uncomfortable about it almost from the beginning. But when that nature was virtually made flesh before him in the person of the frightened little Jew in his railway compartment attempting to flee the country and being hauled back ruthlessly in quivering terror, he could understand, and, understanding, he could not fail to speak what he saw, in "I Have a Thing to Tell You," one of the most effective attacks on Nazi Germany.

To a surprising extent, the provincial's middle-class dream of democracy remained with him, however much it was betrayed by the character of the Depression world in which he lived. Despite the old Tim Wagners and the Piggy Logans, despite the seeming pessimism of the fate of the faceless C. Greens, despite the corruption of the Rumford Blands, Wolfe's America was not a nightmare of the absurd nor did it have the terror of a Kafkaesque meaningless malignity. For him it had causes—relatively simple causes and ones based in the economic system.

In a vignette that defines his position well he wrote of Libya Hill, effectively embodying in a series of images what seems to have been a fundamental position for him:

the air brooded with a lazy, drowsy warmth. There was the last evening cry of robins, and the thrumming bullet noises in undergrowth and leaf, and broken sounds from far away—a voice in the wind, a boy's shout, the barking of a dog, the tinkle of a cow bell. There was the fragrance of intoxicating odors—the resinous smell of pine, and the smells of grass and warm sweet clover. All this was just as it had always been. But the town of his childhood, with its quiet streets and old houses which had been almost obscured below the leafy spread of trees, was changed past recognition, scarred now with hard patches of bright concrete and raw clumps of new construction. It looked like a battlefield, cratered and shell-torn with savage explosions of brick, cement, and harsh new stucco. And in the interspaces only the embowered remnants of the old and pleasant town remained —timid, retreating, overwhelmed—to remind one of the liquid leather shuffle in the quiet streets at noon when the men came home to lunch, and of laughter and low voices in the leafy rustle of the night. For this was lost!

But for Wolfe it was not permanently lost, for he could still declare: "So, then, to every man his chance—to every man, regardless of his birth, his shining, golden opportunity—to every man the right to live, to work, to be himself, and to become whatever thing his manhood and his vision can combine to make him—this, seeker, is the promise of America."

The nightmare merely interrupts the Dream for him. He declares:

I think the life we have fashioned in America, and which has fashioned us—the forms we made, the cells that grew, the honeycomb that was created—was self-destructive in its nature, and must be destroyed. I think these forms are dying, and must die, just as I know that America and the people in it are deathless, undiscovered, and immortal, and must live. . . . I speak for most men living when I say that our America is Here, is Now, and beckons on before us, and that this glorious assurance is not only our living hope, but our dream to be accomplished.

These positive assertions come in a book whose essential theme is not the triumph but the betrayal of the Dream, and they come as direct assertions, however powerfully effective their rhetoric may be, rather than by more convincing dramatic actions. This difference shows how much knowing and feeling about the nature of his native land were at variance in Wolfe, and how very much that variance tears at the structural integrity of *You Can't Go Home Again*.

Focus on Eugene O'Neill's
The Iceman Cometh
The Iceman Hath Come

FREDERIC I. CARPENTER

As everyone has agreed, the real subject of Eugene O'Neill's *The Iceman Cometh* is "pipe dreams." O'Neill himself answered an early question about the play's significance: "All I can say is that it is a play about pipe dreams." The hostile Mary McCarthy complained that "the word *pipe-dream* recurs about two hundred times during the play." Almost every critic, friendly or hostile, has described *The Iceman* in terms of its pipe dreams, and many have quoted the introductory speech of Larry Slade: "To hell with the truth! As the history of the world proves, the truth has no bearing on anything. It's irrelevant and immaterial, as the lawyers say. The lie of a pipe dream is what gives life to the whole misbegotten mad lot of us, drunk or sober." In my book *Eugene O'Neill* (Twayne, 1964), I have traced the theme of dream and delusion through all the author's plays; in "O'Neill, the Orient, and American Transcendentalism" (*Transcendentalism and Its Legacy*, edited by Myron Simon, University of Michigan Press, 1966), I have pointed out the peculiarly Oriental and quietistic nature of O'Neill's dreams: they contrasted sharply with the earlier pragmatic dreams of Emerson, Thoreau, and the American transcendentalists. It should be easy to show that the pipe dreams in *The Iceman* were almost un-American in their Oriental quietism.

But *The Iceman*, I have found, will not stand still. From its first production, the play has continued to grow in significance and to increase in stature. In 1956, its revival proved much more successful than its first performance in 1946, and in the two decades since, dozens of articles and essays on it have been published. In 1968 John Henry Raleigh edited a

158

volume of *Twentieth Century Interpretations of "The Ice-man Cometh,"* some of which illuminated new and unsuspected aspects of the play. Moreover, in 1968 some strange things happened to force a revision of earlier interpretations. I have decided to summarize my earlier ideas briefly, then describe what had forced a modification of them, and end with a new interpretation of *The Iceman.* The very self-consciousness of this technique might suggest the many-layered depth of the play's significance and define more sharply some aspects of the American Dream itself.

From the beginning, all of O'Neill's plays have celebrated the dream of an ideal beauty "beyond the horizon." The hero of his first full-length play spoke of "the beauty of the far off and the unknown, the mystery and spell of the East which lures me in the books I've read, the need of the freedom of the great wide spaces" (*Beyond the Horizon,* 1920). And all of O'Neill's later plays describe this dream so as to emphasize its impossibility. Like the mythical fountain of youth which gave subject and title to *The Fountain* (1923), this dream has remained, by definition, antirealistic. Thus, O'Neill's heroes, "wandering on and on" in search of some impossible fountain, have all had their dreams turn to nightmares. Now *The Iceman* seems again to underline this nightmare unreality by means of its constant repetition of the phrase "pipe dreams." The delusions of a humanity degraded by some opiumlike addiction, these dreams seemed both unreal and impossible. And *Long Day's Journey into Night* (1956), of course, specifically dramatized the actual opium addiction of Mary Tyrone.

Soon after the first production of *The Iceman,* O'Neill personally contrasted these pipe dreams with what he conceived to be "the American dream." In an interview with Hamilton Basso (the *New Yorker,* 1948), O'Neill exclaimed: "We talk about the American dream, and want to tell the world about the American dream, but what is that dream, in most cases, but the dream of material things?" In his interpretation, that is, "the American dream" imagined only practical success in the material world. What James Truslow Adams had defined as "the dream of a better, richer and happier life for all our citizens of every rank," O'Neill now limited to a "richer" life. And he pointed out that riches have never brought happiness: "We are the greatest example of 'For what shall it profit a man, if he shall gain the whole world and lose his own soul?' "

At this time O'Neill had already spent five years writing a great "cycle" of plays whose title was to be *A Tale of Possessors Self-Dispossessed*. This was to describe the success story of an Irish-American family through history. But of this cycle, only *A Touch of the Poet* (1957) and *More Stately Mansions* (produced in 1967) have survived, and these two plays centered upon the Thoreau-like character of an American dreamer who abandoned poetry (*A Touch of the Poet*) to marry an Irish girl and to build *More Stately Mansions* in nineteenth-century America. Unlike the historic Thoreau, O'Neill's American dreamer desired only a "richer" life for his Irish bride, and disillusionment resulted. But the cycle failed, and O'Neill turned to his final autobiographical plays. *The Iceman Cometh* focused exclusively on pipe dreams, while *Long Day's Journey into Night* used the actual success story of his father to illustrate the tragic effect of "the American dream of material things" on the younger generations of twentieth-century America.

To an American scholar brought up on Emerson, Thoreau, and Whitman, this denial of the pragmatic values of the American Dream seemed false. Certainly Thoreau had never dreamed of material things; and if Emerson and Whitman had proclaimed their "hope" of a future America, it had not been the hope of material riches. This American dream was antihistorical; worse—it was antirealistic. The pipe dreams of his characters seemed to prevent them from dramatic action on the stage: O'Neill's denial of all pragmatic values led to a kind of dramatic paralysis. *The Iceman* seemed to exist only in a trancelike world of drink and dream.

The structure of the play contributes to this impression of trancelike inaction and unreality. Most of the drama consists of the conversation of the minor characters who inhabit Harry Hope's saloon: the "No Chance Saloon, Bedrock Bar." Although this conversation is both drunken and long-winded, it achieves dramatic conviction because of O'Neill's firsthand knowledge of his drunken bums and his fine ear for their dialogue. But the structural framework of the play is determined by its one major character, Hickey, who enters regularly about the middle of each act to wheedle and to dominate these minor characters, and—finally—to confess himself to them. This major character is not based on O'Neill's actual experience and observation, but is created by his imagination to act out a kind of modern myth. Therefore Hickey often seems somewhat artificial and even unbelievable.

The story of this traveling salesman who killed his wife because she loved him too much is, obviously, not very probable. Understandably, O'Neill devoted his first three acts to dramatizing the resistance of all the minor characters to Hickey, and to emphasizing their natural disbelief in his action. At the end of each act Hickey suggests more of his story. And O'Neill regularly counterpoints this unlikely tale with details from the life of Don Parritt, who had earlier betrayed his own mother to the police because she was an anarchist and because she practiced free love. Then at the climax of the last act, Hickey confesses his inner hatred of his loving wife: "Well, you know what you can do with your pipe dream now, you damned bitch!" And soon Parritt echoes his words: "You know what you can do with your freedom pipe dream now, don't you, you damned old bitch!" Not only does the violence of the language seem melodramatic, but the parrot-like repetition emphasizes the artificiality of the myth.

If the logic of these criticisms seems unanswerable, several events have occurred which, for me, dictate new answers—not in terms of logic, but of history.

Around the time when I first wrote about *The Iceman*, I visited countries in Asia and Africa and heard other Americans exclaim at the "unbelievable" poverty. Yet the poverty we saw was mild compared to what we did not see; and compared to anything in Asia or Africa, the worst American poverty (which our great society was then legislating against) seemed almost affluent. That is to say, "the American dream of a better and richer life for all our citizens of every rank"—if measured by any relative standards of material well-being—has already been realized in America.

Of course our American affluence did not make us love in the non-Western world. Nevertheless, whenever we talked with natives, they asked repeatedly about the late President Kennedy. Over these troubled lands the memory of the young American President who had recently been murdered hung like a benediction. To them he had seemed the very symbol of youth and hope in the new world. In Africa, especially, his policy inaugurating aid to the emerging nations was remembered, while his Peace Corps had brought personal friendship and hope. Since his assassination these people seemed bemused: had the American Dream, symbolized for the emerging nations by the young President, been murdered too?

Back in America the answer seemed to come, punctuated by the repeated shots of assassins. First Martin Luther King was murdered, then a second Kennedy. And as the shock of horror at the news slowly subsided, I thought I could hear the assassins shouting: "You know what you can do with your pipe dream now, you Catholic son of a bitch!" Or again: "You know what you can do with your freedom pipe dream now, don't you, you black bastard!" O'Neill had asserted more than forty years ago that "in times of great stress, life copies melodrama." Now the improbable myth of his allegorical Iceman seemed to have been realized by history. Life had imitated his melodrama.

Indeed, the more I pondered it, the more real the myth became. For Hickey, as O'Neill had specified, had been a hardware salesman—a salesman of material things. And his hardware had included guns. He had explained: "I'd given her a gun for protection while I was away and it was in the bureau drawer. She'd never feel any pain, never wake up from her dream. So I . . . So I killed her." Symbolically, the hardware salesman had killed the dream of love; and Parritt, his echo, had killed the "freedom dream."

If "the American dream of material things" has already been realized, and if the American Dream of freedom has been killed, what hope remains? This question numbs the mind. Then I attended the graduation ceremony of a granddaughter from grade school. As we sang "The Star Spangled Banner," the adult voices faltered or fell silent, while the children's voices climbed confidently to the higher octaves. After the usual orations, the school choir then rendered the theme song from *The Man of La Mancha*. And again the young voices soared easily to the higher octaves: "To dream the impossible dream, / To fight the unbeatable foe . . . / To right the unrightable wrong . . . / To reach the un-reach-a-ble star. . . ." Sourced in the perpetual fountain of youth and celebrated by the choir of children's voices, the impossible dream remained. But the Iceman remained also. Both in history and in the imagination, he had come, and come again.

Just what does *The Iceman Cometh* mean? The title means, I think, that the dramatic action of the play is not meant to be actual, but psychological or prophetic. The meaningful action of O'Neill's tragedy does not take place on the stage, but offstage, both physically and in the reader's mind. And the final "moment of truth" or tragic "recognition" occurs not even in the conscious mind, but in the unconscious. Just after Hickey has confessed: "I'd always wanted to say: 'Well, you know what you can do with your pipe dream now, you damned bitch!' (*He stops with a horrified start, as if shocked out of a nightmare. . . .*)"

The tragic truth which the play illuminates is also the truth of the American Dream. For this dream, as the word implies, is ultimately subconscious, and the American nightmare is a part of it. Our modern nightmare is caused not so much by any practical disillusion with the dream of a richer material life (which has already been partly realized) as by our recognition of the double nature of the dream. Irrationally we all idealize Hickey the happy warrior, but reject the truth of his dark unconscious hatreds as "insanity." We prefer the pipe dreams of Harry Hope's saloon.

This question remains: O'Neill chose the names of his chief minor characters for obvious allegorical reasons: Harry Hope and Don Parritt. Why then did he name the central character of his tragic myth Hickey? The name seems meaningless to modern ears. In 1912, however, the year when O'Neill was drinking with the actual bums who inhabited Jimmy-the-Priest's (Harry Hope's) saloon, a minor popular novelist named Owen Johnson was achieving national fame with a series of juvenile fictions which celebrated "The Prodigious Hickey." And this Hickey was an engaging but somehow repulsive adolescent who became a folk hero to his idolatrous fellow students at Lawrenceville School. Moreover, in the adolescent slang of the day, the work "hickey" meant a pustule, or boil, which all too often disfigured American adolescents. So "The Prodigious Hickey" of O'Neill's youth had been a mythical carbuncle of a character, not unlike Hickey of *The Iceman*.

Perhaps O'Neill chose the name "Hickey" for its association with "The Prodigious Hickey" and because it suggested mythical overtones. But it also suggested comedy, not tragedy. Did O'Neill mean to imply that, as in all his later plays, comedy preceded tragedy? Or did he mean that the adolescent rebellion of the earlier Hickey prophesied the rebellion of our adolescent society? Or do all the adolescent aspirations of our "impossible dream" inevitably lead to tragic disillusion?

The old slang meaning of the word "hickey" involves further problems. The prodigious "hickey" of early slang was a disfiguring pustule, which would naturally be cured by a better diet, or by time. But the disease of Hickey in *The Iceman* was deadly, rather than merely disfiguring. And *The Iceman* prophesied death, both dramatically and psychologically. Did O'Neill choose this name carelessly? Or did he mean to imply that even the inner violence and adolescent rebellion of Hickey might eventually be cured by the bringing to consciousness of the subconscious hatreds of our society and by growth toward psychological maturity? Perhaps. It is hard to think of O'Neill as an optimist.

As Larry Slade said, "the truth is irrelevant and immaterial. . . . The lie of a pipe dream is what gives life to the whole misbegotten mad lot of us." If *The Iceman* prophesied death, it also celebrated pipe dreams: *"the pipe dream is what gives life."* Perhaps even the American nightmare may lead to life, if one is "shocked out of it" in time.

Focus on Arthur Miller's
Death of a Salesman
The Wrong Dreams

CHESTER E. EISINGER

The structural principle of Arthur Miller's *Death of a Salesman* (1949) is the antithesis between dream and reality, and the play concerns competing dreams and the identity crisis. One dream schema is the urban dream of business success. The other is the rural-agrarian dream of open space, a right relation to nature worked out in terms of the garden concept. In the play, dream is also self-delusion, or the serious entertainment of aspirations impossible of fulfillment because they are based on false conceptions of one's talents and capacities. In such a case, reality shatters dream. And out of such misapprehensions of one's potential for achievement, of possibilities and opportunities, arises the identity crisis. Reality falls short of the dream in part because man chooses the wrong dream. And man chooses the wrong dream because he does not know himself. Willy Loman is lost because he does not know who he is. His son Biff is lost through most of the play, but he finds himself; he achieves a sense of personal dignity and comes to understand his rightful place in society.

The stage directions at the beginning of the play tell us that *Death of a Salesman* is about dreams. An air of the dream clings to Willy's house. Willy is a man of massive dreams and turbulent longings. What are the dreams Miller calls upon in the play? They are conceptions as old as America. The business-urban-success dream begins with the Puritans' doctrine of the calling, which was a codification of the Protestant ethic, designed for an essentially mobile middle-class people whose primary interest was in the economics of trade and production. Franklin's secularization of the Protestant ethic made it available to every business-industrial community in the country. And Franklin fulfilled in his own life the middle-class dream of the shopkeeper whose shop came to keep him; he rose in wealth and eminence through the application of the middle-class virtues of thrift, industry, and prudence which had passed to Poor Richard by way of Puritan treatises like Cotton Mather's *Essays to Do Good* and Defoe's *Essay Upon Projects*. The apotheosis of worldly success through business and industry accords with the Hamiltonian view of the national destiny and reached its highest pinnacle after the Civil War under the sanction of individualism. The businessman, living in accordance with Franklin's worldly ethic, was a viable American hero until the collapse of the economy in 1929.

The rural-agrarian dream begins with the freehold tenure policies of the Puritans who made land freely available to settlers from the Old World, with all the economic and moral implications inherent in the state of yeomanry. In the eighteenth century, Jefferson was the great spokesman for the agrarian dream and Crèvecoeur its poet. Between them they held forth a vision of a nation of independent yeoman farmers who, in the Lockean tradition, had a natural right to the land. The bright idea of property meant that the farmer, owning his land, could guarantee his own economic well-being, and indeed in fertile America achieve that cornucopia-like abundance that underlies the serenity of such versions of rural well-being as "Snow-Bound" (1866). Beholden to no man, the farmer was the mainstay of democracy, enjoying a state of independence that the factory worker, dependent for his job and his bread upon an employer, could not afford. Farmers were the chosen people of God because they worked under His benevolent gaze, out in the open where they could establish a right relationship with His natural world. Their occupation guaranteed their moral, spiritual, and physical health. Closely associated with this vision is the ideal of craftsmanship, the notion that a man must be able to work with his hands and that such work is not only real but superior to the nonproductive work of thinking or selling. This dream survived in the slogan that the farmer was the backbone of the nation, and it accounts for the often frenzied but futile effort today to save the family-size farm as though it were a national asset. It accounts in part for the disproportionate political power wielded by rural areas in state and national governments up until very recent years. It survived in literature in fiction like Willa Cather's "Neighbor Rosicky" (1932) and John Steinbeck's *Grapes of Wrath* (1939) and in a cultural movement like Southern agrarianism, which set forth its principles in *I'll Take My Stand* (1930).

In *Death of a Salesman* Miller gives us various versions of the urban-business-success dream. Dave Singleton and Charley represent its ideal form. In Willy's sentimentalized view, Singleton was the eighty-four-year-old drummer who in twenty or thirty different cities used to go to his hotel room, put on his green velvet slippers, and sell his line simply by telephoning buyers. He was a model for Willy, because he showed that a salesman could be remembered, loved, and helped in many different places in the country. Success, esteem, and affection are all embodied in Dave, and these are goals that Willy wanted to achieve. Charley is, apparently, a successful businessman who is giving Willy enough money to live on, who offers Willy a job in an effort to shore up Willy's self-respect, and who has in the past counseled maturity and sanity in Willy's life. Nothing is ideal about this character, except that without dreaming he has achieved the terms of the business dream, a good man who has found a stable way of life and financial security and whose son, a source of pride to him, has grown up to practice law before the United States Supreme Court. Although Willy has been jealous of Charley and irrationally impatient of him, Charley has remained Willy's friend and professes to understand what he was. He explains Willy to Biff at the end of the play, after Biff has said that Willy never knew who he was: "Nobody dast blame this man. You don't understand: Willy was a salesman. And for a salesman, there is no rock bottom to the life. He don't put a bolt to a nut, he don't tell you the law or give you medicine. He's a man way out there in the blue, riding on a smile and a shoeshine. And when they start not smiling back—that's an earthquake. And then you get yourself a couple of spots on your hat, and you're finished. Nobody dast blame this man. A salesman is got to dream, boy. It comes with the territory." This is an incongruous speech for a practical man like Charley to make, summoning up, as it does, the ineffable and intangible mystique of salesmanship. It serves well enough as an epitaph, but it carries little conviction, so obviously is it a romanticized conception of the salesman.

Willy Loman himself gives us the corrupted version of the urban-business-success dream, for which Uncle Ben and Howard, Willy's boss, are the hard and compelling symbols. At the heart of this dream in Willy's factitious rendering of it is the cult of personality. It is necessary to make a good appearance and to be well-liked. Appearance is a key concept, for a salesman must appear to be more than he is: better liked, more successful, more optimistic, more necessary to the life of his firm. Then the police will protect his car when it is parked on the streets of any New England town, and the doors to the buyers' offices will swing open when he appears. Techniques of personality and human manipulation replace substantive contributions, and the salesman wins friends and influences people after the pattern that Dale Carnegie has formulated, and he exercises charm in the manner of some model drawn from the films. The mythic version of the success dream is Uncle Ben's: "When I was seventeen I walked into the jungle, and when I was twenty-one I walked out. And by God I was rich." The air of exoticism and terror that clings to Ben's achievement rests on the same sense of mystery that Conrad (more effectively) evokes in *Heart of Darkness* (1899). Mystery surrounds the getting of money, a secret is involved which Ben can explain only cryptically and Willy cannot guess. Violence and trickery are necessary, as Ben shows when he spars playfully with Biff. Suddenly he is standing over the boy with the point of his umbrella at Biff's eye: "Never fight fair with a stranger, boy," he says. "You'll never get out of the jungle that way." Finally, Howard gives us the dehumanized version of the dream, for he shows us the heartlessness of the business ethic. When Willy can no longer make money for the firm, Howard fires him, despite his long years of service, because "everybody's gotta pull his own weight" and "you gotta admit, business is business."

Development of the rural-agrarian dream begins in the first paragraph of the stage directions; Miller tells us that a melody is heard played on a flute, "telling of grass and trees and the horizon." Music of the flute opens and closes the play; it is Willy's music and it attaches him at once to growing things and to the out-of-doors. Willy owns a single-dwelling house in the city. The house itself is marginally attached to the rural-agrarian dream, affording the family a place of its own and a sense of belonging, of social status and pride. Willy's hope had been for a home shaded by magnificent elm trees, graced by a lawn and a garden. This ambience for his house is what really attaches Willy to the out-of-doors. It is Willy's effort to create a fruitful relationship with the world of nature by which he would satisfy aesthetic and spiritual needs; the garden will serve the primitive urge to grow his own food. So deeply powerful is Willy's impulse to buy seeds and plant a garden that he follows it, almost without volition, at the most desperate hour of his need— when he has been fired from his job and when his sons have deserted him. Or it might be said that he has recourse to sowing his garden, this ancient ritual by which man sustains himself, when all else has failed him. Miller gives us that painful scene in which Willy wanders out in his yard at night, trying to plant by flashlight.

Further, Willy is a self-reliant man who can work with his hands. He can build his own concrete porch or put up his own ceiling. He believes that a man who cannot handle tools is not a man. This notion of masculinity is perhaps related to the Loman family tradition of westering—Willy's father took him as far west as South Dakota, at least, and Ben had gone to Alaska. This western orientation has encouraged the freedom and individualism of Willy's life style, a style that leads him to resist the confining demands of the city. He has inherited from his father that large optimism characteristic of the frontier. These details suggest rather than constitute a pattern of rural-agrarian aspiration both in their positive identification with elements of this dream and in their anti-urbanism.

The predictable difficulty is that the city and business blight the fulfillment of Willy's rural-agrarian dream. Ironically, he comes fully to own the little house, which is like the homestead, only on the day he is buried, when the last payment on the mortgage is finally made. It was not his, and more, it is alien in the city, surrounded and intimidated by the huge structures around it. These shut off air and light, so that no grass, not even carrots, will grow. Builders have chopped down the elm trees. The fragrance of peonies and daffodils, once so intoxicating in the spring, is now only a memory. The independence and virility of life beyond the horizon becomes, in the city, a "measly manner of existence," as Biff says: "To get on that subway on the hot morning in summer. To devote your whole life to keeping stock, or making phone calls, or selling or buying. To suffer fifty weeks of the year for the sake of a two-week vacation, when all you really desire is to be outdoors, with your shirt off. And always to have to get ahead of the next fella." The city and the pursuit of success enforce a way of life that is essentially corrupting, distorting the human personality. All the Loman men have been the victims of such distortion.

Under the pressure to succeed in business, the appearance of things is always more important than the reality, and the truth about one's accomplishments is never impressive enough; it is, consequently, necessary to delude everyone, even oneself, so often that lying becomes the habitual mode of discourse and hypocrisy the accepted moral stance. Or so Willy thinks. In the perverted and desperate affirmation of his optimism, he assures himself and Linda, his wife, that he is vital to his firm in New England. He exaggerates the volume of his sales; actually, he is not selling enough to justify his continued employment; he had always teetered on the thin edge of failure. He lies to himself and others about Biff's business accomplishments, also. The value scheme induced by this pressure pervades Willy's life. He sanctions Biff's thefts and his cheating at school, because these are the prerogatives of the popular schoolboy athlete and leader. He denigrates the need for learning in the name of a higher good, personality.

Willy carries on a sordid adultery, a painfully conventional affair between the traveling salesman and the other woman. He is driven into this relationship because of his own inadequacies and insecurities. He is lonely on the road, and his loneliness is intensified by his fear of business failure. When he fails to measure up to the model which he believes society to have constructed and which he accepts—the American businessman as rugged, independent, and successful—then he seeks comfort in his sordid little sin and wrecks his sentimental hope for familial bliss.

The erosion of Willy's character under the pressure to succeed eats away the moral center of the Loman family. In their home the two sons breathe in the easy morality of their father. The air there is polluted by the empty optimism and the phony maxims of the business ethic that Willy mindlessly repeats. This kind of home training makes Biff a thief and drives Happy to a refuge in easy sensualism and self-aggrandizing lies. The boys hold menial jobs but tell others and believe themselves that they are persons of consequence in the business world. So thoroughly has Willy indoctrinated them with dreams of success that they are victims of illusions. They work up totally impossible schemes for making money: an escape to the great West where they will become ranchers or the selling of sporting goods through the formation of rival athletic teams that will play each other throughout the country. These schemes are infantile; Willy's corruption prevents his sons from achieving a mature manhood.

Biff is aware of the corruption wrought in him by the impact of the business-success dream on the family. That corruption inhibits his quest for adulthood, which is related to his quest for identity. In the course of the play, he succeeds in stripping himself of illusion and self-deception, in coming to a knowledge of who he is and of coming to terms with that person. When he recognizes the total compulsion to evaluate himself, an act Miller speaks of in commenting on his own play, he provides the contrapuntal release to life that we must set over against Willy's defeat in suicide.

The crucial event that leads to Biff's self-knowledge is his visit to his former employer, Bill Oliver, to borrow money. The scheme is childish; Biff had been a shipping clerk in Oliver's business and had stolen a carton of basketballs from the firm, hardly the basis on which to ask for a ten thousand dollar loan. Oliver refuses Biff, and the latter then takes a pen from Oliver's desk. In one sense the theft is the act of a frustrated and humiliated man. In another it is simply further evidence of Biff's tendency toward habitual stealing. But why does he take a pen? A third way of regarding this act is to see the pen as a phallic symbol and Biff's theft of it his unconscious effort to become a man. Oliver's pen may be regarded as Oliver's surrogate penis. To possess the pen is to have at one's command the potency of Oliver, a successful man. Biff hopes in this theft to revive a version of himself as the man he once was: football hero, idol and lover of high school girls, leader of the neighborhood gang. He hopes to become the man his father wished him to be: a man in a man's world, a business success, a man with status. Because he is lost and impotent, Biff needs to re-man himself, and he tries now to do it in the image that his father and his own past have made available to him. His athletic glory has been gone for a long time; Biff is thirty-four when he commits this theft. He has lost his confidence in the pursuit of women. He has no recognizable place in the economic world. He is not only a failure, alienated from the conventional world of business; he is also a boy because he has no part in this world. He regards himself this way, and on separate occasions his father and his mother say he is like a boy. He seizes the pen, the phallus of a successful man, to throw off boyhood and assert manhood.

If Biff's effort had been successful, he would have become the man his sensual brother and his misguided father would have admired. But he fails. As he runs down the stairs of the office building with the pen, he realizes that he cannot claim his manhood in any synthetic way. The revelation comes to him that he can be a man only under the open sky, working with his hands. He cannot and need not rely on a mere symbol of manhood. This conviction transcends the phallic value of the pen and sustains Biff in his honest self-knowledge at the end of the play.

Nothing saves Willy. To the end he is guided by the ethics of opportunism that mark the corrupt pursuit of business success. He has been contemplating suicide throughout the play. When his affairs reach their apparent nadir, he seems to hear the voice of Ben counseling him to kill himself in such a way that his insurance money will go to Biff. He believes that he is sacrificing himself so that Biff may have twenty thousand dollars to begin his career. He goes to his death confident in Biff's love, but still believing in Biff's capacity to succeed in business. He misjudges his son as surely as he misjudges himself. Biff passes judgment on him at the grave: "He had the wrong dreams. All, all, wrong."

The culture, as we have seen, presented Willy with two dreams, and it thereby imposed upon him the burden of choice. A wise man might have selected the kind of life and promising fulfillment of his needs and aspirations appropriate to his capacities. But Willy is a confused and inadequate man. He never achieves a sense of personal dignity and of his rightful place in society because, not knowing who he is, he cannot make the right choices. The theme of the play, then, seems to be that every man must come to know himself or he is lost. Biff succeeds in the quest for self-knowledge but Willy fails.

Yet this statement of the meaning of the play may be too simple, for it rests on the assumption that if Willy, out of an acute understanding of his character, had chosen the rural-agrarian dream, he would have fulfilled himself and achieved the ideals of family and home that he wanted. This assumption must derive from Miller's uncritical acceptance of the myth of the garden. The culture has a strong emotional, really sentimental, attachment to this myth, an attraction which is in part a product of our nostalgia for primitivistic innocence. And we have, complementarily, a long history of anti-urbanism, as *The Intellectual Versus the City* by Morton and Lucia White demonstrates. But contemporary American culture does not honor the two dreams equally as viable alternatives. Our genius is technological and industrial. The processes that flow from these characteristics have transformed the farm and rendered the rural-agrarian dream obsolete.

Even in the play, there are intimations to be drawn from Biff's career that the satisfactions of the rural life may be limited. Miller has revealed the presence of two dreams in American culture, but it is not at all clear that he has given Willy a genuine choice. Instead he seems to be saying that the dichotomy in the culture in which the business-success dream is corrupt or corrupting and the rural-agrarian dream pure and life-giving is pregnant with paradox, because it is only the corrupt dream that we are expected to follow seriously. It is Willy as salesman whom Charley honors at the graveside and whom Linda accepts. Nothing is wrong with Willy as salesman except that he fails, and much that is wrong with Willy stems from the fact that he does fail. In the liberal tradition we are predisposed to regard Willy as the victim of business—this is the case, I suspect, with reader and author alike. Yet Miller is not uniformly hostile to business: Charley is a decent and patient man who has succeeded in business. To be sure, Willy is victimized by Howard, a gadget-minded and heartless businessman who is immune to appeals based on loyalty and long service, which constitute the refuge of a man who dares not make a case based on merit. But Howard is no more typical or symbolic than Charley.

The play, then, romanticizes the rural-agrarian dream but does not make it genuinely available to Willy. Miller seems to use this dream merely to give himself an opportunity for sentimentality. The play is ambiguous in its attitude toward the business-success dream, but does not certainly condemn it. It is legitimate to ask where Miller is going. And the answer is that he has written a confused play because he has been unwilling or unable to commit himself to a firm position with respect to American culture. Miller prepares us for a stock response—relief in escape to the West and the farm; firm satisfaction in the condemnation of the tawdry business ethic—and then denies us the fulfillment of our expectations. The play makes, finally, no judgment on America, although Miller seems always on the verge of one, of telling us that America is a nightmare, a cause of and a home for tragedy. But Willy is not a tragic hero; he is a foolish and ineffectual man for whom we feel pity. We cannot equate his failure with America's.

Choice
Ironic Alternatives in the World
of the Contemporary American Novel

ALVIN GREENBERG

What does the dreamer do when he gets to the end of his dream? At best, he brings forth from it something that will be creative and useful to himself and his society: his dream projects a future, or a range of future possibilities, and from his vision of these possibilities he can try to shape the reality to which he awakens. Perhaps the most lucid spokesman for such a productive view of the dream was Henry David Thoreau, who, of course, never intended that his dream, however idyllic, should become a permanent dwelling place: "I left the woods," he tells us in his final chapter, "for as good a reason as I went there." But at the other extreme, the dreamer wakes to a nightmarish, pirandellian world in which the coordinates established in his previous state no longer make any sense; and perhaps the best nineteenth-century American spokesmen for this structuring of the dream are the Melville of *Benito Cereno*, in which the innocent dreamer Captain Delano is at the last jolted awake to an awareness of the nightmare with which he must henceforth live, and the later Twain, of "Which Was the Dream?" and "The Great Dark," works whose central dilemma—if it is a nightmare reality to which the dreamer awakes, where can he go from there?—is best illustrated by the fact that Twain was unable to finish them.

And this is, in essence, the dilemma that twentieth-century American fiction has wakened to as well. Somehow the dream, Thoreau's, has become the nightmare; Twain's, and what the contemporary novelist has been left with, by way of an inheritance, has been the need to find a place for man in that dream gone awry. For the nightmare, as a good bit of

175

modern fiction has shown it—*The Sound and the Fury, The Sun Also Rises, The Day of the Locust, The Man with the Golden Arm*, to name only a few—is that of a world run amok, or a world running down, in the midst of which stands the often solitary individual, immersed in a process of frightening disintegration whose end may well be predetermined, whose force seems both irresistible and irreversible. Such qualities, which appear to belong both to his society and to his world at large, mechanistic in their workings and deterministic in their effects, would seem to decree, for the individual abandoned in their midst, the antihumanistic verdict of an essentially antihumanistic universe. And the challenge which the novelist has drawn from such a concept of the contemporary human dilemma has been to explore the questions of whether, and how, in the midst of an apparently meaningless process which threatens to render meaningless all in its grips, man can yet find, or give, meaning to his existence.

The answers, in the context of such a process, have had to be shaped, then, not in terms of ends, which there is perhaps no hope of affecting, but rather of means. However much the forces of that world which the contemporary novelist gives us are revealed as antihumanistic, nonetheless that world, being the world in which man lives, still possesses the capacity for being humanistic, at least while he is there, and in so far as he can make it his. The extent to which he can accomplish these things—remain afloat in the destructive stream of experience and swim, if not in his own direction, at least in his own fashion—defines both his limits and his possibilities. And it is, above all else, choice, however limited the alternatives may be, that gives man, in such a context, the possibility for determining the nature, if not the end, of his experience. "Literature," as Sartre has put it, "is preoccupied with the relation between what man *is* and what he is choosing to make himself within the historical perspective."

Choice, in this sense, becomes not an end (the end being, in the long run, predetermined), but a means: the means to make a meaningful approach to a predetermined end. As an exercise of will which establishes a thing to be done or a direction to be taken, choice implies the humanly possible, the human power over action, including power over the position of the self in the world, and becomes, thus, a humanizing assertion of the self in the world. Such choice,

which operates as a means not to an ending but to a becoming—not a narrowing down but an opening up of possibilities—is alone capable of becoming a meaning-giving process
where, as in the nightmare, no external structure of meaning
can be assumed to exist. And however fantastic such a
desperate struggle to give meaning to human experience may
seem—Sartre, after all, defines the fantastic as "the revolt of
means against ends"—choice so conceived is nonetheless
that way by which man can humanize his world: whatever
the choice he makes, it represents *his* being if *he* chooses it,
nothing if he does not.

In spite of such possibilities, of course, the destructive
process of the nightmare and its end as death remain persistent, unless the novelist is to beg off by violating his assumptions; the effect of these constants is to render all choice, of
necessity, ironic choice. In an absurd universe, characterized
by a vast discrepancy between what is humanly desired and
what is humanly possible, choice comes to possess a certain
absurdity of its own: because of the overall nature of the
process in which they appear, all choices are futile choices,
and yet, at the same time, choice itself is necessary. Because
man can neither accept nor resist the destructive nightmare
to which he has wakened—to accept is inhuman, to resist
impossible—whatever choices he makes are ironical. Because
they arise out of an insoluble situation, they cannot hold
forth any promises of redemption—and hence are not likely
to be of much consolation to Nelson Algren's perhaps apocry-
phal but rather typical complainant who objects to "the
writer who offers me the world's horrors without offering a
solution" (*The Neon Wilderness*, 1960).

And yet, though such choices may permit only alternative
routes to the same end, an end which would arrive equally
well on its own, the significance which arises from them to
create meaning within the nightmare world of the modern
American novel is that they are *human* choices: human alternatives which, however paradoxical, are conceived in full
recognition of the fact that within such a world as the contemporary writer has so frequently seen ours to be, man not
only must justify his existence for himself, but is, moreover,
capable of so doing, through the exploration of those ironic
alternatives that are available to him, that he can make his,
by means of which he can make his world his.

Ralph Ellison's *Invisible Man* provides an encompassing

paradigm for the examination of these ironic alternatives in recent American fiction. While on the one hand this novel indicates the extent to which "great literature is the conscious exploration through the imagination of the *possibilities* of human action in society" (Hugh Dalziel Duncan, *Language and Literature in Society*, 1953), at the same time it conveys a clear recognition of the equal extent to which these possibilities are compromised, rendered paradoxical, by the pervading irony of the world in which they take place. That such is the case here is indicated from the beginning, in fact, through the quotation from Melville's *Benito Cereno* that serves as an epigraph for the novel: " 'You are saved,' cried Captain Delano, more and more astonished and pained; 'you are saved: what has cast such a shadow upon you?' "

For Ellison's hero, life is composed of the process of growing toward a recognition of the shadow that blights the solution, of accepting, finally, the shadow as a necessary aspect of any choice a man can make. One persistent shadow under which the Invisible Man struggles to make the choice that will yield a meaningful life is the deathbed voice of his grandfather, offering the old slave's philosophy of sabotage through agreement: "I want you to overcome 'em with yeses, undermine 'em with grins, agree 'em to death and destruction, let 'em swoller you till they vomit or bust wide open." At every stage of his progress this possibility of ironic acceptance haunts him "like a curse": in his early desires to be "considered an example of desirable conduct—just like my grandfather had been"; at the Negro college, where he is lectured on how to "act the nigger" and profit from conformity and self-submergence in ritualistic social game playing; at the paint factory, where the Negro "swollered" within only assures the continual emergency of a perfect white on the surface, and where a failure to conform only leads to the nightmare of a lobotomy designed to make certain that "society will suffer no traumata on his account"; and even, finally, in the idealistic Brotherhood, which demands the sacrifice of individuality to the impersonal force of history. The irony of such acceptance, for the Invisible Man, is that it functions not as a means of subversion or regeneration, but only as a treadmill, the echo of his childhood dream: "To Whom It May Concern . . . Keep This Nigger-Boy Running." On the unruffled surface of things, no signs of his grandfather's predicted eruptions appear; neither are there any responses to the crises of the individuals submerged within.

On the surface, however, where direct action and change appear more possible, the Invisible Man cannot accept the apocalyptic alternative offered by Ras the Destroyer and his black nationalists. The razing of Harlem (Chapter 25), which becomes, for the moment, a very real choice, ironic because it posits destruction as a mode of salvation, is likewise rendered a futile alternative within the context of social control. All too soon the Invisible Man recognizes it as only another trap set by a society which "needed this *destroyer* to do their work," thus making "you guilty of your own murder, your own sacrifice"—once again destroying the possibility for *self*-realization through choice.

Beyond this second alternative, the Invisible Man moves toward his final paradoxical choice, that whose viewpoint frames the entire novel: withdrawal, carefully defined as neither a flight nor an end in itself, but in fact a beginning. Having explored the wasteland of the nightmarish outside world, and experienced its ways of depriving him of valid choices for a meaningful existence, he turns at last inside, withdrawing into the dark hole of the self. Here he uses whatever he can take from the outside world (e.g., his battle with Monopolated Light and Power, over whether human progress is to be merely a commercial venture or is to illuminate the individual self) as well as whatever he can add from his own interior perspective—"all life seen from the whole of invisibility is absurd"—as means of preparing for a significant re-emergence: "having tried to give pattern to the chaos which lives within the pattern of your certainties, I must come out, I must emerge."

Such withdrawal becomes not an escape from but a viewpoint for understanding the world and man's position in it, and hence serves itself as a significant way of being in that world. From the vantage point of this final choice, he can see clearly the ironic structure on which all rests: not only the earlier alternatives of conformity or destruction—in whose center he recognizes the ironic "joke" of his being "*part of them* as well as apart from them and subject to die when they died"—but all human forms of choice and hope, including his own: "don't let me trick you, there *is* a death in the smell of spring and in the smell of thee as in the smell of me." But at the same time, it is a choice that enables him to escape the narrow borders of social reality, to explore instead a realm of "chaos . . . or imagination" that enables him to synthesize, out of the multitudinous fragments of tragedy and despair that have populated his experience, a final, regenerating sense of possibility. By virtue of the very fact that this new, ironic viewpoint has freed him from the old "assumption that the world was solid and all the relationships therein," he can now say of the world, no longer limited by what it can do to him but broadened by what he can be in himself, that "its definition is possibility." Even this final choice is ironic, because incomplete, and yet from it emerges the potentiality that validates it as choice. It is thus that Ellison's *Invisible Man* posits the realm of ironic alternatives in the contemporary novel: conformity, destruction, or withdrawal, all three of them difficult and paradoxical choices.

First, one may deliberately choose to conform, to participate voluntarily in the meaninglessness of the universe and accept the way of the world as how it is and how, for the time, it has to be. Yet even this apparently simple, if painful, choice may be seen as balanced between a despondent conformity on the one side, perhaps a product of futility and the self-willed collapse of all other alternatives, and a romantic conformity on the other, product of the subversive hope of reforming from within. This latter, of course, is the version of conformity urged throughout the *Invisible Man* by the voice of the protagonist's grandfather as not only preferable but necessary, since it affirms the principles of human existence while permitting the individual to work from within — perhaps the only arena within which progress can be achieved — against the distorted applications of those principles. Yet such a choice also creates the danger of having to go beyond itself, losing the possibilities of ironic conformity in the hopelessness of total submergence not just among the principles but also among their distortions: "Had he seen that for these too we had to say 'yes' to the principle, lest they turn upon us to destroy both it and us?"

Thus the principle of hope is consistently undermined by the unremitting irony of the world; and yet the choice, though rendered impossible as solution, remains necessary and potential as a consideration, a paradoxical choice open to a situation where *some* way out must be found, sufficiently full of possibility to leave Ellison's protagonist, though he himself has selected another alternative, holding it open to question. And it is the answer found in *Catch-22* (1961) by the protagonist's friend Dunbar, who attempts to subvert the destructive process of reality by making his life conform as closely as possible to the tedious and unbearable structure of that reality; paradoxically, life is sustained by willingly submitting it to the most uncomfortable aspects of the world, a condition under which Dunbar insists that life actually "*is* longer" though at times he is found "working so hard at increasing his life span that Yossarian thought he was dead."

What is implied by the ironic nature of conformity is the danger that it will yield a submission from which there is no recall, a submergence of possibility in the muck of impossibility. Such seems to be the recognition of Saul Bellow's Dangling Man, who ends the long holdout during which he has held all commitment in abeyance by shouting "Long live regimentation!" (*Dangling Man*, 1944). Though this no doubt represents choice made in despair, irony is sustained in the acceptance, willingly but without belief, of that whose acceptance might otherwise be enforced as part of the way of the world. This is also, perhaps, the way in which Mailer's Rojack comes to accept the norm of violence in his perversion of *An American Dream* (1965). Yet to choose even conformity, regardless of what determines the choice, is to acknowledge by the very fact of making a choice that there are other possible choices and so to contribute to the definition of the human condition as one of possibility. Perhaps, by rejecting those alternatives which appear to offer an immediately fuller sense of human possibility, to conform is even to participate more fully—in the whole of one's actions —in the tragic irony that underlies this human condition: the vast disparity between the way man is and the way he ought to be.

But if conformity, under any terms, is totally unacceptable, then *one may, at the extreme opposite, choose the way of destruction*, seeking apocalyptically to answer the tragic irony of the human condition by the apparently simple device of doing away with that condition: attempting, that is, to shortcut the disintegrative process. The ironic potentiality contained within this alternative is that of dignifying humanity through the destruction of that which degrades it. And once again, the choice has its own two poles: that demonic wrath that would salvage the human by razing the inhuman but faces the paradox that what is to be saved is inextricably bound up with what is to be destroyed; and that beatific apocalyptic frenzy which seeks destruction as a mode of escape and prays for the resurrection of humanity somewhere up above all the disintegrative clutter.

This latter, angelic version of the apocalypse is the quest of Kenneth Patchen's *Journal of Albion Moonlight* (1941) — the quest for the second coming of a savior who will purge the world, making the violence of the quest itself a kind of purification by fire. This is the heavenly quest finally (inexplicably) achieved at the end of Patchen's *Memoirs of a Shy Pornographer* (1945), where, through the collapse of the ironic view upon which any valid concept of alternatives depends, the goal arises unconvincingly as pure and clear within a structure where purity and clarity cannot be believed in except through a suspension of the only (worldly) reality that could make such virtues significant. In the final symbolic chapters of Jack Kerouac's *Doctor Sax* (1959) the beat apocalypse takes the form of the Divine Bird, descending "surrounded by a great horde of white Doves" to reveal how "The Universe disposes of its own evil" by destroying the great Snake that threatens the world with a wholly demonic Judgment Day: "There was still hope!" The end of this version of apocalypse comes through the intervention of a *deus ex machina*, after whose descent "the bloody worm was ousted from his hole, the neck of the world was free" — but in whose action human need is raised mysteriously above human reality and man himself is suddenly deprived of the possibility of giving significance to his own life.

The demonic version of the redeeming cataclysm that appears in Ellison's *Invisible Man* in the person of Ras the Destroyer directing the burning of Harlem appears a far more meaningful alternative within the consistently ironic context of such a novel, for its effect, in the recognition Ellison's protagonist achieves that we are *"part of them* as well as apart from them and subject to die when they died" is to contain the dilemma of choice wholly within its nature as a human dilemma, making this alternative, then, valid within the wholly human terms that alone can make it meaningful as choice. In both *The Man with the Golden Arm* and *Never Come Morning*, Algren's characters give evidence of a lust for precisely this choice of a demonic destruction of the degraded and degrading human milieu. In the former, Sophie is seen "tracing, with one forefinger upon the dust of the unwashed pane, the single word: *Perdition*. Just as she finished tracing it the sirens sounded, the hook-and-ladder pulled past and patrol cars, insurance cars and all the frantic traffic of a 4–11 alarm fire came crashing by with a sense of imminent doom. She wheeled to the door and shrieked up the stairwell to Violet, 'It's goin' up! Loop 'n all! It's goin' up!'" (*The Man with the Golden Arm*, 1949). Unfortunately, though Sophie's prayers seem for a moment to have been answered, the fire turns out to be confined to a warehouse basement. Just as her desire is aborted by reality, so is Steffi's similar desire ironically confined, however necessary it seems in terms of her world, within the limits of a dream in which the world, which she conceives of as one vast penitentiary where all are entombed, is destroyed by fire: "a great stone penitentiary with all the exits barred and no sign of smoke or disorder without, no sound of crackling flame; but only the steady murmur of the machine shops within. Guards paced the wall steadily and regularly so that no one in the whole outside world could guess that the cells within were blazing, tier upon tier within the very stone, that the smoke was in the lungs of a thousand chained men. That the very bars they grasped were melting within the stone" (*Never Come Morning*, 1942). The very title *Never Come Morning* gives evidence to the choice of the destructive alternative.

Only in Nathanael West's *The Day of the Locust* (1939) does the dream of the demonic apocalypse, Tod Hackett's slowly developing mental image of the picture he wants to paint of "The Burning of Los Angeles," approach the possibility of reality. The final scene of mob violence parallels the destruction of Harlem in *Invisible Man*; and in it Tod envisions art become reality, his own painting become life:

He could see all the rough charcoal strokes with which he had blocked it out on the big canvas. Across the top, parallel with the frame, he had drawn the burning city, a great bonfire of architectural styles, ranging from Egyptian to Cape Cod colonial.

Through the center, winding from left to right, was a long hill street and down it, spilling into the middle foreground, came the mob carrying baseball bats and torches. For the faces of its members, he was using the innumerable sketches he had made of the people who come to California to die; the cultists of all sorts, economic as well as religious, the wave, airplane, funeral and preview watchers—all those poor devils who can only be stirred by the promise of miracles and then only to violence. A super "Dr. Know-All Pierce-All" had made the necessary promise and they were marching behind his banner in a great united front of screwballs and screwboxes to purify the land. No longer bored, they sang and danced joyously in the red light of the flames.

Outside the art vision, too, these are the people and this the action surrounding West's protagonist, the apocalyptic re-demption in the process of destroying the redeemers, who are free from their nightmare at last only by virtue of not being at all any more. It is to this election of the cataclysmic alternative that Alan Reynolds Thompson's analysis of the "spiritual ironist" best applies: "We conclude that spiritual ironists are sick souls, and that irony as a weapon is usually a method of destruction. But the reason that the ironist's soul is sick is that he has visions of a better world than the existing one, and the destruction of present evils gives oppor-tunity for future good" (*The Dry Mock: A Study of Irony in Drama*, 1948). It is the paradox of this second ironic alterna-tive that sickness becomes a form of health, and destruction an understanding of possibility.

And finally, *one may make the choice of withdrawal*, with all its concomitant ironies of the impossibility of a full, real, and lasting withdrawal, of the painfulness of the withdrawal symptoms, of the possibility that there may finally be noth-ing there where one has withdrawn to, of the self-evident futility of withdrawal as a thing in itself. Though its very definition as disengagement threatens to render such an alternative meaningless, withdrawal nonetheless represents the quest for some area that will give meaning to the mean-inglessness outside. Simply as an alternative implying other alternatives, withdrawal too turns choice into possibility, and again it opens in two directions: either toward the use of withdrawal as preparation for return or toward the explora-tion of the full possibilities inherent within this choice itself. Either way, withdrawal may be arrived at by the need of the ironic protagonist, in the face of a disintegrative world which offers him only the either/or of totally destructive (to self in conformity or to self and world in apocalypse) involvement or potentially meaningless *dis*engagement, to choose the latter.

"The main manoeuvre used to preserve identity under pressure from the dread of engulfment is isolation" (R. D. Laing, "Ontological Insecurity," in *Psychoanalysis and Existential Philosophy*, 1962). It is this maneuver which, finally, the Invisible Man chooses, and it is this choice which is Henderson the Rain King's, also. Faced with engulfment—self-destruction—in a world that has become intolerable to him, Henderson's flight to Africa stands as a withdrawal from that other, threatening world. Yet it is not merely a flight, but, as he explains, "really kind of . . . a quest" in which, no longer wishing "to live by any law of decay" like that which the processes of the external world decree, he turns, like the Invisible Man, to seek within the principle of order necessary for making life outside meaningful. It is here, during this withdrawal, during a time in which he has been "discontinuous with civilization," that Henderson is *called from nonexistence into existence*" (Saul Bellow, *Henderson the Rain King*, 1959). And it is from this withdrawal that Henderson is reborn, having both come to himself and become homesick for the world which he has left, but able now to find meaning and purpose in the return to that world, like Ellison's protagonist in his recognition that "having tried to give pattern to the chaos that lives within the pattern of your certainties, I must come out, I must emerge" (*Invisible Man*).

But whereas both Ellison and Bellow present withdrawal as the choice which opens up the possibility of a final, more meaningful re-emergence, for Heller the withdrawal itself becomes final, a means to something *within* itself rather than a return to the without. In *Catch-22* the either/or alternatives with which the ironic protagonist is faced become either/Orr; Orr himself, the thinker-tinker and, though only Yossarian's tentmate in a very real way the hero of the novel, embodies the principle of that withdrawal which, however ironic and ultimately impossible, serves at last, when his actions are finally understood, to impregnate the rapidly disintegrating world of this novel with renewed meaning and fresh possibility. Orr's disappearance occurs simultaneously with the novel's plunge into the depths of disintegration, a world where, for Yossarian, "death was irreversible, he suspected, and he began to think he was going to lose," and where he has been left behind, alone, with only "Orr's marvelous stove" to keep him warm. But it is a world suddenly rejuvenated first by the discovery that Orr, believed to have died in a plane crash while returning from a bombing mission, has actually escaped to Sweden from the destructive arena of war and then by Yossarian's sudden recognition that Orr had "planned it that way from the beginning. He even practiced getting shot down. He rehearsed for it on every mission he flew." Orr, with his "look of stupid innocence that nobody would ever suspect of any cleverness," turns out to be the one who, carefully planning, has suddenly opened up the choice of withdrawal as a possibility for survival in a world where survival no longer seems possible. Even the Chaplain, whose declaration that Orr's survival is a miracle is countered by Yossarian's explanation of it as the product of careful planning, declares that "It's still a miracle, a miracle of human intelligence and human endurance. Look how much he accomplished!" And Yossarian, made conscious of the possibility of human achievement in the recognition that Orr, that most careful planner for survival—as man must be —"knew what he was doing every step of the way," leaps himself, at the very end of the novel, beyond the knife-wielding arm of the destructive world, toward that same choice of withdrawal. It is within this world of withdrawal, that Swedish utopia that cannot possibly be reached by lifeboat from the Mediterranean as Orr has done—within, in fact, the ironic choice to pursue such an impossibility—that human possibility is to be found and the possibility of a meaningful life to be explored.

In such withdrawal, at least, resides the possibility that the self may be able to provide the necessary meaning that is elsewhere totally undermined by the world of nightmare and disintegration; or that the choice itself may yield meaning simply because, however futile and hopeless, it is at least a choice that opposes the destructive process, affirming possibility in the paradoxical recognition that, as Ellison says in the epilogue of *Invisible Man*, "humanity is won by continuing to play in the face of certain defeat." The will to go on, then, and the will to make a choice when choice seems impossible, define the context of all these ironic alternatives, which appear, like the choice of withdrawal, at the end, to be narrow and uncomfortable little rooms, difficult and painful to enter, but may, once entered, turn out to be funnel-shaped, open-ended. "The significant writer today," says Hazel Barnes in *The Literature of Possibility* (1959), "presents in his imaginative works characters . . . confronted with the necessity of making a definite choice, but the conflict is always such that the solution is somehow a commitment to the nature and possibilities of man."

In the twentieth-century American novel such commitment is, to the nature of man *as* possibility, a commitment achieved in the face of forces that would rather seem to decree impossibility. But the effect of this struggle is only to make the commitment, in all its paradoxical nature, more humanly meaningful than could be any non-ironic solution arrived at with an ease and permanence invalidating the struggle. "Alfred North Whitehead once underscored the dilemma," says Wylie Sypher in *Loss of the Self in Modern Literature and Art* (1962), "by saying that the radical inconsistency in modern thought is our firm belief in man as a self-determining organism and our equally firm belief in the validity of deterministic laws." Within these novels, however, Whitehead's "radical inconsistency" is redefined as a "radical necessity" demanding, and lending meaning to, the ironic alternatives as significant acts of will—acts by which man does indeed become a self-determining organism even in a deterministic universe. Even in its paradoxical, unresolving resolution upon such a principle of ironic choice, then, such literature wholly affirms that sense of human possibility embodied in Lionel Trilling's statement in *The Liberal Imagination* (1957) that "the novel at its greatest is the record of will acting under the direction of an idea, often an idea of will itself."

Focus on Ralph Ellison's *Invisible Man*
American Nightmare

ALLEN GUTTMANN

With every manifestation of black discontent, Ralph Ellison's novel *Invisible Man* (1952) seems more prophetic, rings truer when sounded by our sense of American society at the present moment. Drawing imaginatively from the symbolic arsenal of literary modernism, Ellison has written more realistically than Richard Wright. About the many lives of American Negroes, he tells us more than Gunnar Myrdal and a great deal more than Franz Fanon. It is not that the medium guarantees the message; surrealism, as a literary mode, is in no way superior to realism. It is simply that Ellison, on the basis of a single novel, can be called a great writer.

Although Ellison has often maintained that his study of modern writers is what made possible the transformation into art of his experience as a Negro, his familiarity with the *surréalisme* propounded by André Breton has not been established. Nonetheless, Breton's argument that surrealism draws its images directly from the unconscious mind, in the manner of a dream, is relevant to a discussion of *Invisible Man*.

The most dreamlike moments are the most significant, the most dramatic. The action is broken into a sequence of dreams, each more memorable than the prosy narrative that connects them. In an interview conducted by the *Paris Review*, Ellison commented, "I despise concreteness in writing, but when reality is deranged in fiction, one must worry about the seams." The seams still show, like the incongruities of a dream or of a myth, but they are as quickly forgotten.

The first page of the Prologue explicates the title: "I am invisible, understand, simply because people refuse to see me." The narrator, nameless throughout, is a man "of substance, of flesh and bone, fiber and liquids." *His* invisibility is a function of *their* blindness (and blindness is undoubtedly one of the most basic and obvious metaphors of the novel). The precision of the title's vagueness is important—*Invisible Man,* without the definite article. This particular invisible man is one of many, not all of whom are Negroes. As Ellison insists in the introduction to *Shadow and Act* (1964) and in his *Harper's* essay, "A Very Stern Discipline," his intention was to write as a man who is also a Negro. The Prologue plays with the narrator's color when he writes that he's not "a spook like those who haunted Edgar Allan Poe," but the narrator wants "to put invisibility down in black and white" because invisibility can be white as well as black.

Accordingly, the epigraphs are nicely paired. The first is from *Benito Cereno*: " 'You are saved,' cried Captain Delano, more and more astonished and pained; 'you are saved: what has cast such a shadow upon you?' " In the unquoted reply, Benito Cereno answers, "The Negro." Neither of Melville's characters was able to *see* the manhood of Babo (the slave who led the mutiny against Benito Cereno). The second epigraph, taken from Eliot's *Family Reunion*, reminds the reader that white men can also be invisible. To miss this is—in a metaphor from the *Harper's* essay—"to allow the single tree of race to obscure our view of the magic forest of art." In the present political crisis, the point needs to be made, but once made, it can be dropped.

The narrator is a Negro and the forms and stuff of his invisibility (if we can speak so) are part and parcel of the experience of Negroes in the United States, created from their defeats and humiliations, their humor, their ecstasy, their language, their culture. In his odyssey, the narrator acts out the stages of Negro history from the Emancipation to the present.

The first stage is apparent acquiescence, but chapter 1 is deceptive. The narrator's grandfather had given him some deathbed advice: "I want you to overcome 'em with yeses, undermine 'em with grins, agree 'em to death and destruction, let 'em swoller you till they vomit or bust wide open." These words, periodically remembered, seem like the answer, initially shunned, which must finally be accepted, but when the narrator *does* act upon these words, the result is a tragicomic holocaust, the race riot described in chapter 25. At first, however, the narrator puzzles over his grandfather's advice and follows the strategy of Booker T. Washington, whose Atlanta Address of 1895 is alluded to in the hand-finger metaphor of the second paragraph and quoted in the narrator's valedictory speech. He says of himself, "I visualized myself as a potential Booker T. Washington." He believes in the myth of Horatio Alger, in the American Dream —and sees the American flag obscenely tattooed on the belly of the soft-thighed dancer whom "the most important men of the town" use to tantalize Negro youths. The initial chapter's progression from the dancer to the "battle-royal" of the blindfolded Negro boxers to the electrified rug to the narrator's Washingtonian speech is a nightmare of humiliation made more horrid by the narrator's delight, after this descent into Hell, in receiving a scholarship to the state college for Negroes. (This and other episodes are related to Dante's descent, alluded to in the Prologue.)

Whether or not Alabama really resembles the Waste Land, the opening section of chapter 2 is an unmistakably Eliotic pastiche of broken fountain, dead grass, sunken rock, and dry winds. The college itself is very like Tuskegee, at least in its situation. (Ellison himself studied music at Tuskegee.) The Founder is drawn from Booker T. Washington, whose rhetoric the narrator continues to accept.

Allowed to chauffeur Mr. Norton, a white trustee, he foolishly fulfills Norton's repressed desires. He takes him to see Trueblood, a Negro who had done what Norton has longed to do, a man who has committed incest with his own daughter. From Trueblood's farm, the narrator goes to the ironically named roadhouse, The Golden Day, where transcendentalism is a mob of maniacs, a collection of the Ids who overwhelm Supercargo, their keeper, their superego. This nightmare, like the others, has its comic aspect. Brushing Norton's white hair, the prostitutes reverse racial stereotypes: "Girl, don't you know that all these rich ole white men got monkey glands and billy goat balls? These ole bastards don't never git enough."

Returning with great difficulty to the school, the narrator learns that Bledsoe, the director, is no Trueblood. He is rather a Machiavellian who sees the world as a "power set-up. . . . But I've made my place in it and I'll have every Negro in the country hanging on tree limbs by morning if it means staying where I am." The confrontation of cynicism and innocence follows the marvelously rhetorical speech of Homer A. Barbee, the preacher whose web of sentiment and exhortation is ripped to shreds by the brutal reality of Bledsoe.

Dismissed from school, the narrator retains his innocence. He heads for New York, "not a city of realities, but of dreams," and is too naïve to open the "letters of introduction" given him by Bledsoe. Still convinced that the white man's ethic of success fits the black man's condition, he is his own Procrustes. The hunt for a job is tiresome reading, but it leads to the satire of the interview with young Mr. Emerson, a homosexual who urges the narrator to meet him at Club Calamus (clearly an allusion to Whitman), who pants to be Huckleberry Finn with this apparently delectable Jim. In what must be a burst of mingled pity and lust, Emerson shows the narrator one of the letters of introduction. It is, of course, a condemnation, another betrayal of innocence and trust.

The next stage is a comedy of colors, in which things look whiter when black is added, in which the Government is the chief purchaser of "Optic White," made by Liberty Paints, used for monuments and other symbols of inauthentic authority. This chapter too is another descent into the Underworld, where aged Lucius Brockway runs the complicated machinery that makes the whitewash possible. The fantasy ends in a fight and an explosion, in a death followed by a rebirth.

The rebirth is simply the renaissance of illusion. The badly injured narrator is now victimized by modern technology as applied by bureaucratic organization. More concretely, he is strapped and wired and electrically shocked by company doctors who see him only as an object. (The electrical shocks are also a reminder of the rug in chapter 1.) He is eventually released to stumble along Lenox Avenue, until he is rescued by Mary Rambo, an Aunt Jemima figure who offers sanctuary rather than a possible identity. She is, in a sense, his Calypso (with no sexual transactions implied).

On his way to the next stage of the sequence, the narrator encounters an aged, unashamedly Negro yam-vendor. The episode is hysterically allusive with hints of Ben Franklin's self-celebrated entry into Philadelphia. The narrator gobbles yams because he *likes* them, and the scene contrasts with the breakfast eaten when he first arrived in New York, the breakfast at which he shunned Southern foods as "an act of discipline." Now he eats defiantly: "I no longer had to worry about who saw me or about what was proper. To hell with all that." He imagines Bledsoe confronted by chitterlings: "Bledsoe, you're a shameless chitterling eater! I accuse you of relishing hog bowels!" Buying more yams because he's a "serious yam eater," he proclaims, "I yam what I am!" Whether this is an echo of the voice on Mount Sinai or a quotation from Popeye the Sailor Man, or both or neither, is left to the reader. But the marvelous moment is followed by a letdown. The third yam is frostbitten—identity isn't that easy to come by.

Then, without intending to, the narrator whose dreams of heroism led only to disgrace becomes a hero. Finding a crowd already angered by an eviction in progress, he speaks to calm them, and incites them to action, for which he is complimented by a strange man and a strange woman, members of the Brotherhood (which is, of course, a Marxist group remarkably like the Communist Party to which Ellison had at one time been attracted).

For the narrator, as for Richard Wright and many other Negro intellectuals, political activity in cooperation with radical whites seemed a likely answer, at least for the moment. The narrator receives a new name from Brother Jack, a new role, and a new identity. He discovers that people treat him not equally but preferentially. Men admire him, women offer themselves to him. But, in gathering the Brotherhood at a building called the Chthonian, Ellison implies that this too is a descent into the Underworld. Brotherhood is illusory. Success breeds envy. Brother Jack, with the aid of the aptly named Brother Wrestrum, soon turns against his protégé. Because of his leadership in Harlem, the narrator is sent downtown to speak on the Woman Question.

He turns exile to advantage. He finds that he is an effective speaker, but for the wrong reasons. " 'Brotherhood, darling,' she said, gripping my biceps with her little hands. 'Teach me, talk to me. . . .' " She hears tom-toms in his voice. While the narrator spreads the gospel of brotherhood in this ancient way, hard-won political gains are lost.

He is recalled and returned to Harlem, where he discovers the degradation of Tod Clifton, the only Negro leader, within the Brotherhood, with abilities remotely near his own. Clifton has become a street-corner merchant of Sambo-dolls, obscene little paper symbols of loss of identity. Upset perhaps by the narrator's angry reaction (he spits on the doll), Clifton loses his head and strikes a policeman. The policeman kills him. As Harlem approaches detonation, the narrator attempts to defuse the situation through funereal ritual —procession, drums, orations.

He learns, when the Brotherhood gathers, that he has misinterpreted History. "Under your leadership, a traitorous merchant of vile instruments of anti-Negro, anti-minority racist bigotry has received the funeral of a hero." When he answers that he acted on his personal responsibility, he is derided—as he was in the first chapter derided and threatened when he spoke, accidentally, of social equality rather than of social responsibility. The Brotherhood is as cynical as Dr. Bledsoe. "We do not shape our policies to the mistaken and infantile notions of the man in the street. Our job is not to *ask* them what they think but to *tell* them." During this encounter, Brother Jack's glass eye tumbles out—eerie symbol of the reiterated theme of blindness.

After the meeting, the narrator wanders the streets of Harlem. When followers of a Black Nationalist leader, Ras the Exhorter, pursue him, he buys himself dark glasses and a hat—and attains still another identity, that of the man of disguises. Now he is mistaken for Rinehart, the numbers-racketeer, the lover, the cynic, the zoot-suited joker, the ghetto-based reincarnation of Melville's Confidence Man. Rinehart's world "was possibility and he knew it. . . . A vast seething, hot world of fluidity, and Rine the rascal was at home in it." Dropping the Hegelian-Marxist notion of freedom as the recognition of necessity, the narrator defines freedom as the recognition of possibility. Now his blindness is ended. Now he will recognize his invisibility and use it to deceive others. "They want a machine? Very well, I'd become a supersensitive confirmer of their misconceptions." But this solution too is a dream.

The narrator conforms to expectations and, as he knew it would, Harlem explodes. It is a Walpurgisnacht through which he moves. "The moon was high now and before me the shattered glass glittered in the street like the water of a flooded river upon the surface of which I ran as in a dream."

He joins the looters, leaves them, sees Ras the Exhorter, now become "Ras the Destroyer upon a great black horse." Suddenly the narrator realizes that he's been duped again—the Brotherhood *wanted* the riot for the martyrs it produced, for its demonstration of the "error" of premature violence.

Ras is not ready to accept the Prodigal Son. He flings his spear at him, misses, sets his men on him. The narrator flings the weapon back, spears Ras through both cheeks, and flees. He finds safety underground, first in a coalchute, where blackness is disguise, where he symbolically burns the deceptive documents and papers he had lugged through his career in the briefcase given him by his high school principal. Like Theseus, he finds his way out, but he stays underground, builds himself the well-lighted hole described in the Prologue.

In the Epilogue, he takes up the affirmative images of the Prologue; he *seems* to remain faithful to the American Dream which most white Americans have betrayed. He ponders his grandfather's advice (and the rhetoric becomes excessively Faulknerian): "Did he [grandfather] mean to affirm the principle, which they [the whites] themselves had dreamed into being out of the chaos and darkness of the feudal past, and which they had violated and compromised to the point of absurdity even in their own corrupt minds? Or did he mean that we had to take the responsibility for all of it, for the men as well as the principle, because we were the heirs who must use the principle, because no other fitted our needs? Not for the power or for the vindication, but because we, with the given circumstances of our origin, could only thus find transcendence?" The principle, the dream, is unquestioned throughout a long paragraph of questions. The assumption is that the unrealized American Dream is not an impossible one.

He repeats, "My world has become one of infinite possibilities." He applies Whitman's rhetoric to the theory of cultural pluralism: "America is woven of many strands; I would recognize them and let it so remain. . . . Our fate is to become one, and yet many—This is not prophecy, but description." These affirmations are supported by the metaphor of hibernation, defined, in the Prologue, as "a covert preparation for a more overt action." In the Prologue, the narrator compares himself to a bear and the bear to the "Easter chick." Now, in the Epilogue, he announces that the hibernation is over: "I must shake off the old skin and come up for breath." But he smells a stench which might be "the smell either of death or of spring—I hope of spring. But don't let me trick you, there *is* a death in the smell of spring." Like the Whitman of "When Lilacs Last in the Dooryard Bloom'd," he seems to realize that spring and winter are reciprocals, that winter is a prerequisite for spring just as death is a prerequisite for rebirth. He is a chastened and illusionless man who prepares now to emerge to play his "socially responsible role."

Or is he? The narrator's ingenuousness has survived so many disillusionments that we are reluctant, as readers, to believe in his final affirmation. He has cried "Wolf!" so often (or "Sheep!") that the reader is liable to respond with the skepticism lacking in the narrator. Marcus Klein comments on this problem: "There is a constant increase of wattage, but what is to be seen remains the same." I.e., the acceptance of invisibility, the determination to use this invisibility for some unspecified but socially responsible purpose.

What is the role the narrator now must play? By universalizing the significance of the adventures ("Who knows but that, on the lower frequencies, I speak for you?"), Ellison has put himself in the position of a man maintaining—if he ends affirmatively—that solutions exist for problems which are political, social, and psychological rather than literary. The Epilogue concerns the narrator's state of mind, but it includes an implicit judgment of the State of the Nation.

Given the present State of the Nation, it is hard not to read the conclusion as ironic. Perception *n* must be as illusory as perception *n-1*. But we know, from external evidence, that Ellison did *not* mean irony. In his *Paris Review* interview he says: "In my novel the narrator's development is one through blackness to light; that is, from ignorance to enlightenment: invisibility to visibility. He leaves the South and goes North; this, as you will notice in reading Negro folk tales, is always the road to freedom—the movement upward. You have the same thing again when he leaves his underground cave for the open." The scheme, taken from Kenneth Burke, is tripartite—purpose, passion, perception. It is the smoke and ashes of burned cities that make the Epilogue seem ironic when it is not.

The relation of a novel to its cultural context resembles the narrator's room, with its 1,369 lights lit by current stolen from Monopolated Light and Power. Novels—and especially *this* novel—draw much of their power from the context to which they indirectly refer. Good novels, in turn, illuminate the society in which they are written. But Ellison's context has changed, or has seemed to change. A statistically obvious *improvement* in the situation of American Negroes has been accompanied by a greater sense (in many) of deprivation and frustration. The unparalleled (in America) openness of the present conflicts between blacks and whites has made the novel seem prophetic in its nightmares and innocent in its small measure of optimism.

But perhaps it is useful to consider a contrary proposition. If the narrator has, like Trueblood, looked into chaos and survived, if he really has descended to the Underworld and returned, then—perhaps—his affirmations are a clue to the labyrinth of American society in the sixties. Ellison may not be our Theseus, but there are other writers on the loose, doomsayers, who resemble Minotaurs.

Focus on Norman Mailer's
Why Are We in Vietnam?

> Now, we have such a marvelous loss of boundaries that your
> criticism of a happening could be a piece of music or a scien-
> tific experiment or a trip to Japan or a trip to your local
> shopping market.
>
> John Cage

1

About Mailer, criticism must be brave and cunning.

He has created an expensive Legend, and the Legend has become part of his Work. Other writers—Byron to Heming-way—have done the same. We all know the risks: a sleek Legend turns cannibal, and devours both Man and Work. We all know the risks, but it is the writer who takes them.

One of the quirks of a Legend is this: readers respond to it and pretend that their response is to the Work. Mailer haters hate his Legend—they do not know *him*—and conclude that his Work is bad. While the reverse is also true, men, alas, rationalize their hates better than their loves.

The joke may be on everyone. What if the Legend were a fiction as exacting and merciless as the Work? What if the Man needed to create a Legend in order to live—with dan-ger, with generosity, with rage—and so create the Work? What if the reader required a fiction to include himself (Reader plus Man) and the writer (Author plus Man)? Thus literature makes itself, and the imagination transmutes our needs into shadow play, without walls, without lights.

But here the joke suddenly ends: all good fictions pay a ransom to reality in daily courage, and so become true.

2

What are the requirements for reading *Why Are We in Vietnam?* None. I offer, nonetheless, a small exercise in hurtful meditation. Let us recall one or more of these:

1] The liquids of love.
2] A pimple invisible beyond adolescence.
3] Adrenalin, vintage a few seconds.
4] The aroma of our burial urn.
5] Sweat gathering in the palm of the hand.
6] An animal with yellow or green eyes.
7] America now.

3

Norman Mailer has never been to Vietnam. Neither have I. Fact and fiction have now become the same, and they require from us a new consciousness. The novel as history, history as fiction. Precisely Vietnam.

4

Obscenity is crucial to this novel.

Obscenity repels us first, then it disturbs. When we say that it bores us—how debonair!—we try to keep ourselves intact. We are, after all, what we are because we have transformed outwards its demands.

Obscenity is protest. We are right to fear it; vengeance befouls its breath. The return of the repressed. Obscenity begins as protest, ends as assault. Afterwards, release.

Obscenity reminds us of corporeal experience. Unheroic man, clowning between food and excrement, blood and semen. This is the comic element.

Obscenity celebrates; there is sacramental power behind its reductive rage. Nothing merely personal, nothing perishable. The force of obscenity moves the stars.

Obscenity reaches for the root of language, clutches the mystery. When the thick sap rushes upwards, symbols explode. This is also the force of obscenity.

Obscenity, Henry Miller says, seeks "to awaken, to usher in a sense of reality. In a sense, its use by the artist may be compared to the use of the miraculous by the master."

Obscenity, in Mailer's novel, repels and releases. Does it also constrict? Rarely. Its spirit is genital, procreative. Unlike Sade, Beckett, or Burroughs, Mailer conceals no horror of the womb; his excremental language denies itself. Ass means, to D. J., human vulnerability, exposure and self-exposure; he remembers his father who bites him viciously in the rump. Shit means the deadness of the world, defeat. The initiation of D. J. takes him beyond the vulnerability of ass and the deadness of shit. This boy knows how to put us on, pretending to be "marooned on the balmy tropical isle of Anal Referent Metaphor!"

5

It takes an America lover to recognize another.

Mailer is a deep lover of America. Anyone who cannot see this may be hiding something worse than treason from himself. Read the "Terminal Intro Beep and Out," dirge and epiphany to "North America, that sad deep sweet beauteous mystery land. . . ." D. J. is speaking, but the poetry is Mailer's. And how many others still remember the Alamo, Texas courage, "the kink which resides in the heart of the Lone Star?"

Deep lovers of America see its depths. Even Rusty, who can be right, senses the paradox: "But I think it's a secret crime that America, which is the greatest nation ever lived, better read a lot of history to see how shit-and-sure a proposition that is, is nonetheless represented, indeed even symbolized by an eagle, the most miserable of the scavengers, worse than a crow." This to D. J. who senses more than his father knows; D. J. sees the depths.

America as scavenger. Why are we in Vietnam?

D. J. knows more: "electric come machines"; sex among red-blooded Americans—"one can't come unless he's squinting down a gunsight, and the other won't produce unless his wife sticks a pistol up his ass"; the mysterious mastermind who runs America, with "a plastic asshole installed in his brain whereby he can shit out all his corporate management of thoughts"—G. P. A. for Great Plastic Asshole; cowardice in the core of violence—"Rusty bit his ass so bad because he was too chicken to bite Hallelujah's beautiful butt—she'd have made him pay half a million dollars for each separate hole in her marble palace"; will and wonder and the death ray off men like Charley Wilson or Robert McNamara; "Independent, Autonomous, Non-pattern-directed Ductile-type Magnification and Expansion Assertions in Non-Operational Gravitational Ultra-Multi-Mach Ellipsoid Program-Oriented Satellite Capsule Negotiations"; wild life gone crazy in Alaska, howitzer and helicopter hunting; shattered love and respect for the fathers in America; civilization and syphilization; p. 110 f., all the paranoia of the land bursting in sex and race and politics; morticians, necrophilia, formaldehyde; Texas and Harlem.

Why are we in Vietnam? "Vietnam, hot damn."

D. H. Lawrence saw America to these depths, loved it less, cursed, chanted, and wrote: "The essential American soul is hard, isolate, stoic, and a killer. It has never yet melted."

Truth is terrible when it is less than complete.

6

Everywhere force, flux, power visible and invisible, magic, improvisation, you make it on the distractions, dynamite in Rusty's groin, in Hallie's womb, D. J. up tight with the concept of Dread but heaving language with Harlem madness, the whole State of Alaska one nervous system, air is the medium, the message, Toynbee coefficient, challenge and response, Faustian man gone haywire, Big Ollie placating all the wolves of creation nose to a twig, saxifrage cracking rock, magnum guns to bust an elephant or hollow a tunnel, the psycho magnetic fields of the North broken, grizzers roaring, avalanche of fur or "hell in a whirlwind," "no man cell in him can now forget that if the center of things is insane, it is insane with force, heuuuuuu, . . ." and the dying gold brown eyes, "seen through a ruby crystal ball," of Grizzly giving off unearthly intelligence to D. J., "Baby, you haven't begun," the message received, the crystals, the forms, always receiving from less-form, from life, "Urine is a pipe running the dissolution of all unheard messages," the boys, Tex and D. J., training for "special powers" on ghoul surgery and closet fucks but waiting for the Pole, all needles pointing to heart of ire, telepathy, superconductivity, "magnetic-electro fief of the dream," Aurora Borealis and the jumping lights in the Brooks Range, Manichean Mailer reversing the field as "God or the Devil takes over in sleep," hate waves jamming the murder in white wolf, mother nature "big and dangerous and mysterious as a beautiful castrating cunt when she's on the edge between murder and love," sunspots, God talking in the frozen light, "yeah God was here, and He was real and no man was He, but a beast, some beast of a giant jaw and cavernous mouth with a full cave's breath and fangs, and secret call: 'come to me,' and force everywhere, from beginning to end, 'come to me,'" that's a kind of love.

7

Why Are We in Vietnam?, like some crazy crystal, is a form that receives on one frequency and emits on another. This is a question of cunning. Call it, if you wish, technique.

1] The narrative is in the first person, D. J., "disc jockey of America," speaks, sustains his monologue, crackling, obscene, weird, through two hundred pages. He really wants to tell the simple truth, like other adolescents from Huck Finn to Holden Caulfield. But who is he? D. J., son of Rusty and Hallie Jethroe, Texan, or some genius Spade up in Harlem? Does he lie, does he dream? Who can witness his story? "The fact of the matter is that you're up tight with a mystery, me, and this mystery can't be solved because I'm the center of it and I don't comprehend, not necessarily, I could be traducing myself." The monologue is a fantasy, and therein lies its peculiar license and truth. What D. J. cannot know—say Ruby Lil—he invents. Thus was the American nightmare also invented. And $\sqrt{-1}$.

2] The narrative is also memory. Two years have passed, Mailer repeats, since the Alaska hunt, and D. J. is sitting in a "Dallas ass manse" on his eighteenth birthday; "form is more narrative, memory being always more narrative than the tohu-bohu of the present. . . ." Mailer waves to Proust. The transformation of D. J., his initiation, requires a new consciousness to give it form. It is a successful initiation if D. J. can tell it the way Mailer does.

3] The "Intro Beeps" alternate with the "Chapters." This works better in the beginning than in the end where memory and reflection merge. The more D. J. knows, the more his actions and his thoughts converge. But Mailer has a good story, adventure and hunt, to pull us through the songathon of America's own wandering troubadour. Mailer slows the pace, swells the rhetoric, but cries, "wait and see, wait and see." Drama and suspense, heroic action with tongue in cheek.

4] The parodic tone criticizes everything without destroying the possibilities of heroism. Spoof, spoof, rime, and pun. But bravery and truth remain. Professor Mailer says: "Comedy is the study of the unsound actions of the cowardly under stress, just as tragedy is equal study time of the brave under heroic but enigmatic, reverberating, resonant conditions of loss. . . ." But the novel is neither comedy nor tragedy. Call it heroic parody, which means that it must also parody itself, undercut itself. "Nonetheless, if you are really reading this and I am really writing it (which I don't know—it's a wise man who knows *he* is the one who is doing the writer's writing). . . ."

5] The language hops and bops, a new, obscene, metaphysical language full of wit, conceit, learning, defiance, misery, insight and self-delight, hallelujah and hallucination, mad-dog viciousness, full of smell, full of touch. Mailer knows that the hierarchy of senses tumbles from sight to hearing to taste to smell to touch—the more primitive, the more ineluctable. The senses are here. This is why the language rarely lapses into anti-language, neon color, or stroboscopic sound.

8

A novel lives its fullest life in certain dramatic scenes: Julien Sorel brandishing a sword at Mlle de la Mole (*The Red and the Black*), Prince Andrei waiting for a shell to explode on the fields of Borodino (*War and Peace*), etc.

Two scenes in Mailer's novel possess, in part, that quality:
A] The great bear dies, conveying his knowledge to D. J. while Rusty betrays his son: "Final end of love of one son for one Father."
B] Tex and D. J. under the Aurora Borealis, feeling their murder and their love for one another, purified at last from themselves and the greed of America.

Such scenes crash through $\sqrt{-1}$ to the archetypes of our race. Man and Beast and God, Father and Son and Brother, the Spirit of Place, come through.

9

Revolution is no longer radical enough.

The imagination is the teleological organ of evolution. It predicts and fulfills change. At the center of every fancy, a fact waits to be born.

Your violence: the ultimate resource of your enemy.

Creation is the masterwork of Eros, and its Form is Change. Metamorphosis is paedamorphosis.

Guilt: the obscene debt we owe our ancestors. Guilt is to responsibility what onanism is to love.

Choose Life. But choose Death over Immortality. Evil is the flower of Immortality as vampires and werewolves know.

Silence: the alteration of consciousness.

10

Dear Norman:
You said there were Barons and Counts among men. I said there is Faustian and there is Orphic heroism. We can agree on "the aristocracy of achieved talent," and the enhancement of life in its struggle with itself. But the warring vision can have its snobberies too. The sweat or blood we shed waters the laurel tree from which leaves are taken to crown prettily our head.

More: the time has come for man to break the syntax of his dreams, and speak a language stones and gods can hear. Harlem and Dallas are not the same though every night they meet secretly in our dreams. The stones are dumb to their converse, and the gods yawn.

Who knows but at the silent, magnetic Pole America still waits for Columbus to be born?

Sincerely yours,
Ihab

Gift to the World

The Average American—the benevolent fellow who has a
wife, a car, a TV, a mortgage, and 2⅖ths children, and gives
to his church, the Community Chest, the annual Firemen's
Ball, and various charity drives—fervently believes that democracy is an American invention. It was the creation of
Franklin and Washington, who were early and less polished
simulacra of Barry Goldwater and Richard Nixon. Since he is
truly average, he is a college graduate, but although he
avoided the liberal arts, he has heard of Thomas Jefferson,
whom he regards as a weak sister, tolerated by the Founders.
There are always weak sisters around—Adlai Stevenson and
Senator Eugene McCarthy, for example. Rather given to
needlework as thinkers, they do no harm so long as they
know their place and don't try to get above it. But it was the
practical men, Franklin and Washington—*and* Hamilton, he
nearly forgot Hamilton—who made America and the Constitution, which is Democracy.

To suggest that democracy is as old as Greece, and that
the concept had many modifications and amplifications before it reached the Founding Fathers is to court the charge
of treason or communism, or possibly both. Yet the Founding Fathers, who were more numerous than our Average
Friend remembers, unlike him were great readers and knew
practically every writer and thinker who had busied himself
with the concept of democracy. What is more, they cited
these predecessors in letters to their friends, to one another,
and in the formal debates through which they shaped their
thinking. In burrowing and digging for ideas, they found
some names that even well-informed persons do not think of
as contributors to anything politically American. For example, Thucydides, Polybius, Epictetus, Epicurus, Lucretius,
Tacitus, Justinian, Grotius, Nedham, Neville, Hawles, Som-
ers, Burlamque, Shaftesbury, Bolinbroke, Blackstone, Price,

and Volney. When familiar contributors, like Plato, John Locke, Montesquieu, and Pufendorf are added to the list, one may fairly question whether the Founders had an original idea. Certainly they rejected all the extreme ones. In a large sense, their Constitution was a synthesis of their serious reading—something that Americans have almost ceased to do, thus becoming less and less like the Founding Fathers.

It is not here proposed to analyze the original Constitution for its democratic elements, which were largely confined to the Preamble, the section establishing election by the people (as determined by the states) to the House of Representatives, and the carefully guarded right of amendment. But one thing is very clear—it was not in the heads of the Founding Fathers to give the people through this instrument a democracy. *The Federalist Papers*, as has been pointed out time and again, hawked the Constitution as creating a sounder and safer thing—a republic. James Madison describes the conflict of interests in any society as an inevitable breeder of "factions," or dissenting minorities (words he does not use), and touts the Constitution for its capacity to keep them in check. "Should a popular insurrection happen in one of the confederate States," Alexander Hamilton adds, "the others are able to quell it." All contend that the system of checks and balances cunningly contrived for the separate containment of the legislative, executive, and judicial powers makes the Constitution a safe and enduring instrument. Against the republic which they had fashioned, they held up only a "pure" democracy—a cumbersome thing in which the voters assembled *viva voce* to do their business. Did anyone contend for it, or was it a straw horse easily knocked down? They argued speciously that the more persons a representative stood for in this representative republic the more there were to check on his conduct. Yet the saving grace of *The Federalist Papers* is their constant reiteration of "the people are the only legitimate fountain of power," for if they championed a document more notable for fences than vistas, they had these words to confound their cautions.

The Founding Fathers came by their cautions legitimately: they were astute students of history (as we have seen) and could check off more failures of democracy in history than successes. Further, their experience and that of their ancestors put them in fear of disorders and tumults. Cromwellian days, when the people took things into their own hands, were a common inherited and unhappy recollection. So were the hundred uprisings, rebellions, and petty revolutions Professor Andrews has recorded in colonial history. Seven years of war and the riots which occurred in the states when they were bound loosely together by the Articles of Confederation were powerful admonitory factors to any idealisms held by the framers, most of whom had had some share in framing their state constitutions, on which, save possibly that of Virginia, the federal Constitution was an improvement. Nevertheless it can be argued that what made the Constitution acceptable was not the merits of the document but the universal resolution for peace and order. New York expressly instructed its delegate at the Convention to "produce *a firm national government.*" Firmness was also stressed by some of the other states. Caution and resolution, however, have left us with an electoral college, a disproportionate representation from the agrarian states, and the strangulation of legislation through seniority rule in Senate committees, a power granted it in the right to determine its own procedures.

American democracy, as we know it today, is not really a product of the original Constitution, but it is partially a product of our experience of living with it and modifying it by amendment and executive act and by interpreting it through the courts. The first ten amendments created a Bill of Rights; Amendments XII–XV freed the slaves and forbade the abridgment of the rights of male individuals by the states; Amendment XVII broke up the "millionaires' club" and made the popular election of senators mandatory; and Amendment XIX extended suffrage to women. For over a century the Supreme Court was the instrument of the "rigid constructionalists" of the Constitution—it has been observed that the Court found every piece of social legislation in the nineteenth century unconstitutional; Theodore Roosevelt growled that the Founding Fathers had no intention of making the Constitution "a strait jacket." Influenced by the rise of the new social jurisprudence and led by Holmes, Brandeis, Cardoza, and Warren, the Court in the twentieth century has taken into account the consequences of its rulings as well as the precedents it had for those rulings. The result has been a liberal Court whose decisions have pushed further in the direction of equal opportunities for all than the Founding Fathers ever dreamed that this society would. When the Court looked to the free public schools and the state universities, it looked to America's most important original contribution to democracy. In destroying the "separate but equal" concept of the school and in insisting on complete integration, the Court created a mini-democracy that should develop, as its youths mature, into a full democracy. Meanwhile, the extralegal concept of "the right to work" had been exploited in the Great Depression, largely through daring executive leadership, to create the CCC, the WPA, and the PWA, so that that right could be exercised. Halting our enumeration of things that have been done to secure a better society, if not a good one, with minimum wage laws, social security, and medicare, though there is more that could be included, we can easily discern that the pragmatic contributions to our current conception of democracy have been far greater than the gift of the republic, which was the gift of the Founding Fathers. Which does our Average Citizen have in mind when he speaks of American democracy?

He probably hasn't any very clear idea, but relying on his averageness, we may suppose it an amorphous thing made up of vague elements from both categories, minus a gamut of pronounced prejudices, much more definitely defined than his preferences. It may, however, include his passion for *things*, noted especially as typifying by Galbraith, which are a product of our enterprise, an enterprise he is certain is one of the sure results of our democracy—if, indeed, cause and result are not reversed. An awkward package, but one he proposes to leave on the doorstep of the world. Vietnam is one nightmare consequence of our dream of making the world safe for democracy.

For he is obsessed as ever with Wilsonianism (though he doesn't call it that) and wants to make the world safe for democracy, while in our present chaos, it would be far better if democracy were made safe for the world. The Cold War and the success of Russia and China in manufacturing the atomic bomb have increased his apprehension about the future of the world and his resolution that democracy, *our* democracy, shall prevail in it. To him, communism is monolithic, acting everywhere in perfect concord, with the destruction of democracy as its single aim. Unfortunately early in this century the Comintern did a better job indoctrinating the Average American than it did with the Serbs and the Croats, the Poles and the Czechs. Half of the physical world may be Communist, but it is divided into nations much more aware of, and eager to preserve, their national identity than they are to obey the dictates of either Moscow or Peking. The differences between those two centers of power, displayed openly in many instances, are duplicated in the majority of intercommunist relations. Arthur Schlesinger, Jr., has forcefully maintained that, since World War II, intense nationalism has been more characteristic of the nations in the Communist sphere than concerted effort to advance their polity. Even the experienced revolutionist Ché Guevara failed miserably in distant and "ripe" Bolivia primarily because he did not concede enough to Bolivians of his persuasion.

The fears of the Average Citizen have not only backed American witch-hunts, particularly in the Joe McCarthy era, and dubiously labeled every protest movement in this country as "Communist-inspired," but have supported a dangerous and self-defeating foreign policy that has cost this country some of its natural allies and alienated a list of others. The enormously expensive and dangerous policy of "containment" may have had some merit in the Stalinist era, but it has become a policy of folly since that time. No one in the State Department apparently gave any heed to Khrushchev's announced policy of "peaceful coexistence," yet with listening posts in every consulate, it should have been aware of the struggle between Russia and China for leadership in the Communist movement, taken note of the power plays within the coalition, been conscious of the stiffening nationalism, and developed a different policy. Instead, we persisted in the policy of "containment"—which was one policy for all Communist countries, save Yugoslavia. This had the splendid merit of simplicity—one mental exercise did everything, that is, there was no need to contemplate adjustment of policy to each country and to know all the facts on which to base such a policy. Everything could be carried under the not-too-capacious hat of the Secretary of State. Meanwhile, in the U.N., our ambassador not infrequently operated at cross-purposes with the Secretary, giving rise abroad to false hopes and revealing at home the need of some fundamental reorganization of our cumbersome department.

Reflecting the paramount fear of the Average Citizen, we created three great alliances, in Western Europe, Southeast Asia, and in the Western Hemisphere to make "containment" effective. They were supported by promises of military aid and much money. These are menacing alliances, as menacing to Poland, Cuba, and North Korea as they are to Russia and China. They freeze our foreign relations and make vis à vis treatments extraordinarily difficult. If they cannot now be liquidated, we should look to the time when they might be. With World War I we began sending money, arms, and supplies to our friends and defeated enemies; after World War II our munificence skyrocketed. Never in history has there been such largesse. In so far as he could regard this as a patent demonstration of the success of democracy, our Average Citizen grumbled but supported the effort. But he expected "them foreigners" to get on their own feet very soon. And he expected gratitude and devotion. It never occurred to him that the recipients were aware of his terror and looked on all that he gave as an expression of protective self-interest. When it did for them what he wished, they naturally regarded him as paid in full. Affection cannot be purchased in international relations—in fact, it does not exist.

Our Average Citizen has always been a benevolent fellow at heart. He has always been so entranced with his democracy that he has wanted to make a gift of it to the world. It is the most enduring made-in-America fantasy. Senator Thomas Hart Benton advocated extending our western border "to China"; Walt Whitman wished to include "Kanada" in "these States"; Joaquin Miller would have adopted Mexico and Panama. So there is an historical background to what our Average Citizen regards as his philanthropy and his dream for a democratic world. To a more dispassionate appraiser of his urges and gifts, they seem more like compulsions and gestures to a *new imperialism*. It is perhaps not so frank as that of Theodore Roosevelt and Albert J. Beveridge, but it is the same thing essentially.

Indeed, if we apply the classic tests of imperialism, as stated by John A. Hobson in 1903, to the international conduct of the United States since World War II, we fulfill them much more completely than did Great Britain. Basic to Hobson's interpretation is the underconsumption of capital at home with the compulsion to invest it abroad, in colonies, in Hobson's view, though that has been challenged by D. K. Fieldhouse, who thinks that much of Britain's surplus capital was invested in the United States and elsewhere. Consider our foreign aid program as not solely beneficent but to relieve the glut of capital and inflation in America through taxation and distribution (rather than the device of foreign investment, though there was much of that in countries like Germany and England where American models of foreign cars could be manufactured) and some of the benignity of our munificence is washed away. Is one to suppose that the acute foreign observer was unaware of the way in which this worked? Secondly, Hobson felt that the relief of overpopulation was another cause of imperialism. If again we look upon the "containment" policy of America as the new imperialism, our stationing of troops abroad fulfills another test of imperialism. How many troops have we had stationed in Germany, France (prior to their rejection by De Gaulle), England, Spain, and Turkey since World War II? How many in South Korea? Vietnam? What would have been the effect on our economy of returning them all at once with their newly acquired skills, a hostile critic might inquire. The third test is the acquisition of new acreage—the protection of which the British found so costly as to offset the advantages, perhaps completely. Our acreage gains, mostly in the islands taken from Japan, we are gradually returning to their former possessor, save possibly Taiwan, but consider our acquisition of *choice* acreage for bases and airstrips, the maintenance of which is as great as those of England's army and navy and Foreign Office before the war.

England's imperialism produced a class of parasites dependent on its perpetuation. Is there not a sense in which much of the army officialdom of the United States is parasitic and dedicated to perpetuating the policy of "containment"? And what about the Central Intelligence Agency? The activities of this organization are secret, but enough has emerged about those activities to disturb thoughtful Americans, if not the Average Citizen, who probably is not ready to force a greater accounting than is at present enforced. The confession that the Washington end of the agency is eight weeks in arrears in reading the dispatches of its agents points to the inflation of its activities and the uselessness of much of its espionage. Pity prevents us from placing the Peace Corps among these organizations: perhaps it is no more than an expression of the naïve good will that characterizes American action in foreign affairs. We cannot say that, while it ameliorates the policy of "containment" outside the area contained, it is parasitic in the sense that the CIA is.

It is idiotic to try to fix the blame for our involvement in Vietnam on any one individual, either in the State Department or the White House, so long as the policy of "containment" is ardently desired by our Average Citizen. Vietnam is an inevitable consequence of that policy; so is the seizing of the *Pueblo*. Americans will furiously assail the conduct of our affairs in that bomb-and-rocket-blighted country ("We had to destroy Ben Tre in order to save it") who will not even whisper a word against the policy which has produced our frustration there and has the potential of producing endless involvements elsewhere. "Containment" is the ineffectively disguised form of a new imperialism, matching the definition at every point. It is the thing we mocked England for and vowed that, as a nation, we would never indulge in. Yet here we are. It provides the exhausting conflicts, the bleeding incisions on the body politic characteristic of imperialism, through which the historical good will of America is drained away. It contributes to the moral frustration of Americans at the present time, which Archibald MacLeish, perhaps wrongly, assigns to our lack of control over our technology and science.

No sensible person advocates a return to isolationism, but a vis à vis relationship with each individual country, one of mutual regard, is a policy that much commends itself and was in the main the practice of our State Department before World War I. It is one, now that our Average American has seen demonstrated the consequences of a lumping, undiscriminating, monolithic policy, he should prefer. It will not always be successful, but it has a greater chance of success than the policy presently in vogue, which has cost us, in Vietnam alone, over forty thousand young men and the distrust of the world. In accepting a vis à vis relationship, however, we must also accept the idea that to impose democracy on another country is against the very nature of democracy itself. It is not a gift that can be wrapped up for the world. We did not achieve it ourselves as a result of our revolution. It was, as we have seen, a slow, pragmatic development of over a century of growth after that revolution and after the adoption of the Constitution. As weaknesses in, or hindrances to, our aspirations for a better society were revealed, we manufactured solutions that have in a degree satisfied us, at least till we have more experience with them. Democracy lies in the method as much as in the results, and method, born in a sense out of each occasion, has to be learned and cannot be freely transferred. We must let other countries alone to originate their own form of government. We should particularly check the CIA, which apparently has a penchant for dangerous, undemocratic meddling. There may be instances where a dictatorship might develop a primitive people faster than a blundering attempt to initiate sophisticated democratic forms. A dictatorship, for example, would probably be more capable of reducing graft and wholesale corruption, such as exists in South Vietnam, than is the devious "democracy" we have sponsored there. If that country ever has an effective government, it must be of the people's choosing and development. One should not despair if the National Liberation Front comes to dominate it, for it may adopt eventually democratic measures (with others) that will serve the Vietnamese better than any imposed forms, whatever their origin. The best American gift is hands-off as soon as possible. Of Wilsonianism, only one aspect has validity: the self-determination of peoples. It is dubious if we should even send "advisers" unless they are requested. In any cold appraisal, we have been as great meddlers as the Russians in their sphere of influence since 1945.

A vis à vis relationship is not isolationism. Its end is mutual understanding and mutual effort to improve all manner of relations between the two nations treating with each other; nor does it inhibit international conferences for the general good. As a super-power, America needs to acknowledge only one other super-power, Russia. The recent successful international conference which produced the so-called nuclear nonproliferation treaty was successful because the super-powers thought alike and worked to a common end. It is a hopeful sign that the USSR and the U.S. could enter into an agreement which was limiting to themselves, even if it were more limiting to others. Further, both look to imposing still other mutual controls. We have never appreciated how much Khrushchev altered the whole policy of Russia — how the aggressive communism of Stalin has given way to "peaceful coexistence," or how much Stalinism is itself despised in Russia. We must remember that between ten and fifteen million Russians perished in the torture chambers of the N.K.V.D. while Stalin was in power. If one could trust our Average Citizen to read, one would commend to him Andrei D. Sakarov's *Thoughts on Progress, Peaceful Co-existence, and Intellectual Freedom.* Dr. Sakarov, a prominent physicist and member of the Russian Academy of Sciences, obviously is thoroughly acquainted with the recent histories of Russia and the United States and has reflected deeply on postwar, senseless confrontation. He sees that a collision between them would destroy the world. But everybody sees that. What makes Sakarov illuminating to the West, particularly to the U.S., is his dismissal of the old Stalinist dogmatisms: capitalism doesn't necessarily enslave the worker — revolution in a country like the U.S. would presently do the worker more harm than good. And above everything else, he wants more intellectual freedom and democracy in Russia. He sees rapprochement between the socialist system of Russia and the capitalist system of America as not only possible but imperative. He is for cooperation between the super-powers to aid underprivileged peoples and to reduce poverty, pollution, and disease everywhere. Plainly he is not speaking for himself alone, but for a considerable intelligentsia in the USSR.

But Sakarov mentions a neo-Stalinism in Russia and denounces several of that ilk by name. If we continue to press "containment," we shall strengthen this repudiated element in Russian society, but if we can reach a vis à vis relationship with that country, the whole world will profit. If we do not, the reactionaries, the Stalinists, will prevail, not merely in Russia, but in Poland, East Germany, and Hungary, where they still rule, and we shall have other Czechoslovakias. The gift for which the world hungers and which, at least, it is partially in our power to give, is peace.

Notes

The Dream Metaphor—HEILMAN

1. One thinks, however, of Joyce, who declared "history . . . a nightmare from which I am trying to awake" and went on to entertain a dream containing all history.

2. *Tess of the D'Urbervilles*, chapter 11. Hardy might have found a secular version of the same doctrine in Horace's *Delicta maiorum immeritus lues*: you, guiltless, will pay for the misdeeds of your forefathers.

3. See the chapter "Ersatz Religions" in *Science, Politics, and Gnosticism* (Chicago: Regnery, 1968), pp. 85–88.

4. Incidentally, Thomas Hardy presents *Tess of the D'Urbervilles* as a "dreamy" girl, and he manages to portray in her the doubleness of the dream: the imaging of a goal, and the faulty grasp of uncooperative or hostile circumstance. Compare also Clym Yeobright and Jude Fawley.

5. This is evident in Carolyn See's essay, "The Hollywood Novel: The American Dream Cheat," in *Tough Guy Writers of the Thirties*, ed. David Madden (Carbondale and Edwardsville: Southern Illinois University Press, 1968), pp. 199–217. In this essay, however, it appears sometimes to be the dream itself which is the cheat, sometimes the society which cheats the dreamer. Miss See notes that the "dream girl" (my term, not hers) is an element in "the dream." The title character in Elmer Rice's *Dream Girl* (1945) dreams rather than is dreamed. In O'Neill's *The Dreamy Kid* (1919) a young Negro tough is named "Dreamy"; the name is simply an ironic commentary on his commonplace end—arrest for unheroic murder. Wright Morris' characters appear repeatedly to be actuated by "the American dream" in its more commonplace sense; at least the term appears regularly in David Madden's *Wright Morris* (New York: Twayne, 1964). See pp. 20, 27, 29, 61, 65 ff., 74, 102, 132, 136, 144.

6. Cf. Walter J. Meserve, *An Outline History of American Drama* (Totowa, New Jersey: Littlefield, Adams, 1965), p. 358: "Both *The Sandbox* (1960) and *The American Dream* (1961) show the emptiness of the American dream." The same idea has a central place in Frederick Lumley's general discussion of Albee

in *New Trends in 20th Century Drama: A Survey Since Ibsen and Shaw* (New York: Oxford, 1967), pp. 319 ff. According to Lumley, George's "killing" of the son in *Who's Afraid of Virginia Woolf?* reveals "the truth, the whole truth, that the American dream doesn't exist" (p. 319). Again, "dream" is undefined.

7. The quotation is from Howard M. Harper, Jr., *Desperate Faith* (Chapel Hill: University of North Carolina Press, 1967), p. 124. I am indebted to Harper's general discussion of Mailer.

8. A comparable sense of duality appears almost casually in the language of observers of the American scene. Mailer speaks of "that combination of ecstasy and violence which is the dream life of the nation" (quoted by Howard M. Harper, Jr., in *Desperate Faith*, p. 130). David Madden mentions "the urge to violence that is the Siamese twin of the American urge to peace and tranquility" (*Tough Guy Writers of the Thirties*, p. xxix). The word *violence* used by both writers will do as a synonym of destructiveness; "ecstasy" and "peace and tranquility" are different statements of the other side of the dream.

9. Thinking primarily of the American Stalinists of the 1930's, Alfred Kazin writes warmly of the inhumanity of people who were "merely the slaves of an idea." See *Starting Out in the Thirties* (Boston: Little, Brown, 1965), pp. 139–41.

Sinclair Lewis and Western Humor—AUSTIN

1. Lewis acknowledged his early reading of Dunne and Ade in "My First Day in New York," *The Man from Main Street* (New York, 1953), p. 58. My use of Minnesota newspapers in this essay was made possible through the assistance of the Minnesota Historical Society and especially of Mr. Edward Swanson, Head, Newspaper Division, and through the support of the Research and Projects Committee of Southern Illinois University, Edwardsville.

2. In *A Time of Harvest: American Literature, 1910–1960,* ed. Robert E. Spiller (New York, 1962), pp. 54–64.

A *Selective Bibliography*

1. Novels and Stories

Adams, Henry. *Democracy: An American Novel.* New York: New American Library, 1961.

Anderson, Sherwood. *Poor White.* New York: Horace Liveright, 1920.

———. "The Egg." In *The Triumph of the Egg.* New York: Horace Liveright, 1921.

Arnow, Harriette. *The Dollmaker.* New York: Macmillan, 1954.

Barth, John. *The Sot-Weed Factor.* Garden City, N. Y.: Doubleday, 1960.

———. *Giles Goat-Boy.* Garden City, N. Y.: Doubleday, 1966.

Bellow, Saul. *Dangling Man.* New York: Vanguard Press, 1944.

———. *The Victim.* New York: Vanguard Press, 1947.

———. *The Adventures of Augie March.* New York: Viking, 1953.

———. *Seize the Day.* New York: Viking, 1956.

———. *Henderson the Rain King.* New York: Viking, 1959.

———. *Herzog.* New York: Viking, 1964.

Berger, Yves. *The Garden.* New York: George Braziller, 1963.

Blechman, Burt. *Stations.* New York: Random House, 1964.

Burroughs, William. *Naked Lunch.* New York: Grove, 1959.

Cahan, Abraham. *The Rise of David Levinsky.* New York: Harper, 1917.

Conroy, Jack. *The Disinherited.* New York: Covici, Friede, 1933.

Cooper, James Fenimore. *The Oak Openings.* New York: Burgess, Stringer, 1848.

———. *The Prairie* (1827). New York: Rinehart, 1950.

Davis, Clyde Brion. *The Great American Novel.* New York: Farrar & Rinehart, 1938.

Dos Passos, John. *U.S.A.* New York: Harcourt, Brace, 1939.

Ellison, Ralph. *Invisible Man.* New York: Random House, 1952.

Fast, Howard. *The American.* New York: Duell, Sloan & Pearce, 1946.

Faulkner, William. "The Bear" in *Go Down, Moses.* New York: Random House, 1940.

Ferber, Edna. *American Beauty.* New York: Doubleday, 1931.

216

Fitzgerald, F. Scott. *The Great Gatsby*. New York: Charles Scribner's Sons, 1925.

———. *Tender Is the Night*. New York: Charles Scribner's Sons, 1934.

Foster, Michael. *American Dream*. New York: William Morrow, 1937.

Friedman, Bruce Jay. *Stern*. New York: Simon & Schuster, 1962.

Gold, Michael. *Jews Without Money*. New York: Horace Liveright, 1930.

Greenwood, Joanne. *The Monday Voices*. New York: Harcourt, Brace & World, 1966.

Hawkes, John. *The Beetle Leg*. New York: New Directions, 1951.

Hawthorne, Nathaniel. "Earth's Holocaust" (1844), "The Maypole of Merrymount," "The Artist of the Beautiful." In *Hawthorne's Short Stories*, ed. Newton Arvin. New York: Alfred A. Knopf, 1946.

———. *The Scarlet Letter* (1850). New York: New American Library, 1959.

Hemingway, Ernest. *The Sun Also Rises*. New York: Charles Scribner's Sons, 1926.

James, Henry. *Portrait of a Lady* (1881). London: Macmillan, 1921.

———. "Europe." In *The Short Stories of Henry James*, ed. Clifton Fadiman. New York: Modern Library, 1945.

———. *The Ambassadors* (1903). New York: New American Library, 1961.

———. *The American* (1877). New York: Holt, Rinehart & Winston, 1964.

Jones, LeRoi. *The System of Dante's Hell*. New York: Grove, 1965.

Kafka, Franz. *Amerika* (1938). New York: New Directions, 1946.

Kazan, Elia. *America, America*. New York: Stein & Day, 1962.

Kerouac, Jack. *On the Road*. New York: Viking, 1957.

Kesey, Ken. *One Flew Over the Cuckoo's Nest*. New York: Viking, 1962.

Lewis, Sinclair. *Main Street*. New York: Harcourt, Brace, 1920.

———. *Babbitt*. New York: Harcourt, Brace, 1922.

Lockridge, Ross, Jr. *Raintree County*. Boston: Houghton Mifflin, 1948.

McCullers, Carson. *The Heart Is a Lonely Hunter*. Boston: Houghton Mifflin, 1940.

Mailer, Norman. *An American Dream*. New York: G. P. Putnam's Sons, 1965.

———. *Why Are We in Vietnam?* New York: G. P. Putnam's Sons, 1967.

Malamud, Bernard. *The Natural* (1952). New York: Farrar, Straus & Giroux, 1964.

———. *A New Life*. New York: Farrar, Straus & Cudahy, 1961.

Melville, Herman. "The Bell-Tower," "The Paradise of Bachelors and the Tartarus of Maids," "The Two Temples" (1856). In *The Complete Stories of Herman Melville*, ed. Jay Leda. New York: Random House, 1949.

———. *Pierre, or The Ambiguities* (1852). New York: New American Library, 1964.

Miller, Henry. *Tropic of Capricorn* (1939). New York: Grove, 1961.

———. *Black Spring* (1936). New York: Grove, 1963.

Morris, Wright. *Wright Morris: A Reader*. New York: Harper and Row, 1970.

Nabokov, Vladimir. *Lolita*. New York: G. P. Putnam's Sons, 1955.

Poe, Edgar Allan. "The Black Cat" (1843), "Ligeia" (1838). *In Tales of Mystery and Imagination*. New York: Tudor, 1939.

———. *The Narrative of Arthur Gordon Pym* (1838). New York: Hill & Wang, 1960.

Rand, Ayn. *The Fountainhead*. New York: Bobbs-Merrill, 1943.

———. *Atlas Shrugged*. New York: Random House, 1957.

Rechy, John. *City of Night*. New York: Grove, 1963.

Salinger, J. D. *The Catcher in the Rye*. Boston: Little, Brown, 1951.

Selby, Hubert. *Last Exit to Brooklyn*. New York: Grove, 1964.

Southern, Terry. *Candy*. Paris: Olympia, 1958.

Stegner, Wallace. *The Big Rock Candy Mountain*. New York: Duell, Sloan & Pearce, 1943.

Steinbeck, John. *The Grapes of Wrath*. New York: Viking, 1939.

———. *East of Eden*. New York: Viking, 1952.

Tevis, Walter. *The Hustler*. New York: Harper & Row, 1959.

Twain, Mark. *The Adventures of Huckleberry Finn* (1884). New York: Harper, 1912.

———. "The Man Who Corrupted Hadleyburg." In *The Man Who Corrupted Hadleyburg and Other Stories and Essays*. New York: Harper, 1917.

———. "The Mysterious Stranger" (1916). In *The Mysterious Stranger and Other Stories*. New York: Harper, 1922.

Updike, John. *The Poorhouse Fair*. New York: Alfred A. Knopf, 1959.

Wallant, Edward Lewis. *The Pawnbroker*. New York: Harcourt, Brace & World, 1961.

Warren, Robert Penn. *All the King's Men*. New York: Harcourt, Brace, 1946.

West, Nathanael. *The Complete Works.* New York: Farrar, Straus & Cudahy, 1957.

Wharton, Edith. *The Age of Innocence.* New York: D. Appleton, 1920.

Wolfe, Thomas. *You Can't Go Home Again.* New York: Charles Scribner's Sons, 1940.

Yates, Richard. *Revolutionary Road.* Boston: Little, Brown, 1961.

Yerby, Frank. *The Foxes of Harrow.* New York: Dial, 1946.

2. Poems

Aiken, Conrad. "The Kid." In *Collected Poems.* New York: Oxford University Press, 1953.

Blake, William. "America—A Prophecy" (1793). In *The Complete Writings of William Blake,* ed. Geoffrey Keynes. London and New York: Oxford University Press, 1966.

Crane, Hart. *The Bridge.* New York: Horace Liveright, 1930.

Ferlinghetti, Lawrence. *A Coney Island of the Mind.* New York: New Directions, 1955.

Frost, Robert. "The Gift Outright." In *The Complete Poems of Robert Frost.* New York: Holt, Rinehart & Winston, 1962.

Ginsberg, Allen. *Howl and Other Poems.* San Francisco: City Lights, 1956.

Jeffers, Robinson. *Selected Poetry of Robinson Jeffers.* New York: Random House, 1937.

MacLeish, Archibald. *America Was Promises.* New York: Duell, Sloan & Pearce, 1939.

Pound, Ezra. *The Cantos of Ezra Pound.* New York: New Directions, 1948.

Sandburg, Carl. *The People, Yes.* New York: Harcourt, Brace, 1936.

Stallman, R. W. "The Figurehead." *The New Republic,* 138 (Jan. 20, 1958), 16.

Tate, Allen. "Records." In *Poems: 1928–1931.* New York: Charles Scribner's Sons, 1932.

———. "The Wolves," "Autumn: II, Seasons of the Soul," "The Buried Lake." In *Poems.* New York: Charles Scribner's Sons, 1960.

Whitman, Walt. *Leaves of Grass* (1855). New York: New York University Press, 1965.

Williams, William Carlos. *Paterson.* New York: New Directions, 1948.

3. Plays

Albee, Edward. *The American Dream.* New York: Coward-McCann, 1961.

Garson, Barbara. *MacBird!* New York: Grove, 1967.

Ghelderode, Michel de. "Christopher Columbus." In *Seven Plays*, vol. 2, trans. George Hauger. New York: Hill & Wang, 1964.

Kopit, Arthur L. *Oh Dad, Poor Dad, Mamma's Hung You in the Closet and I'm Feelin' So Sad.* New York: Hill & Wang, 1960.

Laurents, Arthur. *Gypsy.* New York: Random House, 1960.

McClure, Michael. *The Beard.* New York: Grove, 1968.

Miller, Arthur. *All My Sons* (1947). In *Collected Plays.* New York: Viking, 1957.

———. *Death of a Salesman.* New York: Viking, 1949.

Moody, William Vaughn. *The Great Divide* (1906). In *Best Plays of the Early American Theatre*, ed. John Gassner. New York: Crown Publishers, 1967.

Odets, Clifford. *Golden Boy.* New York: Dramatists Play Service, 1937.

O'Neil, George. *American Dream.* New York: Samuel French, 1933.

O'Neill, Eugene. *The Iceman Cometh.* New York: Random House, 1946.

Sackler, Howard. *The Great White Hope.* New York: Dial, 1968.

Serling, Rod. *Patterns.* New York: Simon & Schuster, 1957.

Van Itallie, Jean-Claude. "America Hurrah." In *Eight Plays from Off-Off Broadway.* Indianapolis: Bobbs-Merrill, 1966.

Williams, Tennessee. *The Glass Menagerie.* New York: Random House, 1945.

4. Nonfiction: Criticism, History, Biography, and Autobiography

Aaron, Daniel. *Writers on the Left.* New York: Harcourt, Brace & World, 1961.

Adams, Henry. *The Education of Henry Adams* (1907). Boston: Houghton Mifflin, 1961.

Adams, James Truslow. *The Epic of America.* Boston: Little, Brown, 1931.

———. *The American: The Making of a New Man.* New York: Charles Scribner's Sons, 1943.

Agee, James. *Let Us Now Praise Famous Men.* Boston: Houghton Mifflin, 1941.

Aldridge, John. *After the Lost Generation.* New York: Noonday, 1951.

———. *Time to Murder and Create.* New York: David McKay, 1966.

Allen, Gay Wilson. "The Influence of Space on the American Imagination." In *Essays on American Literature in Honor of*

Jay B. Hubbell, ed. Clarence Gohdes. Durham, N. C.: Duke University Press, 1967.

Allen, Walter. *The Urgent West: The American Dream and Modern Man*. New York: E. P. Dutton, 1969.

Arnow, Harriette. *Seedtime on the Cumberland*. New York: Macmillan, 1960.

————. *Flowering of the Cumberland*. New York: Macmillan, 1963.

Babcott, C. Merton. *The American Frontier: A Social and Literary Record*. New York: Holt, Rinehart & Winston, 1965.

Baldwin, James. *Nobody Knows My Name*. New York: Dial, 1961.

Baskett, Sam S. and Strandness, Theodore B. *The American Identity*. Boston: D. C. Heath, 1962.

Baumbach, Jonathan. "Paradise Lost: The Novels of William Styron." *South Atlantic Quarterly*, 63 (Spring, 1964), 207–17.

————. *The Landscape of Nightmare*. New York: New York University Press, 1965.

Beard, Charles A. and Mary R. *The Rise of American Civilization*. New York: Macmillan, 1949.

Bewley, Marius. *The Eccentric Design*. New York: Columbia University Press, 1957.

Blankenship, Russell. *American Literature as an Expression of the National Mind*. New York: Henry Holt, 1931.

Bolitho, William. *Twelve Against the Gods*. New York: Simon & Schuster, 1929.

Boorstin, Daniel. *The Image, or What Happened to the American Dream*. New York: Atheneum, 1962.

————. *The Americans: The National Experience*. New York: Random House, 1965.

————. *An American Primer*. Chicago: University of Chicago Press, 1966.

Bradbury, John. *Southern Renaissance*. Chapel Hill, N. C.: University of North Carolina Press, 1963.

Brogan, D. W. *The American Character*. New York: Random House, 1944.

Brooks, Van Wyck. *Three Essays on America*. New York: E. P. Dutton, 1934.

————. *The Flowering of New England*. New York: E. P. Dutton, 1936.

Cain, James M. "The Pathology of Service." *American Mercury*, 6 (November, 1925), 257–64.

Cargill, Oscar. *Intellectual America*. New York: Macmillan, 1941.

Carpenter, Frederic I. *American Literature and the Dream*. New York: Philosophical Library, 1955.

Carpenter, Frederic I. " 'The American Myth': Paradise (to be) Regained." *PMLA*, 74 (December, 1959), 559–606.

Cash, W. J. *The Mind of the South.* New York: Alfred A. Knopf, 1941.

Caudill, Harry. *Night Comes to the Cumberlands.* Boston: Atlantic Monthly Press, 1963.

Chinoy, Ely. *Automobile Workers and the American Dream.* New York: Random House, 1955.

Cleaver, Eldridge. *Soul on Ice.* New York: McGraw-Hill, 1968.

Clebsch, William A. *From Sacred to Profane America: The Role of Religion in American History.* New York: Harper & Row, 1968.

Commager, Henry Steele, ed. *Was America a Mistake?* New York: Harper, 1967.

Conroy, Frank. *Stop-time.* New York: Viking, 1967.

Cornuelle, Richard C. *Reclaiming the American Dream.* New York: Random House, 1965.

Cowley, Malcolm. *Exile's Return.* New York: Viking, 1951.

Crèvecoeur, J. Hector St. John de. *Letters from an American Farmer.* New York: E. P. Dutton, 1912.

Croly, Herbert. *The Promise of American Life.* New York: Macmillan, 1909.

Dahlberg, Edward. *Can These Bones Live?* New York: New Directions, 1940; rev. ed., 1960.

Davis, Kenneth. *The Hero: Charles A. Lindbergh and the American Dream.* Garden City, N. Y.: Doubleday, 1959.

Eisinger, Chester. *Fiction of the Forties.* Chicago: University of Chicago Press, 1963.

Emerson, Ralph Waldo. "The American Scholar" (1837) and "Self-Reliance." In *The Complete Writings of Ralph Waldo Emerson.* New York: H. W. Wise, 1929.

Federal Writers' Project. *These Are Our Lives.* Chapel Hill, N. C.: University of North Carolina Press, 1939.

Feidelson, Charles. *Symbolism and American Literature.* Chicago: University of Chicago Press, 1953.

Fiedler, Leslie. *An End to Innocence.* Boston: Beacon Press, 1955.

———. *Love and Death in the American Novel.* New York: Stein & Day, 1960.

———. *The Return of the Vanishing American.* New York: Stein & Day, 1968.

Filler, Louis. *The Anxious Years.* New York: Capricorn Books, 1964.

Fisher, Marvin. "Melville's 'Bell-Tower': A Double Thrust." *American Quarterly*, 18 (Summer, 1966), 200–207.

Fishwick, Marshall. *The Hero: American Style.* New York: David McKay, 1969.

Fitzgerald, F. Scott. *The Crack-Up*. New York: New Directions, 1945.

Frank, Waldo, *et al.*, eds. *America and Alfred Stieglitz: A Collective Portrait*. Garden City, N. Y.: Doubleday, Doran, 1934.

Frank, Waldo. *Our America*. New York: Boni & Liveright, 1919.

——. *The Rediscovery of America: An Introduction to a Philosophy of American Life*. New York: Charles Scribner's Sons, 1929.

——. *Chart for Rough Water: Our Role in a New World*. Garden City: Doubleday, Doran, 1940.

Geismar, Maxwell. *The Last of the Provincials*. New York: Hill & Wang, 1949.

Guerin, Wilfred L. *et al. Handbook of Critical Approaches*. New York: Harper & Row, 1966.

Gurko, Leo. *The Angry Decade*. New York: Harper & Row, 1947.

Hart, James D. "Platitudes of Piety: Religion and the Popular Modern Novel." *American Quarterly*, 4 (Winter, 1954), 311–22.

Hassan, Ihab. *Radical Innocence*. Princeton, N. J.: Princeton University Press, 1961.

Hazard, Lucy. *The Frontier in American Literature*. New York: Barnes & Noble, 1927.

Hicks, Granville. *The Great Tradition*. New York: Macmillan, 1933.

Hoffman, Frederick J. *The Twenties*. New York: Viking, 1955.

Holbrook, Stewart. *Dreamers of the American Dream*. Garden City, N. Y.: Doubleday, 1957.

House, Kay. *Reality and Myth in American Literature*. Greenwich, Conn.: Fawcett, 1966.

Howard, Leon. *Literature and the American Tradition*. Garden City, N. Y.: Doubleday, 1960.

Howe, Irving. "Anarchy and Authority in American Literature." *University of Denver Quarterly*, 2 (Autumn, 1967), 5–30.

Hoyt, E. P. *The Guggenheims and the American Dream*. New York: Funk & Wagnalls, 1967.

James, Henry. *The American Scene* (1907). New York: Horizon Press, 1967.

Jones, Howard Mumford. *The Theory of American Literature*. Ithaca, N. Y.: Cornell University Press, 1948.

——. *O Strange New World*. New York: Viking, 1964.

Kazin, Alfred. *On Native Grounds*. New York: Harcourt, Brace, 1942.

Klein, Marcus. *After Alienation* (1962). Cleveland: World, 1965.

Lawrence, D. H. *Studies in Classic American Literature*. New York: Thomas Seltzer, 1923.

Lerner, Max. *America As a Civilization*. 2 vols. New York: Simon & Schuster, 1957.

Levin, Harry. *The Power of Blackness*. New York: Random House, 1958.

———. "The American Voice in English Poetry." In *Refractions: Essays in Comparative Literature*. New York: Oxford University Press, 1966.

Levitas, Mitchel and Magnum Photographers. *America In Crisis*. New York: Holt, Rinehart & Winston, 1969.

Lewis, R. W. B. *The American Adam*. Chicago: University of Chicago Press, 1955.

Lynn, Kenneth. *The Dream of Success: A Study of the Modern American Imagination*. Boston: Little, Brown, 1955.

———. *The Comic Tradition in America*. Garden City, N. Y.: Doubleday, 1959.

Macdonald, Dwight. *Against the American Grain*. New York: Random House, 1962.

Madden, David. *Wright Morris*. New York: Twayne, 1964.

———, ed. *Proletarian Writers of the Thirties*. Carbondale, Ill.: Southern Illinois University Press, 1968.

———, ed. *Tough Guy Writers of the Thirties*. Carbondale, Ill.: Southern Illinois University Press, 1968.

———. "Wright Morris' *In Orbit*: An Unbroken Series of Poetic Gestures." In *The Poetic Image in Six Genres*. Carbondale, Ill.: Southern Illinois University Press, 1969.

Martin, Jay. *Harvests of Change*. New York: Prentice-Hall, 1967.

Marx, Leo. *The Machine in the Garden*. New York: Oxford University Press, 1964.

Matthiessen, F. O. *American Renaissance*. New York: Oxford University Press, 1941.

Mencken, H. L. *Prejudices: Second Series*. New York: Alfred A. Knopf, 1924.

Miller, Henry. *The Air-Conditioned Nightmare*. New York: New Directions, 1945.

Miller, Perry. *The Life of the Mind in America*. New York: Harcourt, Brace & World, 1965.

Morris, Willie. *North Toward Home*. Boston: Houghton Mifflin, 1967.

Morris, Wright. *The Territory Ahead*. New York: Atheneum, 1958.

Nevins, Allan. *James Truslow Adams: Historian of the American Dream*. Urbana, Ill.: University of Illinois Press, 1968.

Noble, David W. *The Eternal Adam and the New World Garden: The Central Myth in the American Novel Since 1830*. New York: George Braziller, 1968.

Parkes, Henry B. *The American Experience*. New York: Alfred A. Knopf, 1947.

Parkinson, Thomas, ed. *A Casebook on the Beat*. New York: Thomas Y. Crowell, 1961.

Parrington, V. L. *Main Currents in American Thought*. New York: Harcourt, Brace, 1930.

Pearson, Norman Holmes. "The Nazi-Soviet Pact and the End of a Dream." In *America in Crisis*, ed. Daniel Aaron. New York: Alfred A. Knopf, 1952.

Podhoretz, Norman. *Making It*. New York: Random House, 1967.

Rand, Ayn. *For the New Intellectual*. New York: Random House, 1961.

————. *The Virtue of Selfishness*. New York: New American Library, 1964.

Rideout, Walter B. *The Radical Novel in the United States: 1900–1954*. Cambridge, Mass.: Harvard University Press, 1956.

Riesman, David. *The Lonely Crowd*. New Haven, Conn.: Yale University Press, 1953.

Rourke, Constance. *American Humor: A Study of the National Character*. New York: Harcourt, Brace, 1931.

Rubin, Louis D. and Moore, John Reese. *The Idea of an American Novel*. New York: Thomas Y. Crowell, 1961.

Salzman, Jack, and Wallenstein, Barry. *Years of Protest*. New York: Pegasus, 1967.

Sanford, Charles L. *The Quest for Paradise*. Urbana, Ill.: University of Illinois Press, 1961.

Sevareid, Eric. *You Can't Kill the Dream*. Richmond, Va.: John Knox Press, 1969.

Simpson, Lewis P. "Boston Ice and Letters in the Age of Jefferson." *Midcontinent American Studies Journal*, 9 (Spring, 1968), 58–76.

Smith, Henry Nash. *Virgin Land: The American West as Symbol and Myth*. Cambridge, Mass.: Harvard University Press, 1950.

Spengler, Oswald. *The Decline of the West*. 2 vols. New York: Alfred A. Knopf, 1926.

Spiller, Robert. *American Literary Revolution, 1783–1837*. New York: New York University Press, 1967.

Stearns, Harold B. *Civilization in the United States*. New York: Harcourt, Brace, 1922.

Sultan, Stanley. "Call Me Ishmael: The Hagiography of Isaac McCaslin." *Texas Studies in Literature and Language*, 3 (Spring, 1961), 50–66.

Swados, Harvey. *The American Writer in the Great Depression*. Indianapolis: Bobbs-Merrill, 1966.

Thoreau, Henry David. *Walden* (1854). New York: New American Library, 1961.

226 A SELECTIVE BIBLIOGRAPHY

Tipple, John. *Crisis of the American Dream: A History of American Social Thought, 1920–1940.* New York: Pegasus, 1968.

Tocqueville, Alexis de. *Democracy in America* (1835–1840). New York: Schocken Books, 1961.

Trachtenberg, Alan. *Brooklyn Bridge: Fact and Symbol.* New York: Oxford University Press, 1965.

Turner, Frederick Jackson. *The Frontier in American History.* New York: Henry Holt, 1920.

Tyler, Moses Coit. *History of American Literature, 1607–1765* (1878). Ithaca, N. Y.: Cornell University Press, 1949.

Van Zandt, Roland. *The Metaphysical Foundations of American History.* Gravenhage: Mouton, 1959.

Viereck, Peter. "Vachel Lindsay, The Dante of the Fundamentalists: The Suicide of America's Faith in Technology." In a forthcoming book on Lindsay.

Webb, Walter Prescott. *The Great Plains.* Boston: Ginn, 1931.

Williams, Stanley. *The American Spirit in Letters.* New Haven, Conn.: Yale University Press, 1926.

Williams, William Carlos. *In the American Grain.* New York: New Directions, 1933.

Wolfe, Don. *The Image of Man in America.* Dallas: Southern Methodist University Press, 1957.

Young, Philip. "The Mother of Us All." *Kenyon Review,* 24 (Summer, 1962), 391–415.

———. *Ernest Hemingway: A Reconsideration.* University Park, Pa.: Pennsylvania State University Press, 1966.

Index